LENT

A Guide to the Eucharist and Hours

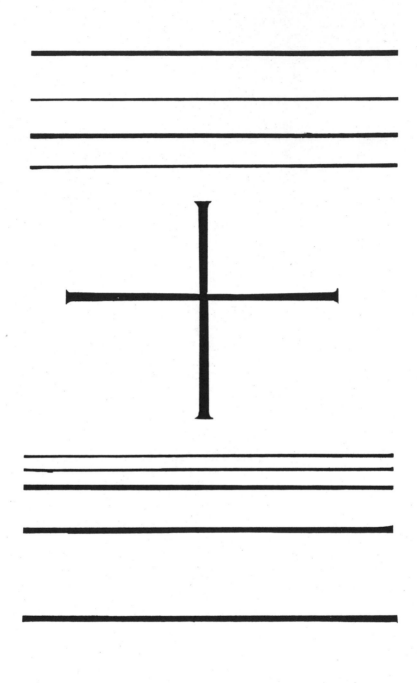

The Liturgical Seasons

LENT

A Guide to the Eucharist and Hours

Kevin W. Irwin

PUEBLO PUBLISHING COMPANY

New York

To Anthony Ciorra, O.F.M. Cap.

Contents

Introduction to the Series

This book is one of a three-volume series on liturgical seasons; it provides a daily commentary on the eucharist and the liturgy of the hours. Intended as a help for all who celebrate liturgy, it would be of particular use for those who plan or preside at liturgy in a variety of settings including parishes, schools, and religious communities. The series emphasizes the important place that the liturgy plays in our individual and communal spirituality.

Unlike preconciliar liturgical commentaries (such as the important works of Pius Parsch and Amiliana Löhr), which were based on a fixed ritual, these commentaries emphasize the variety and flexibility of the rites revised since Vatican II. They try to balance the rhythm and pattern that is inherent in liturgy with the different needs of varying celebrating communities.

As a liturgical commentary, this book discusses the readings, prayers, gestures, and symbols of the eucharist and hours within the context of a given season. This means that exegesis and interpretation is influenced by the actual use made by the liturgy of texts and symbols. As a spiritual commentary, this book tries to show how our lived experience links up with what is celebrated in liturgy and how the liturgy influences our appreciation of how God works in our lives. Through the liturgy we remember God's saving action in Christ through the power of the Holy Spirit. Through this communal remembering we experience anew the paschal mystery.

Each of the commentaries is divided into six sections:

Liturgical Context—This provides historical background about a particular day or shows how one day relates to another in the present reform. The purpose of this section is to help situate the liturgy of a given day.

Eucharist—This section discusses the Mass texts of the day: the antiphons and prayers from the Sacramentary, and the readings and responsorial psalm from the Lectionary. The purpose of this section is to offer an appreciation of how these texts relate to each other and how they express the spirituality of the season.

Celebration of Eucharist—This section discusses the various textual options: the prayers, preface, eucharistic prayer, and dismissal that can be chosen. It also offers ideas for the intercessions, where to employ additional comments, and how to emphasize the symbols or gestures to be used. The purpose of this section is to help stimulate ideas for ways to adapt the eucharist to specific communities.

Liturgy of the Hours—This section discusses the various parts of the office of readings and morning and evening prayer. These hours were chosen because they offer the most material for communal or individual reflection (readings) and also because they are regarded as those hours that are central to the prayer of the whole church (morning and evening).

Celebration of the Hours—This section offers suggestions for selecting texts, choosing hymns, composing psalm prayers and intercessions, and for the ritual used at these hours. The suggestion to vary the invitatory text and its accompanying psalm sometimes utilizes the phrase placed between the psalmody and the readings at the office of readings. This is to allow for greater variety. The invitatory can be used as the introduction to morning prayer if the office of readings is not celebrated in common. Like the section on the celebration of the eucharist, this section is meant to offer ideas on how to adapt the hours to meet the needs of varying communities.

Reflection—This section takes a theme from the day's liturgy and tries to relate it to our lived experience. It is intended as a point for personal meditation, but it can also serve as a homily idea.

Preface

The season of Lent is meant to refocus our vision on the sacrificial life, death, and glorious resurrection of Jesus. It is meant to clarify our vision of what is truly important in our lives, that is, our conversion to Christ in the community of the church. It reestablishes priorities so that we may live in harmony with our identity, as a people called by and converted to the Lord. This annual forty-day retreat is celebrated liturgically with a wealth of rites, symbols, gestures, and texts. Together these form the church's liturgy, the prayer shared by all her people. This book is about the formative role that the liturgy can play in making Lent the season it should be, a time of renewal and re-creation in Christ.

In its classical form and in its present shape, Lent concerns initiation into Christ's body through the sacraments of baptism, confirmation, and eucharist. This explains why many texts use the symbols of water and light, especially the texts used on the Third, Fourth, and Fifth Sundays in the "A" cycle. For those already initiated, this season is one of reconciliation and a renewed sharing in the sacrament of unity, the eucharist. This process is effected by and symbolized through the sacrament of penance or reconciliation. This explains why many texts of the Lenten liturgy refer to forgiveness and reconciliation.

Lent is a season of memory and of hope. It is a season of memory because through the liturgy we recall Christ's paschal mystery; it is a season of hope because through sharing in the liturgy we gain confidence to live out in our own lives what we celebrate. This means that the Lord's humiliation, suffering, and death are not just realities of the past, or aspects of Christ's experience only. They are our experiences as well. Through the liturgy we experience his victory over sin and death, a victory that gives us the hope and confidence we need to face up to and deal with the bondage, isolation, selfishness, and sin that we all too often experience. The liturgy offers us the liberation, forgiveness, and reconciliation accomplished once-for-all in Christ. It is our present share in this accomplished act of redemption.

A motif that runs through the texts of the eucharistic liturgy during Lent is that of Christ the obedient one. A book that dominates the office of readings during Lent is Exodus, the journey of Israel in response to the Lord's call. I have dedicated this volume to a man who has helped me respond more fully to the Lord's call. His own example and continued encouragement have spoken eloquently of the importance of hearing and responding in obedience to the word of God. For his direction and support from October 1980 to January 1983 I am most grateful. Needless to say, my responding to the word has not ended, and at times this requires that I face up to new temptations and deal with conflict and pain. It is then that I relearn the meaning of perseverance that he taught me. In the words of Aelred of Rievaulx:

"If, then, when you have given up the fleshpots of Egypt, the cares of this world and its striving and quarrelling, in exchange for the poverty of Christ and a life of obedience, do not be surprised if you do not immediately receive God's manna from heaven. You have crossed the Red Sea like a true Israelite; you have chosen solitude and silence, a life of brotherly love and voluntary poverty; you have escaped, in fact, from the tumult of this world. Do not, therefore, murmur against God if you do not yet experience the sweetness of His love. Do not wonder if indeed God is still with you. . . . Yet you need not be surprised that you do not immediately receive heavenly consolation, when you remember Saint Paul's reminder that we cannot enter into the kingdom of God without suffering many tribulations in this life. These trials must not make us waver, he tells us, since they are our appointed lot" (*Mirror of Charity*).

May this book be a way of expressing my thanks to a priest, director, and friend who has helped me along the path of perseverance in the Lord's service.

Feast of the Dedication of the Abbey Church
Saint Anselm Abbey, Manchester, N.H.
July 18, 1984

LENT

A Guide to the Eucharist and Hours

Chapter One

Week of Ash Wednesday

ASH WEDNESDAY

Liturgical Context

Most major feasts and liturgical seasons begin with evening prayer and vigils as ways of anticipating and experiencing the richness inherent in such times of celebration. Lent, however, is unique in that it has no such introduction or preparation. The still popular feasting of Mardi Gras, *carnevale,* and pancake suppers on Shrove Tuesday is not the beginning of Lent. The day of Ash Wednesday begins the forty-day commemoration of Lent, which looks toward the celebration of the first day of the new creation at Easter. While formerly the Roman Rite set aside the preceding three Sundays as a prelude to Ash Wednesday, this custom has been eliminated in favor of emphasizing the season of Lent itself as the time to prepare for Easter, which extends to a season of fifty days. The Lent-Easter liturgy begins with morning prayer or the imposition of ashes made from the palms distributed the preceding year on Passion (Palm) Sunday. Now, almost a year later those palms are burnt, blessed, and imposed to begin another cycle of Lenten liturgy. The "death" of nature in the winter and its rising to new life in the spring is the symbol of the annual commemoration of the death and resurrection of Christ.

The season of Lent is an annual pilgrimage, an annual retreat, an annual time for stock-taking and soul-searching about the meaning of the Christian life—the dying and rising of Jesus and our dying to sin and rising to real life in him. The center of the Christian faith is the paschal mystery of Jesus' death and resurrection that is affirmed and acclaimed each time we celebrate the sacred mysteries at the eucharist. "Christ has died, Christ is risen, Christ will come again." During Lent, we take time out of ordinary, everyday life in order to deepen our identification with and our share in the paschal mystery, that is, dying and rising with Jesus.

The "forty days" of Lent is reminiscent of Christ's sojourn in the desert where he fasted and prayed prior to his public ministry, which ended in his humiliation, death, and resurrection. The fast, prayer, and length of Lent are expressed in the traditional Lenten hymn (ascribed to Gregory the Great) sung at evening prayer:

"O loving Maker of the world,
Hear now the prayers your people raise:
Give us the grace we need to keep
This sacred fast of forty days!

O gentle searcher of the heart,
Our human weakness well you know:
As now we turn again to you,
The grace of your forgiveness show!

Our many sins we now confess,
And trust our sickness to your love:
Now for the praise of your blest Name,
Grant healing mercy from above."

Today's Lenten discipline of fast, abstinence, prayer, and works of charity follows a rich tradition in theology and practice. While the imposition of ashes dates only from the eighth or ninth centuries, it has become and remains a most significant practice for western Catholics. The liturgy of Ash Wednesday offers a significant set of readings, prayers, gestures, and symbols whose purpose is to help orient us to the wise use of these means of personal sanctification. In fact, the liturgy from Ash Wednesday through the following Saturday stresses the notion of conversion (what Lent is all about), the true meaning of the traditional practices as aids to conversion of heart and mind. What is stated about contrition in the General Instruction on the revised Rite of Penance can also be said concerning the discipline and practices of Lent:

"The most important act of the penitent is contrition, which is 'heartfelt sorrow and aversion for the sin committed along with the intention of sinning no more.' 'We can only approach the kingdom of Christ by *metanoia*. This is a profound change of the whole person by which we begin to consider, judge and arrange our life according to the holiness and love of God, made manifest in his Son in the last days and given to us in abundance. . . .' The genuineness of penance depends on this heartfelt contrition" (no. 6).

Fittingly, there is no liturgical "eve" of Ash Wednesday. The liturgy of this day puts into perspective the rest of the Lenten season. Blessing and imposing ashes, observing a fast for the Lord, and gathering for common prayer at liturgy on Ash Wednesday help us realize what Lent and the whole Christian life are all about—turning again and again to the Lord so that our identification with and participation in his paschal mystery might be ever deeper. This process of conversion continues until the day when we are called from this life to the next, where ashes, fasts, and sacraments will no longer be needed because we will be totally assumed into the mystery of God.

Liturgy of the Eucharist

The eucharist on Ash Wednesday begins simply and starkly. The entrance antiphon fittingly introduces the scripture readings by acclaiming God as "merciful" and describing the Lord as one who overlooks sins and loves all he has created. There is no penitential rite today, its place being taken by the blessing and distribution of ashes after the homily. The similarity between the beginning of this liturgy and the even simpler one on Good Friday evinces the fact that the Roman Rite originally had no public penitential rite at the beginning of the eucharist as we do today. The text of the opening prayer is a traditional one that speaks of customary and important Lenten themes: "self-denial" and the "struggle against evil." (Unfortunately the force of the Latin original, which refers to "fast" as part of the discipline of the season is lacking in the present English translation.)

The proclamation of the texts from Joel (2:12–18) and Matthew (6:1–6,16–18) at the eucharist continues a long-standing custom of using these passages to begin Lent. Joel speaks of returning to the Lord with our whole heart. The God to whom we return is gracious and merciful, "slow to anger" and "rich in kindness." The people are to assemble. They are to do penance for their sins and ask the

Lord to take pity on them. This text is indeed appropriate for the first reading on Ash Wednesday, a day of gathering, of hearing the word, of signing with ashes in church and fasting for our sins.

The responsorial psalm, Psalm 51, appropriately sung after this reading from Joel, is also used at other Lenten liturgies (First Sunday "A" cycle, Fifth Sunday "B" cycle, Wednesday of the first week, and Saturday of the third week). It is the Lord who creates clean hearts, who renews our spirits so that they may become more steadfast, and who opens our lips to declare his praise. This same God invites us into the Lenten season to offer him what is of real value, a humble and contrite heart.

The gospel from Matthew (Mt 6:1–6,16–19) is an expansion of the text (Mt 6:16–21) assigned for this day in the Missal of Pius V. The former pericope was limited to fasting (vss. 16–21), while the present selection includes the notion of praying and almsgiving without public fanfares. The readings from Joel and Matthew challenge us to turn to God humbly by prayer and self-sacrifice.

The communal dimension of Lent (implied in the Joel reading) is emphasized in the reading from 2 Corinthians (5:20–6:2) which has been added in the revised Lectionary. In it, Paul reminds us that we are to be reconciled to one another and to God. The "acceptable time" is now; the "day of salvation" is upon us. The church emphasizes the reconciliation theme of Lent (and not only private devotion and fasting) by using 2 Corinthians 5:17–22 on the Fourth Sunday "C" cycle.

The church's traditional Lenten disciplines of fasting, prayer, and works of mercy such as almsgiving are given a prominent place in the liturgy of the word today. We are made to realize that Lent is more than just receiving ashes.

The blessing and giving of ashes take place after the homily, following the brief introduction that speaks of the ashes as "the mark of our repentance." While both formulas for the blessing derive from traditional texts, the variations in these prayers bring out important Lenten themes. The first blessing prays that those on whom the ashes will be imposed will receive the Lord's forgiveness, so that by keeping Lent they may prepare to celebrate Easter. The second blessing prays for pardon and conversion of sinners so that they may be more completely identified with the risen Christ. The eschatological note struck at the conclusion to the prayer ("but to live with the risen Christ") should not be overlooked. The Easter prepared for by Lent and annually inaugurated by Ash Wednesday is the eternal paschal feast in the kingdom forever.

Two formulas are provided for the imposition with ashes. The traditional text of "remember . . . you are dust" recalls the Fall and our need for redemption. The newer option is oriented toward the gospel by reminding believers that Lent concerns personal conversion ("turn away from sin") and growth in faith ("be faithful to the gospel"). The citation of Mark 1:15 in this formula implies that the individual who receives the ashes and the whole church are in need of reform. The gesture of signing the forehead with ashes in the form of a cross indicates that we are redeemed by sharing in both the dying and rising of Christ. After the ashes have been given, all join in the prayer of the faithful. Appendix I to the Sacramentary, Sample Formulas for the General Intercessions, number 5, for Lent I, contains significant terms that ought to be recalled and reiterated throughout Lent: fidelity to the "word," this season as the "acceptable time," "reconciliation," and repentance "with all our hearts."

The liturgy of the eucharist now follows. The prayer over the gifts speaks about the tradition of "Lenten works of charity and penance" and associates this eucharist with the Easter mysteries to come. The fourth Lenten preface, subtitled "the reward of fasting," is prescribed for proclamation. Unfortunately the word "fast" does not appear in the present translation as it does in the Latin original; however the preface emphasizes that it is God who sanctifies us and that Lent is an important time for us to turn to the Lord.

The prayer after communion, as is usually the case with these prayers, joins the celebration of the liturgy with the practice of the rest of Christian life—in this instance with "our Lenten penance."

Celebration of the Eucharist

Today's liturgy should reflect the tradition of the Roman Rite and be simple and direct in speech. The sign of the cross and the greeting are followed immediately by the "let us pray" introducing the opening prayer. A pause for silence here, followed by a deliberately paced proclamation (or singing) of the prayer, can help set the tone for a liturgy that is serious and appropriately reflective. Similarly at the blessing of the ashes (after the homily), the brief introduction to the blessing prayer should be followed by a period of silence and then the proclamation of the blessing. This act of blessing is best done in full view of the community with ashes in a suitable container placed on a small table (not on the altar). Maximizing the visibility of the ashes and being careful in imposing them can go a long way toward making them an effective symbol with which to begin Lent.

In the prayer of the faithful, intentions might include the particular projects in which the community will be engaged this Lent such as evangelization, the catechumenate, scripture study groups, works of charity, almsgiving, and so on. Mentioning these intentions at different times throughout Lent can help a community to strengthen its communal observance of this season. The universal nature of this prayer should not be lost, however, and petitions for the whole church as well as national and civic needs should also be included (see General Instruction on the Roman Missal, no. 46).

The liturgy of the eucharist now follows. Because of its brevity, the use of the second eucharistic prayer would be a good complement to the preface Lent IV prescribed today.

The Lord's Prayer could be introduced by reference to forgiving each other in this season (as provided in the third option), thus underscoring the reconciliation notion in the reading from 2 Corinthians.

Liturgy of the Hours

The balanced approach to the season seen in the texts of the liturgy of the eucharist is also exemplified in the liturgy of the hours. The verse between the psalmody and the scripture text in the office of readings offers the challenge: "Turn back to the Lord and do penance—Be renewed in heart and spirit." Yet the use of Psalm 103 at the office of readings balances this with a reminder of God's tender compassion toward those who abide by his will. Then the powerful text of Isaiah 58:1–12 is proclaimed about the true spirit of fasting. This severe prophetic text points out that fasting is not self-serving. It does not simply mean lying "in sackcloth and ashes." Fasting means releasing those unjustly bound, freeing the oppressed, and sharing food with those in need. It also signifies hungering and thirsting for God alone. Isaiah states that if we do certain things such as "bestowing your bread on the hungry . . . ," then the Lord will "renew your strength. . . ." The liturgy proclaims this text most appropriately on Ash Wednesday in the hours and repeats verses 1–9 in the first reading at the eucharist on Friday and verses 9–14 on Saturday of this week to stress the need for Lenten penance.

The selection from the letter of Pope St. Clement to the Corinthians points out that if we turn to God our Father, we are assured that he will not only give us a hearing, but will forgive us all the evil we have done and strengthen us if we are merciful to others.

This notion of God's call to us is reiterated in the short reading at morning prayer from Deuteronomy (7:6,8–9). We are God's own, having been called into relationship with him as was Israel. God's call and our response is underscored in the short reading for evening prayer from Philippians (2:12b–15a). It is God who inspires, accomplishes, and brings to completion whatever we do. Part of the asceticism of Lent is letting go of the false notions that *we* accomplish penances and earn the forgiveness of our sins. The liturgy reminds us that in the history we call "salvation," it was God who accomplished our redemption. It is this redemption that we share in at the liturgy. The antiphons for the Canticle of Zechariah at morning prayer and that of Mary at evening prayer repeat the admonitions of today's gospel reading about fasting and giving alms humbly and without ostentation.

Celebration of the Hours

The psalms of Wednesday week 4 are prescribed for use at the hours today except at morning prayer, where the psalms, canticle, and antiphons for Friday in week 3 are offered as options. Since the scripture texts for the short readings at morning and evening prayer recur on the same day each week for the first four weeks of Lent, communities which celebrate only these hours in common might want to explore the possibility of making an alternate list of readings to use at these hours throughout Lent. For example, short excerpts from the book of Exodus, which is read semicontinuously throughout the first part of Lent at the office of readings, could be used as short readings by those communities that do not celebrate readings in common. Another option would be to choose an Old

Testament prophet and read excerpts from it semicontinuously at morning prayer. The same could be done at evening prayer. Since most of the responses at morning and evening prayer are seasonal and thematic, they could be used with the substituted reading. Or they could be omitted to allow for a more extended pause for reflection.

In addition, other intercessions may be substituted for those for morning and evening prayer. What should be kept in mind is that at morning prayer the intentions are to dedicate the day to the Lord, and at evening prayer they function as do the intercessions at Mass. Since the intercessions at each of these hours end with the Lord's Prayer, Lent would be a good time to emphasize this prayer by a special introduction and/or by singing it.

Reflection—"Return and Live"

Lent begins today—again. The familiar journey to be traveled again, once more, this year, every year. Why? Because we need this Lent and every Lent to remind us that at the heart of the rituals we call liturgy and the words we call revelation is the mystery of God and our relationship to him. The reason we gather for these forty days again this year is that we are different people from who we were last year and will be different next year because we are always reaching new and different stages of life's journey to complete and total union with God. We hear the same stories, receive the same ashes, make the same gestures, and share in the same eucharist. Yet we do all this somehow differently to the extent that we allow faith to dominate our lives and rule our hearts. It is different because the points of intersection of our lives and the life of God change as we change. We always need to be redeemed; what changes each year are what particular things need redeeming. The call of the prophet to gather the assembly is for us to gather once more to begin anew in the hope the prophet offers that the Lord will save us. We need this Lent to turn, to return, and to turn again and again to God.

With the beginning of Lent today, we profess that we want to follow the Lord more closely. We need Lent and these ashes to remind us of the fragility, the imperfection, the incompleteness of life. But as we use this season and these symbols, we need to remember that they are to lead us nowhere else but to God.

Liturgical Context

The main theme of the liturgy of the days from Ash Wednesday to the First Sunday of Lent is the appreciation of the works of Lenten asceticism. The tradition of the church has given a special liturgical and ascetical emphasis to Wednesdays, Fridays, and Saturdays. This was evident in the celebration of the Ember Days four times a year.

Essentially the liturgy today is about following Christ *daily*. The opening prayer (formerly from Ember Saturday in Lent) states it succinctly: may all that we do begin, continue, and reach perfection in and through the Lord. There is a certain tongue-in-cheek quality to what is celebrated today! Well begun is not half done in Lent; well begun is only the beginning. What is required is consistent prayer and penitential practice, not sudden outbursts of spirituality one day and a return to indifference the next.

The liturgy today speaks about continuing our good works with God's help. They who meditate "day and night on the law of the Lord will yield fruit in due season" (Ps 1:2–3, Communion Antiphon, Ash Wednesday).

Liturgy of the Eucharist

Today's entrance antiphon is traditional and continues to impress upon us the image of a God who hears us, saves us, and supports us especially when our struggle becomes more real and demanding than we would have ever imagined. The Lord is the support and the one who sustains. This same Lord is the one who initiates, continues in us, and brings to completion all good works, especially those we do in Lent. This is reiterated in today's opening prayer.

The selection of scripture passages for the weekdays in Lent follows the principles stated in the Lectionary: "The readings from the gospels and the Old Testament were selected because they are related to each other. They treat various themes of the Lenten catechesis that are suited to the spiritual significance of this season" (Introduction, Lectionary for Mass, no. 98). The catechesis referred to in these texts concerns the *daily* choices we have to make for God, even when and especially because that choice often means carrying our cross(es) in imitation of Jesus. Today's first reading, Deuteronomy 30:15–20, invites us to "choose life," but a life that heeds the voice of the Lord. We are not to choose the superficial and ephemeral things that apparently make life easy; rather we are to make choices that conform our wills to God's. We are not to turn our heart from the Lord, because it is through our heart and spirit that God speaks with us in prayer. The God we worship and adore is the God who was revealed to "Abraham, Isaac and Jacob" and who is ever faithful to his promises. This text, most appropriate for the beginning of Lent, is also suggested as one of the readings for the Rite of Penance (no. 118) and for Christian Initiation of Adults outside the Easter Vigil (no. 388,4) to remind us what the Christian life demands. The use of Psalm 1 as the response, subtitled "two ways of living," reiterates that we are to choose God's ways. Like Israel, we come to know God through his law. For Israel, the law is not primarily a series of statutes or prescriptions, but a means of revealing who God is and what is expected of those who believe in him (see Ps 119).

The gospel from Luke (9:22–25) is introduced by the Deuteronomy text. Jesus says that the pattern of his suffering and death leading to glory must be reproduced in the lives of his followers. The profit from gaining the whole world but destroying one's very self in the process is indeed no gain at all—rather it is total loss. What the world calls loss (suffering, dying for the sake of the gospel) is really gain, for through such means we grow in union with God.

The reference to the "cross" is a significant image for the Lenten season. The sign of the cross with which we begin and end our liturgy and which was used to impose ashes yesterday reminds us that the cross is the standard of our faith. The daily crosses in life are not to be avoided so that we may have more time or strength to carry out our Lenten discipline. Paradoxically part of the asceticism of Lent is to accept the crosses that plague us daily as the *everyday* means of sanctification.

This passage from Luke, also used in Masses for martyrs, helps us focus on what real virtue is: daily choosing God's ways no matter what the cost.

Today's communion antiphon is traditional in the Roman Rite and reminds us that what God desires is a "steadfast spirit" and a "clean heart."

The prayer after communion assures us that the liturgy brings us "pardon and salvation."

Celebration of the Eucharist

Today the penitential rite at the beginning of the eucharist is resumed. An appropriate form would be the second because it is simple and straightforward.

Since this part of the liturgy should lead to the readings and not derogate from them, a brief comment at the beginning of the liturgy about the daily renunciation to be practiced during this season would be helpful.

For the verse before the gospel, Lectionary 224, no. 10, inspired by Luke 8:15, would be a good choice since it speaks of a "generous heart" and yielding a harvest "through perseverance."

In today's prayer of the faithful, it would be good to include petitions for the help and insight needed to face such problems as war, hunger, and injustice. The prayer could also ask that the community's Lenten projects be sustained and brought to completion for the sake of Christ.

Of the Lenten prefaces, the second, subtitled "the spirit of penance," would be appropriate because it shows that by controlling our desires we learn from God "how to live in this passing world/ with our heart set on the world that will never end."

The first eucharistic prayer for Masses for Reconciliation would be a good choice since it refers to the covenant bond, forged and broken (reflecting the urgency of the Deuteronomist's challenge to "choose"):

"Time and time again
we broke your covenant,
but you did not abandon us.

Now is the acceptable time
for your people to turn back to you."

The fourth introduction to the Lord's Prayer about the coming of the kingdom, or an adaptation which underscores "*thy* kingdom come, *thy* will be done" would be appropriate today.

Liturgy of the Hours

The second invitatory verse provided in the liturgy of the hours for Lent (up to Passion Sunday) clearly reflects the central theme of the liturgy today: "Today if you hear the voice of the Lord, harden not your hearts." This is taken from Psalm 95, the classic invitatory psalm, which contains a brief summary of God's dealings with Israel and the command that they obey his word. The combination of the theme of daily application seen in the eucharist and of God's dealing with Israel in the book of Exodus, read at the office of readings throughout Lent, make this verse (and the use of Ps 95) most appropriate.

The first scripture reading, from Exodus 1:1–22, begins a series of continuous readings that will extend to Saturday of the third week of Lent.

The scriptures do not consider the Exodus event merely as a one-time, past happening. Rather it is often recalled and referred to by the prophets, and the Christian liturgy sees in it a foreshadowing of the passage of Jesus from this life to the Father. This reading, and the others from the book of Exodus, remind and inspire us to persevere in the Lord's ways, even in the face of persecution and injustice that make life bitter for us.

The patristic reading from St. Leo the Great speaks of the *"daily renewal"* required to repair the shortcomings of our mortal nature. St. Leo also calls for the renunciation of sin to accompany abstinence, and almsgiving to accompany fasting.

At morning prayer, the reading from 1 Kings (8:51–53a) reminds us of our share in the heritage of Israel as the new people of God. But election carries with it the responsibility to respond ever more faithfully to the Lord who calls. The antiphon for the Canticle of Zechariah reiterates the sentiment of denying self and following Christ.

At evening prayer, the section from the letter of James (4:7–8,10) about submitting to the Lord is read. In submission we draw close to him and he, in turn, draws close to us and brings us ever nearer to the fullness of life in him.

Celebration of the Hours

Today's invitatory and psalm deserve special care in proclamation (or singing) as they set the tone for the day's liturgy. The use of part of Psalm 95 ("Today, listen to the voice of the Lord") as a responsory to the reading from Exodus would be a fitting substitution for that provided.

The intercessions at morning prayer might well reflect our election at baptism and our responsibility to live out that commitment. The doctrine of election carries with it the burden of responsibility and faithfulness. Our common prayer today is an example of our response to being chosen.

At evening prayer the intercessions provided reflect the work of the Holy Spirit in helping us live "through faith and sacrament."

Appropriate hymns to use at the beginning of morning and evening prayer are those that speak about the "forty days" and the discipline of fasting, prayer, and almsgiving, since the intention of the liturgy these days is to begin Lent well.

Reflection—"Daily Cross-carrying"

Today the struggle of Lent really begins. Today's liturgy will be better attended than usual but it will pale in comparison with yesterday's crowds. We have to choose today to continue, to persevere, to carry out what was begun on a large scale yesterday. We know that conforming ourselves to the will of God means pain and suffering. But we do not submit to God's will blindly or with "grin-and-bear-it" stoicism. We do it because we have glimpsed in and through the cross of Christ, his triumphant resurrection to new and eternal life. We are willing to accept our own crosses, and to bear the burdens of others because we believe that obedience to Christ leads us to full, rich, and real life in him.

The prerequisite in making these choices, however, is faith. When things do not go our way or the demands of faith seem altogether too much for us, we need to be reminded that Israel, (the first chosen race) wandered and had to be called back "again and again." It is precisely when we see all our hopes, plans, and human accomplishments eclipsed because of human illness and tragedy that we need to be reminded that all that really matters in this life is our living for God alone and doing things in conformity with his will. After all, the pattern of the life of Christ is defeat before exaltation.

What matters in Lent is the long haul, not flashy starts and finishes. The only start worth making in Lent is the one that leads to a daily (so very "everyday") discipline of fasting, prayer, and works of mercy.

Today's liturgy asks serious questions, questions only answerable in our own hearts before the God who so loved us that he allowed his Son to suffer death so that we might look beyond death in our own lives to the fullness of real life, total union with God.

The *daily* prayer and work of Lent are our means to union with God. The *daily* carrying of our crosses and the bearing of each other's burdens is the way we share in the humiliation Jesus suffered before his resurrection. To carry our cross in this life means sharing Christ's glory in heaven forever.

FRIDAY AFTER ASH WEDNESDAY

Liturgical Context

From the earliest church documents on community discipline (for example the *Didache*), it is clear that the Christian church made Wednesdays and Fridays special days of fasting, a tradition that is continued in many monastic rules today. For all Christians, the tradition of Friday fast and abstinence is encouraged, especially in Lent. Today, the first of the Fridays in Lent, the liturgy continues to emphasize this tradition. The liturgy of Lent thus helps us to deepen our understanding of a spirituality which includes both liturgical prayer as well as fasting and the giving of alms. Each of these is noted and considered fully in today's eucharist and liturgy of the hours. The liturgy of these first days of Lent endeavors to purify our motives, to direct us toward appropriate ascetical practices, and to make us aware of the meaning of conversion to the Lord. Today's first reading shows how the discipline of fasting is related to the virtue of justice:

"This, rather, is the fasting that I wish:
   releasing those bound unjustly,
   untying the thongs of the yoke;
Seeking free the oppressed,
   breaking every yoke;
Sharing your bread with the hungry,
   sheltering the oppressed and the homeless;
Clothing the naked when you see them,
   and not turning your back on your own" (Is 58:6–7).

Liturgy of the Eucharist

The traditional form of today's opening prayer spoke of "the fast we have begun," thus making it a fitting collect on days when fasting was prescribed. The present version substitutes the word "penance" for "fast." This deliberate textual adjustment focuses our attention not only on fasting, but on all Lenten ascetical practices as well. We pray that with God's help we may persevere in carrying them out, a notion that was emphasized in yesterday's liturgy.

Today's first reading (Isaiah 58:1–9) is from a section of the book that is postexilic in authorship and whose complement will be read at the eucharist tomorrow (58:9–14). Isaiah 58:1–12 was already used on Ash Wednesday in the office of readings. Verses 1–15 of this same chapter are suggested as a reading in the reformed Rite of Penance (chapter IV, no. 119); verses 6–11 are suggested as a reading for the common of saints (Lectionary 737, no. 15), and for civil needs (Lectionary 861, no. 3). The reading points out that individual ascetical practices must lead to practical help for others.

The obvious link between today's liturgy and that of Ash Wednesday is strengthened by the use of the same responsorial psalm, Psalm 51. The response is different, however, for today we pray: "A broken, humbled heart, O God, you will not scorn" (vs. 17). The purest sacrifice we can offer is a contrite *heart*. The psalmist rebukes external observance without inner conversion of one's heart to God.

Today's gospel reading replaces that of Matthew (5:43–48; 6:1–4) that appeared in the former Missal. The present Lectionary assigns a text, Matthew 9:14–15, that is in line with the Isaian reading on fasting. Again, Jesus is asked why his followers do not fast while the disciples of John the Baptist and the members of the Pharisee party do fast. Jesus responds that fasting is for the time when he is "taken away." As we await the day when Christ will come again in glory, we remain vigilant for his return by fasting and works of charity. The two scripture readings taken together establish the importance during Lent of fasting (gospel) and instruct us about the kind of fasting that is acceptable to the Lord (Isaiah).

The prayer over the gifts is traditional in the Lenten liturgical tradition. The Latin speaks about our offering the sacrifice of our Lenten observance, a notion that can be seen as refering both to the works of penance undertaken and to the liturgy of the eucharist being celebrated. Understood in this way, the prayer recapitulates the spirit of the Isaiah text. The petition that "we grow in your love and service" indicates once again the importance of our daily efforts to live the gospel outside the eucharistic assembly.

Today's communion antiphon reiterates that it is the Lord's ways and paths that are to be relearned and followed in Lent. The prayer after communion sees the eucharistic mystery as a sacrament that forgives sins. This is especially encouraging in the light of the acknowledgment of sin in today's responsorial psalm.

Celebration of the Eucharist

Because of the strength and force of the first reading today, it would be helpful to use the penitential rite as a way of introducing it.

After greeting the community, the presider (or other minister) could make a brief comment about the wider vision of liturgy and sacraments that includes our relations with each other and with life lived outside liturgical assemblies. Then a period of silence could be followed by the common recitation of the Confiteor (with the important words: "in what I have done and in what I have failed to do").

A sung "Lord have mercy" would lead to the opening prayer with its mention of "love and sincerity." A well prepared proclamation of the Isaiah text will help to emphasize its power and challenge. Singing the psalm response (the familiar Psalm 51) would be another way of emphasizing the first scripture reading today.

The prayer of the faithful might well include petitions for justice in the world, for the alleviation of hunger, for those oppressed and their oppressors, and for purity of intention as we continue the discipline of Lent.

While the fourth Lenten preface is entitled "the reward of fasting," thus making it an obvious choice for a Lenten Friday, the use of the third preface, with the phrase "we are to show to those in need your goodness to ourselves," might well be the better choice to underscore in a subtle way what the liturgy is concerned with today. The Lord's Prayer could be introduced suitably by the third optional introduction about forgiving those who sin against us, a most demanding principle for Christian living.

Liturgy of the Hours

The reading of the book of Exodus continues in the office of readings with the account of the birth and flight of Moses (2:1–22). God's wondrous plan for Israel, where good comes out of questionable and even sinful situations, is alluded to in this passage. A mother who hides her newborn son from the law that would take his life and the miraculous events that continue to protect him reiterate God's loving kindness for his chosen ones.

The patristic text from John Chrysostom is striking because it focuses on the relationship between prayer and the external works of mercy and fasting, which are stressed in the prayers and readings at today's eucharist. Chrysostom's emphasis on prayer gives a unity and wholeness to his vision of the Christian life. It is not a question of either/or for works and prayer. It is a question of balance, harmony, and integration. Both prayer and works are done in the presence of God; both require asceticism and commitment.

Friday as a special day emphasizing forgiveness of sin and the passion of Christ is reflected in the present structure of the four-week psalter used in the hours. At morning prayer on each of the Fridays, the first psalm is Psalm 51. While this is true for ordinary time as well as Lent, the psalm's presence on this first Lenten Friday should not go unnoticed.

The short reading from Isaiah (53:11b–12) on this and succeeding Fridays in Lent (to the fifth week), as well as the first reading on Good Friday (Is 52:13–53:12), refers to the suffering servant who is predictive of Christ and his sacrifice.

The cross is mentioned repeatedly in the intercessions at morning prayer, a usage that should be borne in mind even if these particular prayers are altered and others substituted. The cross as "the tree of life" and as the place where Christ was "lifted high . . . and pierced by the soldier's lance" is a symbol of Christ's death as a victory over sin and resurrection to a new life.

At evening prayer, the reading from James (5:16,19–20) reiterates the communal aspect of Lent in that it exhorts us to pray for each other and to work for each other's salvation.

The intercessions at evening prayer are introduced by the classical liturgical reference to our experience of the paschal mystery: "by dying [Christ] destroyed death and by rising again restored life." This same thought recurs in the second memorial acclamation at the eucharist and in the first preface for Easter. It is appropriate that this early in Lent we are reminded that the whole paschal mystery brings us to life and union with God as we, like him, freely accept the Father's will.

Celebration of the Hours

The second invitatory to the hours today, "Today if you hear the voice of the Lord, harden not your hearts," should be emphasized because it expresses very well the meaning of the season of Lent and epitomizes the review of salvation history in the psalmody used at the office of readings, Psalm 78:1–39. Since few communities sing the whole psalmody for this hour, a sung invitatory with Psalm 95 might be one way of reflecting the events of salvation history recounted in Psalm 78 itself.

Singing Psalm 51 at morning prayer today would help emphasize its place as an important part of Friday in Lent; this same setting (perhaps already used on Ash Wednesday) can also be used at the eucharist today as the responsorial psalm.

At evening prayer, the psalmody emphasizes praise for God's majesty and his continual care for "all who love him" (Psalm 145). This note of praise and confident trust in God might well be reflected in the tones used for singing these texts at evening prayer. The fact that the Friday liturgy emphasizes the passion obviously does not preclude mention of these more positive and hopeful images of the mystery of God. This same balance should be reflected in the invocations at morning prayer and the intercessions at evening that refer to the passion and death of Jesus as that by which we have been freed from sin and raised to life with God.

Reflection—"The Fasting God Wants"

Religious practices always are in need of purification and direction. Today's case in point is fasting. We are told that the kind of fasting God wants is not measured in amounts of food and drink. The kind of fasting God wants results in sharing our bread with the hungry. Depriving ourselves so that others may eat makes individual fasting a good work. But the liturgy goes even more deeply by requiring us to see that concern for others must go beyond their physical needs. To help unburden the oppressed and take up their cause is the challenge faced by God's people today.

This fundamentally communal dimension of religion brings us to the bedrock of biblical religion—that God called a people to himself from "age to age" and that in our observance of Lent what matters is not so much "my penances" and "my prayer" as those penances and prayer forms that will reconcile us with each other and unite all peoples under the lordship of Christ. This is what requires real asceticism and real virtue. The asceticism of fasting means that we give up insisting on our way and our opinions when others (such as the elderly and the young) need to be heard, understood, and loved. The asceticism of fasting means that we deprive ourselves of unnecessary food and drink so that others may share the goods of God's creation. The asceticism of fasting means that we surrender to God all the hurts we have endured and forgive those who have harmed us and caused us pain. The asceticism of fasting means that we will not overindulge and thereby dull our senses and not allow the Lord alone to nourish and sustain us with his presence and love. The asceticism of fasting means that we keep informed about the sources of oppression in our society and our world and seek to alleviate them.

Especially in a world like ours that features gourmet meals and nouvelle cuisine, the countercultural asceticism of fasting should mark the Christian as one who sees beyond this present life and all its good gifts to the life to come and to the source of all that is good and holy. Our fasting should mark us as a people who know that we live in an imperfect world and that we look for the Lord to come again. And when he returns in glory, all manner of estrangement and oppression will finally end for we shall all be invited to the marriage feast of the Lamb in the kingdom. Until that day, however, Christians are to accept the asceticism of fasting in its full dimensions. The kind of fasting that God wants requires that we draw a bold line between pharisaical practices and virtuous deeds. The kind of fasting that God wants should be communal in its expression and divine in its inspiration and fulfillment.

SATURDAY AFTER ASH WEDNESDAY

Liturgical Context

Today's eucharistic liturgy completes the overture to Lent that began on Ash Wednesday. These days the readings and prayers have been concerned with the appropriate ways of observing Lent. What is required is not the mere observance of Lent through customary religious practices, but perseverance in deepening the Christian life during Lent (Thursday). This requires more than superficial compliance with the counsel to fast during Lent (Friday) and an ever deepening conversion in response to the Lord's invitation (Saturday).

Today's liturgy continues to probe into the depth of commitment we have made to the discipline of Lent and to our growing identification with Christ. But uppermost in the liturgy today is the foundation on which all conversion and religious practice is based—the initiative of God. Just as Clement of Rome reminded us of God's overarching love in the text from the office of readings on Ash Wednesday, so too today's gospel and some of the prayers at the eucharist emphasize God's constant call and our response to him.

The continuation of yesterday's first reading from Isaiah takes a more encouraging and positive tone. If we observe the Lord's commands and live according to his word, then we shall experience the fullness of salvation when he comes again. The eschatological hope and vision of the prophet encourage us to deeper conversion knowing that the Lord who has done this great work in us will himself bring it to completion (Phil 1:6).

Liturgy of the Eucharist

The encouraging and positive tone in today's liturgy begins with the entrance antiphon as it addresses the Lord on whose "loving kindness" and "great mercy" we can rely (Psalm 69:17). In the opening prayer, we acknowledge our weakness before God and affirm our trust in his protection and love.

The first reading from Isaiah 58 (vss. 9–14) continues yesterday's text. In it the author offers hope and comfort, provided "you remove from your midst oppression . . . [and] you bestow your bread on the hungry." The test of the true believer, the true follower, is to submit to the Lord "by not following your ways, seeking your own interests" (vs. 13). That the ways of the Lord lead to salvation and blessedness is reiterated in the responsorial psalm (Psalm 86) with the refrain, "Teach me your way, O Lord, that I may be faithful in your sight." God's initiative is stressed for he is acclaimed as "good and forgiving, abounding in kindness to all who call upon you" (vs. 5). The first verse of the psalm, however, offers something of a paradox when compared with yesterday's first reading about sharing with the hungry and oppressed. Yesterday we were challenged to share our goods with those less fortunate. Today's psalm reminds us that even though we have goods to share, before God we are all in need and are all poor. By acknowledging that we own nothing, for all we have is God's, we come before the Lord humbly and honestly to ask for his love and mercy. We come before him in Lent, in true poverty, so that he can once again fill us with the richness of his life, mercy, and peace.

While today's first reading is the traditional text for this day, the gospel (Lk 5:27–32) in the new Lectionary has been selected to reflect the message of the prophet. The wideness of God's mercy demands a real response by one who chooses to follow him. There is a cost, a continuing cost to discipleship. Jesus is pictured at the beginning of the gospel text as calling Levi (himself a "tax collector" and hence an outcast) to follow him. Luke states simply but poignantly that he became a follower by "leaving everything behind" (vs. 28). Once again the psalmist's assertion is reechoed here: Levi had to become poor in order to follow Jesus. Today's gospel reading may be brief, but in these few verses we have a powerful statement of the expansiveness of God's love and the way in which we should respond to the Lord's invitation. We must be poor before God, but our reward is fullness of life, mercy, and peace in him.

That we who celebrate the eucharist stand in need of forgiveness is noted in the prayer over the gifts, a customary place for such petitions in the church's liturgical tradition. The wide expanse of God's mercy is reiterated in the communion antiphon, which is taken from Matthew 9:13 and reflects today's Lukan gospel. This text also points out how the Lord looks on offering sacrifice without showing mercy for others: "It is mercy that I want, and not sacrifice, says the Lord; I did not come to call the virtuous, but sinners" (Mt 9:13). The prayer after communion, which speaks about the present eucharist and about the eternal life we will one day share in heaven, also strikes a traditional note for this type of prayer. The term of all Lent and all eucharist is the eschatological banquet in heaven.

Celebration of the Eucharist

Since the celebration of tomorrow's eucharist will be characteristically more solemn, it would be pastorally suitable to keep today's celebration simple. The penitential rite could be the third form (C), with its first set of sample invocations about Jesus healing the contrite and calling sinners coinciding well with one of the dominant motifs in today's scripture readings.

The gospel could be introduced by using the fifth of the verses before the gospel: "I do not wish the sinner to die. . ." (Lectionary, 224). The intercessions today should include the needs of those who are on the margins of the church, those involved in evangelization programs, and for all the faithful that their Lenten penances may be done with proper motivation and thus be pleasing in the Lord's sight.

The fourth Lenten preface would be a good choice for proclamation today because it speaks of the process of conversion, "you help us grow in holiness," and the end of all human life, "the reward of everlasting life." The second eucharistic prayer, since it is the briefest, would be a good choice today.

Liturgy of the Hours

The first reading for the office of readings today (Ex 3:1–20) tells about the call of Moses and the revelation of the name of the Lord. (Another account of Moses' call, Ex 6:2–13, will be read on Monday.) In this passage from Exodus, God reveals himself as the God of Abraham, Isaac, and Jacob (vs. 6), whose descendants he will save from the oppression they are enduring. He will do this through Moses. Despite the distance between God and his creatures, he promises to be with his people and sustain them.

In the text from Irenaeus, the author speaks about the reward given to those who follow and serve the Lord—"life and immortality and eternal glory." In this reading, Irenaeus strikes a keynote of our Lenten observances: "to *persevere* and *remain* in the service of God." Lent comes once a year, but our service of God is for all the days of our life. And we are to render this service not as slaves but as friends of God.

The brief passage from Isaiah (1:16–18) read at morning prayer is reminiscent of Isaiah 58:1–12, read on Ash Wednesday, about setting free the oppressed, the wronged, the orphan, the widow. By "setting [such] things right," God will forgive our sins:

"Though your sins be like scarlet,
   they may become white as snow;
Though they be crimson red,
   they may become white as wool" (vs. 18).

It is the common practice in the seasonal liturgy of the hours to base the antiphons to the canticles of Zechariah and Mary (morning and evening prayer) on the scripture readings of the day's eucharist. Today, however, the antiphon to Zechariah's canticle is taken from Matthew 6:20: "Store up for yourselves treasures in heaven where neither rust nor moth can destroy." This admonition reflects much of what the season of Lent is all about.

Celebration of the Hours

The same pastoral principle that would call for a simple celebration of the eucharist would also call for a simple celebration of the hours in comparison with the solemnity of tomorrow's Sunday liturgy. The psalmody for the office of readings is the continuation of yesterday's Psalm 78:1–39. Today's verses are 40–72. This review of salvation history keeps us in mind of the Lord's plan to deliver his people from oppression, as recounted in today's reading from Exodus. Even the antiphons speak about God's revelation to Israel as savior. Since other psalm-prayers may be substituted for those given in the text of the liturgy of the hours, the presider might consider adapting today's prayers to acknowledge the revelation of God and his relationship to his people throughout history even to the present liturgical assembly.

For morning prayer, a sung Benedictus would be appropriate as a way of underscoring God's continual offer of salvation and his sustaining presence among his people. So many of the phrases in this gospel canticle reflect the scriptural texts proclaimed in today's liturgy.

Reflection—"The Cost of Conversion"

For us the summons to convert to the Lord comes in Lent. But the conversion never seems to be completed even when Easter comes and we affirm the promises of our baptism. That is why this

Lent (every Lent) is important as a time to deepen our response to the Lord. Lent gives us the chance to give up what we have kept for ourselves. What are this year's things, people, habits, and prejudices of which we have to divest ourselves in order to be more fully converted to the Lord? Do we hold onto things in order to surround ourselves with material possessions because we sense a growing insecurity? The only real security for the believer is to submit to God, and when that is done nothing else really matters. Do we manipulate people to get our own way? What relationships must we detach ourselves from? What are the habits and patterns of behavior that we have grown so accustomed to that perhaps we don't even recognize them as faults that need God's healing and amazing grace? What are the prejudices against people, races, or creeds that we have rationalized so much that prejudicial remarks are part of our normal vocabulary? Do we oppress rather than free others?

Yes, conversion is an ever deepening process that requires care and attention this Lent. We may not be rid of all these inclinations to sin on Easter, but if we have lived this Lent well, we may be further on the way than we were on Ash Wednesday.

May we who celebrate sacred mysteries in Lent pray for the courage to eliminate some of the contradictions in our lives here and now. To do that we need the strength and sustaining presence of the Lord whom we worship and adore. This is the same God who is so committed to us that he is revealed as the God of relationship. This is the same Lord who not only teaches us his ways but sustains us in them through this earthly life. "Answer us, Lord, with your loving kindness, turn to us in your great mercy" (Ps 69:17, entrance antiphon, liturgy of the eucharist).

Chapter Two

First Week of Lent

Liturgical Context

An historical review of the structure of the season of Lent shows that there have been various ways of numbering the days of the season starting either with the first Sunday or with Ash Wednesday. While the custom of beginning Lent with Ash Wednesday dominates our thinking and approach to the season, the fact that the First Sunday has had a special place in inaugurating the season should be recalled today. The restored catechumenate advises that the rite of "election" or "enrollment" of the names of those to be initiated at the Easter Vigil takes place today. The General Instruction, Rite of Christian Initiation of Adults, states:

"The sacraments of initiation are celebrated during the Easter solemnities and preparation for them is part of the distinctive character of Lent. Accordingly, the rite of election should normally take place on the First Sunday of Lent. The time for the final preparation of the *competentes* should coincide with the Lenten season. The celebration of Lent will benefit the elect by reason of its liturgical structure and the participation of the community" (no. 139).

"At the beginning of the Lenten season, during which the final preparation for sacramental initiation takes place, the 'election' or 'enrollment of names' is celebrated" (no. 133).

Liturgical tradition demonstrates the intimate involvement of the bishop in the catechumenate and the rite of initiation. It is he who did much of the public formal instruction during Lent and who celebrated the election and the scrutinies. Even when the catechumenate fell into disuse, the notation in the Roman Missal for the stational liturgy for both the First Sunday of Lent and for the Easter Vigil was St. John Lateran, the pope's "cathedral" and the church made famous by its impressive baptistery. The example of the bishop of Rome involved in initiation was thus not forgotten even when the intrinsic and obvious connection between Lent and initiation was lost.

What is important to understand about adult initiation and the election liturgy this Sunday is that the catechumenate is a communal process of conversion in which both those to be initiated and those already initiated commit themselves to the Lord at this first public liturgy leading to sacramental initiation. To understand that baptism is most appropriately celebrated at Easter is to understand that Lent includes the process by which candidates, sponsors, clergy, and the local church deepen their commitment to each other in Christ and affirm their faith in him at Easter.

The logic and sense of the catechumenate are highlighted by today's rite of election, the scrutinies on the third, fourth, and fifth Sunday of Lent, all culminating in the Easter celebration. It is these liturgies involving the whole community that make initiation a central focus in Lent. It is the works of Lenten discipline and asceticism that expand and develop what is implied in the liturgy— that conversion is a process begun in the catechumenate, ratified and accomplished in sacramental initiation, but which continues throughout the lives of all the baptized. As the proposed introduction to the prayer for the elect states:

"My brothers and sisters, in beginning this period of Lent, we look forward to celebrating at Easter the life-giving mysteries of our Lord's suffering, death, and resurrection. These elect, whom we bring with us to the Easter sacraments, will look to us for an example of Christian renewal. Let us pray to the Lord for them and for ourselves, that we may be renewed by one another's efforts and together come to share the joys of Easter" (no. 148).

The temptation of Jesus in the desert is the theme of the gospel readings in all three cycles of the Lectionary. What better text to use to demonstrate to catechumens the price of professing the faith? What better text for the baptized to hear each year as they renew their baptismal commitment? The church gathers this day to begin again the process of making acts of faith and trust in the Lord. God's own Son was tempted, leaving us a model and an example of how we are to engage in this annual struggle of forty days.

Unlike the texts for Ash Wednesday about fasting, prayer, and almsgiving (the time-honored means of disciplining ourselves during Lent), the scriptures proclaimed today speak of the reality of evil, temptation, and sin in our world and in our lives. The real conflicts in Lent involve the temptations to think too highly of ourselves, to worship gods of our own making, and to mistrust the saving presence of God with us. The temptation gospels proclaimed today encourage us to apply these texts to ourselves and admit to ourselves that these temptations can only be overcome by the grace and mercy of God and through the prayer and fasting of this holy season.

Even at Masses where no rite of election takes place this Sunday, the texts chosen from the Sacramentary and Lectionary should reflect this Sunday's relationship with Christian initiation. This First Sunday in Lent offers more time and opportunities than Ash Wednesday for the parish community to truly "begin" Lent together. The planning and celebration of this day should stress it as a true beginning to Lent.

The Introduction to the Lectionary explains the selection of the first two texts for today and for the rest of the season:

"The Old Testament readings are about the history of salvation, which is one of the themes proper to the catechesis of Lent. The series of texts for each year presents the main elements of salvation history from its beginning until the promise of the New Covenant.

"The readings from the letters of the apostles have been selected to fit the gospel and the Old Testament readings and, to the extent possible, to provide a connection between them" (no. 97).

Therefore, in interpreting the full meaning of the proclamation of the word today, one should pay close attention to the different stylistic traits of each evangelist as well as the light shed on each gospel account by the first two readings and the responsorial psalm. This method is followed in the commentaries in this book.

Cycle "A"

The first reading from Genesis (2:7–9; 3:1–7) places us at the primordial event of the Fall. In mythical language and imagery, the author presents us with the temptation of Adam and Eve to become like God and to know as God knows. The setting is Eden, the characters are those created by God himself, and the temptation involves overstepping the appropriate relationship between creator and creature. The result of the sin was a fall, a definitive breach between God and his creatures, here told in striking literary style. But the result was tragic, for from this point onward all human life would be affected by this primal separation from God.

While the tale is mythical and the language somewhat hyperbolic, the truth told in Genesis is perennially valid and reaches to the depths of every human heart. We are separated from God, and we can only rely on his act of redemption in Christ to bridge that gap. One day we hope and pray that the intimacy lost in the garden and experienced as lost in our lives will be completely bridged when we join the saints victorious in the kingdom forever.

The tree of the garden now and forever remains a symbol of defeat. The tree of the cross on which Christ died becomes a symbol of hope, especially in Lent.

That the liturgy is concerned to have us apply the myth of Genesis to ourselves is demonstrated in the responsorial psalm, the familiar text of Psalm 51. The response is the same as that used on Ash Wednesday and begs God's mercy, for like Adam and Eve "we have sinned."

The second reading is a link between the Old and New Testaments because the Adam/Christ typology so carefully developed by Paul in Romans (5:12–19) is proclaimed today.

Just as we share corporately in the sin of our first parents, so this text affirms that we share corporately in the forgiveness of Christ. Our relationship with both Adam and Christ is clear from our Christian experience. From Adam comes separation, loss, banishment, and condemnation. From Christ (the second Adam) comes intimacy, gain, invitation, and acquittal. The theological refinement and precision of Paul should be noted as a way of exploring what Lent means and how best to interpret what the glory of Easter is all about. These readings proclaimed in the liturgy remind us of how we identify with both Adam and Christ and how we ought to be strengthened and encouraged knowing that Christ has triumphed over the sin we inherit from Adam.

The gospel proclaimed today is the traditional text for this Sunday in the Roman liturgy, and it is suitably introduced by the verse taken from the Matthean text on living not on bread alone but on every word that comes from the mouth of God. That the liturgy wants to emphasize the importance of God's word is seen in the fact that this same verse before the gospel is used in all three cycles of this Sunday's liturgy.

The setting of Christ's temptations is familiar—the desert. Throughout the scriptures the desert wastelands are the place where the chosen ones of God meet trial and are tempted. Christ sums up and personifies these temptations of his people and remains there for forty days and nights, reminiscent of the forty years of Israel's trials in the desert. His fasting makes him hungry (as does ours in Lent) and he is ripe for the devil's lure. Jesus is tempted to misuse his miraculous power to change stones into bread, but he rebukes Satan by stating that we live on the word of God, not just on loaves of what we have come to call the "staff of life." The second temptation is set at the temple because it is a temptation to misuse the texts of scriptures, which are essential elements of worship. Jesus rebukes the tempter once more by quoting another passage (Ps 91) back to him. The proper view of religion is at stake here and Jesus strenuously rebukes any misuse or caricature of it. The final temptation, like the other two, is to power, and again Jesus rebukes Satan by admonishing him to worship and adore the Lord alone. The revealed God of the scriptures is the only God to be honored and revered.

The recounting of Jesus's temptations at the start of Lent offers a fitting introduction to the holy season for the faithful and for those to be initiated. Inclinations to evil in the form of prizing earthly nourishment above heavenly food, or misusing religion for our own purposes, or being tempted to positions of power and prestige are often the common experience of humans, including believers. Today's gospel presents us with a model according to which we can evaluate whether we yield to these or other temptations. Lent is a time to ponder the word of God rather than to overindulge in food and drink. Lent is a time for honest, humble worship before God alone and not before the gods of money, success, power, or influence.

This first set of Sunday Lenten readings point out some of the problems we experience and some of the temptations we endure as we make our way to God. But they are given a hopeful cast in the reading from Romans. If we know well our inclination to be like Adam, the liturgy offers us the opportunity to recall that in Christ we have been redeemed from sin and are strengthened in our struggle against evil. It is this same Jesus Christ who feeds us with the word and the bread of life in the Sunday eucharist to sustain us on our Lenten journey.

Cycle "B"

Where the "A" cycle of readings takes us to the garden of Eden to set the stage for the temptation of Adam and Eve, the readings in this "B" cycle begin by reminding us of God's covenant with Noah. Again the language is hyperbolic and the story is mythical, but what is essential here is the covenant bond between Noah, his descendants, and God. The flood waters that destroyed evil are the same waters that bring cleansing and purification. God's initiative in the Noah story is to save those who have responded to his invitation and to offer salvation to all who would heed his law.

The use of the Noah story here at the beginning of Lent reflects the patristic interpretation of this story as a type and prefigurement of baptism. Hence it is a fitting first reading for a day on which the rite of election takes place.

The responsorial psalm takes up the covenant notion of the first reading and reminds us of our responsibility even in a loving, covenant relationship with God. While this covenant is not a pact relationship between equals, it is a relationship that requires a commitment on both sides. Because of the overwhelming and limit-less love of God for us, we are now enabled to keep our part of the covenant. We pray that the Lord will make his ways known to us. In Lent we commit ourselves to respond to God's love through the help of his grace.

The baptism motif is developed in the text from 1 Peter (3:18–22). The life we live through baptism derives from Christ's work of redemption. The pledge and promise of a gifted, covenant relation-ship with God in Israel is offered to us and sealed in the sacramen-tal bath of baptism. The salvation of Noah and his family (symbol-ized by the ark) from the destroying waters of the flood is fully realized by Christ and offered to us through the saving waters of baptism.

Unlike the accounts of the temptation of Jesus in Matthew and Luke, the evangelist Mark (1:12–15) stresses the fact of Jesus being tempted rather than the specific kinds of temptations. Mark mentions that Jesus was in the "desert," a "wasteland" considered a place where evil spirits dwelled. The "wild beasts" in this passage can be interpreted as the powers of evil that Jesus fights against or exemplars of the new era of peace foretold by Isaiah. "The calf and the young lion shall browse together with a little child to guide them" (Is 11:6,c,d). The angels minister to Jesus as he struggles with the tempter. The stories of Genesis and Exodus are capsulized in this short passage—Jesus restores the kingdom of peace and establishes his reign by triumphing over the temptation of the Evil One.

Another significant fact is that Mark mentions twice the "good news" (the *gospel*) that Jesus came to preach and personify. This emphasis on the good news is a typical Markan touch, for, unlike the other gospels, the first verse of his gospel states clearly: "here begins the gospel of Jesus Christ" (1:1) and at the conclusion Jesus commands his followers: "Go into the whole world and proclaim the good news to all creation" (16:15).

The liturgy of Lent stresses the invitation of Jesus to "reform . . . and believe the good news" (the second formula for the imposition of ashes on Ash Wednesday), and repeats the message in today's gospel reading.

That we are to emphasize gospel living throughout this season is seen in today's verse before the gospel: "Man does not live on bread alone, but on every word that comes from the mouth of God."

The rite of election today captures the challenge, responsibility, and meaning of Lent: that those to be initiated, and the community already initiated, might spend this season in solidarity with Jesus by accepting this time in the desert of self-denial as an opportunity for more faithful hearing and obeying the good news he came to preach.

Cycle "C"

The first reading from Deuteronomy (26:4–10) is a summary of Israel's belief in the favors God granted to their ancestors and to every generation of the chosen people. By his "strong hand and outstretched arm" as well as "by signs and wonders," God led them to the land of promise. Before meeting God they were a marginal people. After being elected they are a nation with a promise, an identity, and a destiny. This text is crucial for understanding the heritage that Israel bore and bears still; it is crucial for our self-understanding as a people whose identity is rooted in Jesus who fulfilled the promise.

Today's responsorial psalm (Psalm 91) acts as a prelude to the gospel reading, in which Jesus conquers the temptation to power and ostentation and thus is not only our model for resisting evil, but helps us to share in his victory.

The second reading from the letter to the Romans (10:8–13) reminds us of the presence of God to us through his word (the Son) and that our salvation comes from both inward faith and outward acknowledgment and proclamation. What is required for salvation is not just a passive faith in Jesus, but an active personal faith leading to salvation. Anyone, not just Israel (the former people of election), can and will be saved if they acknowledge and call on the Lord's name, his very being.

The "confession" aspect of two of today's readings is evident first from the text of Deuteronomy, which is a confession formula (that is, a summary of belief, not an admission of sins) about Israel as chosen of God. The text from Paul states that we must openly express our faith in Christ who brings us to salvation.

The Lukan author gives his own coloration to the account of the temptations of Jesus (4:1–13) by changing the order of temptations found in Matthew. The arrangement enables him to dramatize Jerusalem by making it the focus of the last temptation. Luke stresses "Jerusalem" because it is the place where Jesus goes to die and rise again. In Acts, Luke also shows that the faith is spread to the ends of the earth (from Jerusalem). It is from this holy city that Jesus' triumph over sin and evil will reach out to all generations.

The statement, "not on bread alone shall man live," is from Deuteronomy 8:3. For the Lukan author, these words on Jesus' lips show that he relies on his Father for all he needs. If Jesus is to experience physical hunger, it is so he can grow in reliance on his Father's provident care. Jesus is revealer and suffering servant. We who hear and heed his words must realize that we too have to rely on his Father's provident care for us in the midst of sorrow and temptation.

Jesus' triumph over the devil shows us that where Jesus is at work through the Spirit the power of Satan cannot reign. By recommitting ourselves to God's care in Lent and confessing our faith in Jesus as the Lord of our lives, we preserve ourselves from the power of the devil. As the responsorial psalm assures us:

"No evil shall befall you,
    nor shall affliction come near your tent,
For to his angels he has given command about you,
    that they guard you in all your ways" (vs. 10–11).

Sacramentary Texts

The eucharist today begins on a note of quiet confidence from Psalm 91 (vss. 15–16) as the entrance antiphon. Parts of this psalm also appear in the responsorial psalm in cycle "C."

The opening prayer emphasizes the central theme of the celebration of Lenten liturgy, that we not merely understand or appreciate what happened in Christ's paschal mystery but also that we appropriate its full meaning by reflecting it in our own lives.

The alternative opening prayer reflects the text of Genesis 2 found in the "A" cycle of readings and hence would be an appropriate beginning to the liturgy when the "A" readings are proclaimed.

The prayer over the gifts is based on a traditional prayer from the Ash Wednesday liturgy. The Latin text asks that as we offer our sacrificial gifts at the beginning of Lent, we may practice restraint in the use of bodily food and refrain from harmful pleasures.

The Sacramentary provides a preface for each of the Sundays in Lent as well as four other seasonal texts. Today's preface is a modern composition that is based on traditional texts from the church's Lenten liturgy. It refers to Jesus' fast of forty days as proclaimed in today's gospel. It bids us share in Jesus' eucharistic paschal meal in purity of heart so that we may share in this eternal paschal meal in heaven.

The prayer after communion is newly composed and is based on the texts from Matthew 4:4 and John 6:51. The text joins the word of Jesus with the bread of the eucharist as signs of the life we will one day share fully with him in the kingdom.

Rite of Election

Like all sacramental rites reformed after Vatican II, this particular rite is designed to take place after the liturgy of the word and the homily. The rite involves the presentation of the candidates, the enrollment of names, the admission (or "election"), and finally a prayer for the elect and then their dismissal (see Rite of Christian Initiation of Adults, nos. 143–150). It is significant that the candidates are evaluated on how well they have "faithfully listened to God's word"; "how they have responded to that word" and shared the prayer of the Christian community. The gospel orientation of this examination invites both candidates and the whole community to self-scrutiny as this Lenten season begins.

In the enrollment of names and the election proper, the texts speak of "the Easter sacraments" and being initiated "into the sacred mysteries at the Easter Vigil." This reminds all present of the importance of the Lenten season.

After the intercessions, the celebrant extends his hand over the elect and says one of two prayers. The first, drawn from the Genesis story of creation, speaks of the new covenant that they wish to enter sacramentally. The second asks the Father to help them "to be built into the kingdom" of Christ and to prepare them "to be sealed with the promised Spirit."

This rite assures the candidates that their sponsors, the pastoral staff, and the whole community are praying for and with them that they may be ready to celebrate sacramental initiation at the Easter Vigil.

Celebration of the Eucharist

It would be helpful to set the environment for liturgy this Sunday simply by leaving the altar, lectern, and baptistery without unnecessary candles, flowers, and bright cloths. The Lectionary and Gospel Book may be covered with violet cloth (matching the vestments used throughout Lent). The use of pottery or wooden plates and chalices for communion rather than furnishings of precious metal can all speak of the penitential aspects of Lent.

Keeping the focus on hearing the word (lectern and books) and on the altar from which we receive the bread of life shows that we live "not on bread alone . . . [but] on every word that comes from the mouth of God."

Ample silence maintained after the introduction to the liturgy at the penitential rite, after each of the readings, and after communion is important to mark the sobriety of the Lenten liturgy.

Deciding on one form of the penitential rite and using it on all five Sundays (with a different comment to introduce the liturgy each week) would be helpful. It might be well not to sprinkle the congregation with holy water during Lent since it will be used at baptism during the Easter Vigil and at the renewal of baptismal promises on Easter Sunday. Thus, the use of water at Easter will be more appreciated.

A sung "Lord, have mercy" could emphasize the penitential rite, especially since a sung "Glory to God" could take its place throughout the Easter season.

Singing one responsorial refrain (with the psalm verses changing each week) with the same verse before the gospel on Sundays can also help unify these weeks. Similarly, one simple setting for the acclamations during the eucharistic prayer would help to promote an atmosphere of reflection.

Singing the Lord's Prayer in Lent and introducing it by comment about forgiveness may emphasize the communal sense of reconciliation in Lent.

Singing the Lamb of God to a setting that stresses the "have mercy on us" could be a special reminder of the mercy for which we pray during this season.

The solemn blessing for the passion of the Lord is reproduced in today's Mass text. Its use on all the Sundays of Lent would help unify the season.

Today's intercessions should include a petition for the elect at all Masses so that the whole community may pray for them.

This Sunday the profession of faith and the prayer of the faithful can be left out of the liturgy that includes the rite of election. Doing this would emphasize the importance of the rite itself. Where comments are made during the liturgy and where adaptations are made of the suggested texts of the rite of election, these should be kept very brief and should focus on the liturgical action rather than on catechetical instruction.

With regard to the hymns chosen during Lent, those responsible should be attentive to texts that incorporate the community into the mystery of Christ's death and resurrection as opposed to texts that objectify it. The hymns need not always stress our Lord's passion, for this will be emphasized later as the season comes to its climax in the paschal triduum.

Liturgy of the Hours

The antiphons for psalmody at Evening Prayer I for the First Sunday of Lent reiterate familiar Lenten themes: "humble and contrite hearts," "call upon the Lord and he will hear you," and "Christ died for our sins, the innocent for the guilty." They speak of the assurance of God's presence, the fullness of redemption in Christ (the Second Adam), and the conversion of our hearts to him.

The scripture reading consists of verses 1–4a of 2 Corinthians. The first section (ending with "Now is the day of salvation") forms the conclusion to the second reading at Mass on Ash Wednesday. This proclamation is reiterated this evening to remind us that Lent is the "acceptable time" and "the day of salvation."

The text of the antiphon to the Canticle of Mary echoes the verse before the gospel of today's eucharistic liturgy: "Man cannot live on bread alone but by every word that comes from the mouth of God."

The intercessions provided in the text underscore our need to imitate Jesus' concern for all peoples. Jesus is offered as model and example. Through the celebration of liturgy, we share now in the very being of him who has redeemed us and lives now to intercede for us with the Father.

The concluding prayer this evening is the opening prayer, or its alternative, of tomorrow's eucharist (as is usual in the liturgy of the hours for the seasons). In the present Roman Rite, evening prayer on Saturdays in Lent indicates something of the direction that the liturgy will take on Sunday while at the same time insisting on the priority of general Lenten themes and theology.

At the office of readings, the first reading is a continuation of the book of Exodus (5:1–61) about the oppression of the people and the Lord's command to Pharoah: "Let my people go, that they may celebrate a feast to me in the desert" (vs. 1). During Lent we commemorate and experience anew our freedom from the bondage of sin and offer to the Lord our sacrifice of liturgy and the discipline of this season.

In the second reading from St. Augustine's commentary on the psalms, the full impact of the temptation theme of today's liturgy emerges. Our identification with Christ is emphasized here: "If in Christ we have been tempted, in him we overcome the devil." The saint exhorts us: "See yourself as tempted in him, and see yourself as victorious in him." The Lord who was tempted and whose victory over Satan becomes final in his resurrection offers us hope in Lent.

The antiphons and the reading at morning prayer (Neh 8:9,10), about praising God and rejoicing in him, are fitting for Sunday, the day of the Lord, despite the context of the discipline of Lent. Sunday is always a day free from fasting because it is the day when we commemorate the Lord's rising to new life. However, there is ample reason to be prayerful, reflective, and watchful today for, as the antiphon to the Canticle of Zechariah reminds us, even Jesus was tempted (which text is taken from the introduction to Matthew's gospel read at today's eucharist).

The importance of baptismal themes in Lent is specified in the intercessions at morning prayer, a good introduction to the rite of election.

At Evening Prayer II, the first antiphon is taken from Jesus' rebuke to the tempter while the second speaks of the importance of this season and the third of Jesus' suffering. The scripture text used at evening prayer, not found elsewhere in the celebration of the liturgy today, is from the section of 1 Corinthians (9:24–25) about running so as to win not a perishable prize, but the imperishable crown of life in heaven.

The antiphon at the Canticle of Mary puts into a prayer form the message of today's gospel as applied to us: "Watch over us, eternal Savior; do not let the cunning tempter seize us. We place all our trust in your unfailing help." This theme about the unfailing help of the Lord is reechoed in the intercessions. The intercession referring to Jonah and the city of Nineveh is, as it were, a preview of the reading of Mass on Wednesday of the first week of Lent, which is from the book of Jonah.

Celebration of the Hours

The first invitatory verse, "Come, let us worship Christ the Lord, who for our sake endured temptation and suffering," coincides with today's gospel and should be used at the beginning of the hours. The use of Psalm 24 as the invitatory psalm would be a good choice.

The selection of an appropriate hymn for the hours of morning and evening prayer can help to emphasize what the liturgy celebrates today: the temptation of Jesus and our struggle against evil during Lent.

A period of silence after the psalms and psalm prayers can reflect the general Lenten themes of the hours today. As was noted for the eucharist, the Lord's Prayer might well be introduced by a comment about our relationship to each other and the importance of forgiveness and reconciliation in Lent; and then singing it.

Since today's scripture readings at morning and evening prayer are also assigned through the Fourth Sunday of Lent, other verses from 2 Corinthians 6 could be added to make a longer reading and emphasize Lent as a time to ponder and pray over God's word.

Another option would be to replace these texts with readings from other parts of this epistle or from other biblical sources. The theme of Sunday as a day of rejoicing even during Lent and our persevering to finish the race could be changed next Sunday in order to give variety to the Lenten celebration.

Reflection—"The Temptations of the Chosen"

Today the scriptures take us back both to the idyllic garden of Eden and to the desert wilderness where Christ himself was tempted by Satan. These texts remind us that what happened to Adam and Eve still happens to us—we are tempted to exaggerated self-importance and often we are tempted to think ourselves all-knowing and almighty. We choose to glorify self rather than to glorify God.

Satan tempted Jesus to glorify himself. Jesus resisted his tempter. Yet how often do we wind up following our own desires rather than following Christ? How often do we manipulate situations and people so that we are the center of attention and are glorified? It may well be that we need to spend some time in the "desert" today, at liturgy and in personal prayer, to see to what extent we succumb to self-glorification. Are we like Adam and Eve when it comes to honoring God or are we faithful like Christ to the Lord our God?

We do not begin Lent on a note of self-scrutiny only; we begin on a note of hope and encouragement because through Christ we share a destiny of reconciliation and the forgiveness of our sins. Because we share in the very life of God in Christ, we have the courage to discern in our lives what is truly fertile and green and what is parched and barren. Even for those who have been made new through Christ in baptism, the battle continues and will continue until that day when there will be no more deserts, no more temptations, and no more estrangement from God. But until that day we need this day, this first Lenten Sunday, to discover and acknowledge the temptations and sins in our lives that need the healing of Christ, the victor over Satan, of Christ who is indeed the Second Adam.

Lent offers both the catechumens and the baptized the opportunity to face up to the responsibilities that chosenness and election require. For the catechumens, it involves "purification and enlightenment." For the already baptized, it means purgation and struggle. Only Christ, the Chosen One of God, can transform the deserts of life into oases where everything is once again green and fertile. Here in the liturgy we experience his grace, his triumph, and his forgiveness.

"You who dwell in the shelter of the Most High,
    who abide in the shadow of the Almighty,
Say to the Lord, 'My refuge and my fortress,
    my God in whom I trust.'
No evil shall befall you,
    nor shall affliction come near your tent,
For to his angels he has given command about you,
    that they guard you in all your ways" (Ps 91:1–2,10–11).

MONDAY OF THE FIRST WEEK OF LENT

Liturgical Context

With the beginning of Lent well established last week by the special celebrations of Ash Wednesday and the First Sunday and the regular rhythm established for weekdays from Thursday to

Saturday, we begin a new phase of the season today. The liturgy turns from specific acts of penance (fasting, almsgiving, and prayer) emphasized last week to a deeper and much more demanding level this week—reconciliation with one another. The means used to accomplish such reconciliation are works of penance but the reason for performing them is not only to strengthen ourselves in the fight against sin, but so that we may be reconciled with others through Christ. That our Lenten journey necessarily involves other people is repeatedly stressed this week. The celebration of the rite of election yesterday and the process of the catechumens entering their final phase of "purification and enlightenment" remind all believers that reconciliation with God and neighbor is a necessary part of our Lenten discipline.

In the Lectionary texts for the eucharist this week, all the gospel readings (except Wednesday's) are taken from Matthew. Recalling that the name Matthew is from the Greek word for "follower" may help us to look at these readings as a short course on the part reconciliation must play in the lives of Christ's followers.

For catechumens, sponsors, and the whole community these Lenten weekdays form an essential part of this annual liturgical retreat. The moral life demanded of Christians is more demanding and challenging than even that prescribed in the old covenant. The readings this week build to the demanding text from Matthew on Saturday:

"If you love those who love you, what merit is there in that? Do not tax collectors do as much? And if you greet your brothers only, what is so praiseworthy about that? Do not pagans do as much? In a word, you must be made perfect as your heavenly Father is perfect" (Mt 5:46–48).

Liturgy of the Eucharist

The eucharist begins today with an entrance antiphon that has been frequently used in the tradition on this day—we pray with our eyes "fixed on the Lord our God, pleading for his mercy" (Ps 123:2). In Lent this prayer has a special significance as we become more and more aware of our need for redemption. But it is a confident plea for we know our Lord to be merciful and filled with compassion.

The Latin text of the opening prayer today speaks directly about the work of conversion. The conversion asked for (translated as "bring us back to you") requires a turning away from what causes us to sin and a return to God. God is the source of this conversion, as he enriches us by the works we do in Lent ("our observance of Lent").

The first scripture reading from Leviticus (19:1–2,11–18) reports the revelation of the law to Moses for the newly chosen people of Israel. The Lord's commands conclude with the strong admonition: "love your neighbor as yourself" (vs. 18). Moses received the law from the Lord. Moses then told the community all that the Lord had commanded. And the community, in cultic gatherings, would speak these words again and again in order to remind themselves of their identity as a special and chosen race and their consequent responsibility to show by their actions their relationship to God. This same dynamic is at work in liturgical gatherings. We hear the revealed word of the Lord again and again, ponder it, preach it, and pray over it so that it continues to be the mainstay of our lives.

Today's responsorial psalm (Psalm 19) reflects these themes for it speaks of "the law of the Lord," "the precepts of the Lord."

The gospel today (Mt 25:31–46) is the text traditionally assigned to the Monday after the First Sunday of Lent; it also appears in the revised Lectionary on the last Sunday of the year in the "A" cycle, and as an optional reading in the revised Rite of Penance (no. 185). In this apocalyptic section, Matthew says that just as a shepherd separates the "sheep" from the "goats" (25:32), so the kingly Christ will separate the good from the bad. Church members are thus reminded of the judgment that will occur at the end of time when the criterion for being welcomed into the kingdom will be how they treated Christ's least brothers and sisters. Matthew here uses customary biblical locations to express the final situation of the unrepentant (on the king's left hand) and those admitted to the kingdom (on the king's right hand). The Matthean text speaks of God's judgment and, by extention, of the necessity of living a truly Christian life. Religious practices alone are not sufficient. What is essential is to care for our needy brothers and sisters. Christian love for others is the ultimate criterion for the Christian life.

The prayer over the gifts at today's eucharist is well attested in liturgical tradition for this day. The petition that the liturgy "transform our lives" recognizes that the eucharist is the source of the Lord's mercy, which we are to share with others in fulfillment of the gospel's demand.

The communion antiphon, based on verses 40 and 34 of today's gospel, reinforces Jesus' promise of eternal life for those who care for the poor and suffering.

The prayer after communion reminds us that the eucharistic liturgy gives us a unique share in Christ's "saving love."

Celebration of the Eucharist

Since the liturgy offers such challenging texts, it might be well to begin the liturgy with the first of the penitential rites, the Confiteor, which stresses "that I have sinned through my own fault . . . in what I have done and in what I have failed to do."

The gospel today could be introduced by using number 9 of the verses before the gospel: "Repent, says the Lord, the kingdom of heaven is at hand."

The intercessions today could pray for the catechumens elected yesterday and for their sponsors. Petitions could also be made for the success of community programs that help the needy.

The preface for Lent III, which speaks about our responsibility "to show to those in need your [God's] goodness to ourselves," would be appropriate.

The third eucharistic prayer would be suitable today in view of the following eschatological references:

"Father, calling to mind the death your Son endured for our
    salvation,
his glorious resurrection and ascension into heaven,
and ready to greet him when he comes again,
we offer you in thanksgiving this holy and living sacrifice.
Welcome into your kingdom our departed brothers and sisters, and
    all who have left this world in your friendship.
We hope to enjoy for ever the vision of your glory,
through Christ our Lord, from whom all good things come."

The fourth sample invitation to the Lord's Prayer ("Let us pray for the coming of the kingdom as Jesus taught us") would fit well with the gospel as would the third of the dismissal formulas ("Go in peace to love and serve the Lord").

Liturgy of the Hours

The verse between the psalmody and readings in the office of readings today reminds us of the liturgy of Ash Wednesday. The first part of "Turn away from sin and be faithful to the gospel" (Mk 1:15) is also optional for use at the imposition of ashes. (The second part of the antiphon, "The kingdom of God is at hand," is the first part of verse 15 in the gospel text.) This indirect link between Ash Wednesday and today's liturgy reminds us that even at this early stage of the season, the urgency of Jesus' call to reform ought not be forgotten.

The first reading in the office of readings, Exodus 6:2–13, from the priestly tradition, parallels that of Saturday for both deal with the call of Moses. Today's text stresses the election of Israel: "I will take you as my own people, and you shall have me as your God" (vs. 7). The election of Israel is reflected in the responsory, an adaptation of 1 Peter 2:9,10: "You are a chosen race, a royal priesthood, a holy nation; a people God has made his own."

This reading functions well as a kind of summary of what the book of Exodus is all about and of its importance in the Lenten season. It is read for our instruction—to remind us that we are chosen in baptism, that those who are to be baptized, as well as the already baptized, are required to respond ever more and more to the Lord's revelation and call. The exodus journey of Israel is the model and example of our own journey through this life to the kingdom of God.

The second reading, from Gregory Nazianzen, subtitled "Let us show each other God's generosity," coincides with the gospel reading in today's liturgy of the eucharist. What we have received from God we must share with the needy.

At morning prayer today we use the traditional morning psalm, Psalm 5, and Psalm 29, which contains important references to the word of the Lord, his power to create and to save his chosen. Psalm 29 provides a view of God's kindness and power that challenges us to respond lovingly to his call to conversion.

The short reading from Exodus 19:4–6a is a kind of summary of today's readings about the covenant between God and Israel. The antiphon to Zechariah's canticle, ". . . come and receive the kingdom . . . ," is based on verse 34 of today's gospel.

The psalms at evening prayer reiterate God's support for the just

(Ps 11) and remind us of what is required before one can enter God's "tent"—his eternal dwelling in heaven (Ps 15).

The mystery of God revealed in Christ is at the heart of the familiar canticle from Ephesians 1:3–10.

The short scripture reading at evening prayer, from Romans 12:1–2, reminds us of the relationship between liturgical prayer and living the Christian life. Paul exhorts us: "offer your bodies as a living sacrifice." Unless we offer ourselves in good works, our prayers and actions in liturgical gatherings will profit us little. As at morning prayer, the antiphon to the Canticle of Mary is taken from today's gospel: "whatever you do for the least . . . you do for me" (vs. 40).

Celebration of the Hours

Today the second invitatory antiphon and Psalm 95 could be sung at the office of readings or as the beginning of morning prayer to emphasize the hearing of God's voice and our commitment to respond in repentance. Should morning prayer begin with a hymn, one with a general Lenten text emphasizing our share in God's mercy and love should be chosen.

At evening prayer, the intercessions could reflect the needs of the local and universal church using the familiar categories of the church, the world, the sick, and the dead as guidelines. The more universal and the less individual the intentions, the better. Although the prayer may include local needs, especially those which relate to Lent (e.g., RCIA, works of charity), these local concerns are to be distinguished from purely personal and individual concerns.

Reflection—"The Judgment of God"

The history of Christian art and architecture reveals many varied ways of expressing Christian beliefs and truths. One such example is the building of the great cathedrals of Europe, each of which uniquely expresses facets of the faith shared by those who built and used these houses of worship. Over the main portal of the cathedral at Chartres there is a carving that portrays today's gospel text of the last judgment. Christ the Lord is seated in the center; on the left are those who are damned and on the right are those who will enter the kingdom of God. On either side are angels (good and bad) who lead each group to the assigned place. Among the numbers of the saved are a monk and a bishop. On the other side, the artist depicts the very same types of people, including a monk and a bishop. The artist's point is that the last judgment will be no respector of persons. Rich and poor, big and small, monks and bishops can be among the condemned, just as they can be among the saved.

The artist illustrates the perennially valid message of today's gospel—all will be judged according to the extent that each of us loved as Jesus loved, or refused to love as he did. What matters is not our status or function in this life, or the kind of clothes we have worn, or the position we have held, but the true charity we have shown to others.

What is also interesting about the portal of the Chartres cathedral is that this particular scene is placed above the main entrance to the church. As worshipers enter they cannot help but see depicted over them a continual reminder that it is not only their acts of worship that matter but what they say and do outside the church.

This week in Lent, the church gives us in many challenging ways the message that conversion, turning toward the Lord in faith and love, requires that we not privatize faith and love but live faithfully and lovingly with each other. What will really matter when we are called before the Lord at the end is whether we have lived fully the message and mystery of his love.

TUESDAY OF THE FIRST WEEK OF LENT

Liturgical Context

Today's liturgy continues the emphasis on responding to the love of God through our care for others. We are to cooperate with God's word to accomplish what he wishes us to do (Isaiah). Our concern for each other is expressed especially in the prayer which Jesus taught us (Matthew).

Liturgy of the Eucharist

The entrance antiphon from Psalm 90 expresses hope and trust in God as our refuge. Our celebration of the liturgy is an acknowledgment of his sovereignty and his enduring care for us.

The opening prayer, traditional for this day, expresses the needs of the community (translated as "your children" but the Latin has "your family") as it engages in the fasting and discipline of Lent. That the Lenten penance will "help us grow in our desire for you [God]" is a constant theme in the ascetical teachings of the desert fathers: "Abba Theodotus used to say, 'Abstinence from bread quiets the body of the monk' " (E.A.W. Budge, *Paradise of the Fathers*, New York 1972).

The first reading from Isaiah (55:10–11) is a part of a text (Is 55:6–11) that was traditional for this day. A longer text from Isaiah 55:1–11 will be proclaimed as reading V at the Easter Vigil. The Rite of Penance (no. 117) offers the longer version of this text (vss. 1–11) as an optional reading at the celebration of the sacrament.

When the word of God is proclaimed, the Spirit acts to move the mind and change the heart. That the word is understood as that which causes and sustains our conversion to the Lord is reiterated each time the deacon (or priest) completes the proclamation of the gospel at Mass and says to himself, "May the words of the gospel wipe away our sins."

Psalm 34, used as today's response, will also be used on Friday of the fourth week in Lent and on the Third Sunday of Easter in the "C" cycle. The Lord is merciful yet just and invites our worship, thanks, and praise.

Today's gospel is from Matthew 6:7–15 and contains what was left out of the reading on Ash Wednesday (6:1–6,16–18). This chapter in Matthew's gospel has been carefully constructed to consider such ascetical works as fasting, prayer, and almsgiving. Today's verses offer Jesus' teaching as a model to use for prayer to the Father. A balance between praise and petition, elements of Jewish piety, is sustained here: "hallowed be your name" and "give us today our daily bread. . . ." The Lord's Prayer is the norm for the kind of prayer expected of believers.

The Lord's Prayer has been part of the liturgy of the hours three times a day in monastic communities because it concerns an important aspect of community life—forgiveness of others.

The liturgy of the Roman Rite emphasizes both the Lord's Prayer and the forgiveness of sin in the eucharist. This is demonstrated by the fact that part of the rites leading to communion include the Our Father and, even in the early stages of its evolution, the eucharistic prayer has included the words from Matthew's gospel "that sins may be forgiven." The petition for forgiveness offers a continual challenge to communities that seek to live as reconciled brothers and sisters.

The prayer over the gifts refers to the eucharist as the "food of eternal life" that nourishes and strengthens us as we journey to the kingdom.

Today's communion antiphon from Psalm 4 is traditional for this day and the Psalm itself is a classical psalm for night prayer. It expresses confidence and hope in the God of justice (an attribution already seen in the responsorial psalm today).

The prayer after communion asks that we "restrain our earthly desires and grow in love for the things of heaven." Both the restraint and the growth in love coincide with the liturgy and spirituality of Lent and are achieved through the celebration and the living out of the liturgy.

Celebration of the Eucharist

Since the word plays such a prominent part in the liturgy today, the introduction to the eucharist could be adapted to help orient the community to the power of the scriptures as proclaimed in the liturgy. Using invocations from the variety suggested in form C of the penitential rite (such as, "you are the Word made flesh," "you came to preach the good news of the kingdom," and "you come in word and sacrament to strengthen us in holiness") along with the "Lord, have mercy" would lead the community to appreciate the Word as revealed in scripture and in the person of Jesus. The verse before the gospel (Lectionary 224) could be no. 4: "Rid yourselves of all sins; and make a new heart and a new spirit" (based on Ezekiel 18:31), which would point to the petition of the forgiveness of sins for which we pray in the Lord's Prayer.

The general intercessions at today's eucharist could include petitions asking for a cessation of hatred and hostility among nations, in neighborhoods, and in families, all of which need the reconciling forgiveness of Christ.

Today might well offer the opportunity to use one of the two eucharistic prayers for masses of reconciliation. The text of the first prayer:

"God of love and mercy,
you are always ready to forgive;
we are sinners,
and you invite us
to trust in your mercy."

and of the second:

"Your Spirit changes our hearts:
enemies begin to speak to one another,
those who were estranged join hands in friendship,
and nations seek the way of peace together.

Your Spirit is at work
when understanding puts an end to strife,
when hatred is quenched by mercy,
and vengeance gives way to forgiveness."

are cogent expressions of what is proclaimed in the word and celebrated in eucharist.

The Lord's Prayer could be sung today, or at least should be given a special introduction in view of its prominence in today's gospel reading. A special introduction to the sign of peace could stress the connection between the Lord's Prayer and the gesture of peace. Both of these rites precede communion to make us realize that when we share in the body and blood of Christ we must share the peace that Christ alone can give.

Liturgy of the Hours

Today's first reading in the office of readings is from Exodus 6:29–7:25 and describes the first plague inflicted on Egypt, a clear demonstration (among many to come) of the Lord's power on behalf of his people.

The second reading is taken from Cyprian's treatise on the Lord's Prayer; hence it coincides with the gospel text from the liturgy of the eucharist. Cyprian views the Lord's Prayer as a model for personal and liturgical prayer, a common theme of patristic and spiritual writers.

The *berakah* ("blessing") form of Jewish piety included praise and thanks to God, a declaration (brief or extended) of why we praise him, and then a prayer of petition and a final doxology. This same pattern is evident in the blessing prayers of the present Roman Rite, from the blessing over water at baptism, to the eucharistic prayer itself, to many others such as the nuptial blessing and prayer of consecration at ordination. Since petition can become too dominant a part of our prayer, spiritual writers encourage us to maintain a balance of praise-petition.

The short reading at morning prayer today, from Joel 2:12–13, takes us back to Ash Wednesday when verses 12–18 appeared in the first reading at the eucharist. It is our "whole heart" that should return to the Lord, that is our whole person. Turning the heart to God should result in acts of charity to others.

The antiphon to the Canticle of Zechariah is reminiscent of Luke 11:1, where the disciples ask Jesus to teach them to pray.

At evening prayer the short reading from James (2:14,17,18b) reiterates the now familiar theme of the importance of both faith and good works as evidence of leading the Christian life. Neither one without the other is complete.

The antiphon to the Canticle of Mary is in the spirit of the gospel of the day, and is based on verses from Matthew 6. The admonition to "go to your room, shut the door, and pray to your Father in secret" (vs. 6) warns against a hypocritical use of public prayer, but this is no condemnation of liturgical prayer as such (see above, commentary on Ash Wednesday).

Celebration of the Hours

With the wealth of material offered in the readings and antiphons at the hours, communities may well wish to compose new psalm prayers and/or intercessions, especially at morning and evening prayer. Remembering that the formulas presented for intercessions are not fixed but can be expanded, and that the sample psalm prayers can be changed or eliminated entirely, gives communities great flexibility in adapting the hours to given pastoral situations.

While respecting the separation between the cycle of the hours and eucharist, it still might be helpful to emphasize the use of the Lord's Prayer at morning and evening prayer because of its emphasis in the gospel proclaimed at today's eucharist.

Reflection—"Lent, A Prayerful Season"

In the spiritual life, deeds that reflect thoughts and actions that reflect ideas are essential. Lent is a particularly significant period for reflection on the way actions express belief, for example: fasting to allow the Lord to be the center of life and food for the soul; works of charity to signify that the gospel calls us to real concern for each other. Actions make the "theory" of Christianity explicit, obvious, and part of our lives. We cannot do without actions if we want to be truly Christian.

Today's liturgy also emphasizes prayer. There is the prayer of petition in which we ask God to be present in our lives, especially in situations of need, concern, and anxiety. We open all areas of life to his grace and care and we offer them to him for attention and care. The petition "thy will be done" in the Lord's Prayer makes us look to God not just for favors, but for the grace to accept his will when it is contrary to what we want.

For the modern Christian, this takes a great deal of faith and humility. It takes faith to trust that in the end God is directing all that we do; it takes humility because we are asking God to take over every aspect of our lives, even (especially!) those areas we have under control or think we have in hand. Letting go and letting God direct it all is what is meant by praying the Lord's Prayer.

But there is also the prayer of praise. Lent is not just a time for helping others and forgiving those who have hurt us. It is also a time to praise God for being what he is—all good, all loving, and the One to whom we owe our very lives. This is the all-powerful God we worship in prayer, whose grace we receive through the sacraments, and to whom we offer praise through our Lenten self-sacrifice.

WEDNESDAY OF THE FIRST WEEK OF LENT

Liturgical Context

In the Roman liturgical tradition, the Wednesdays and Fridays of Lent were times of special prayer. But the Wednesday, Friday, and Saturday after the First Sunday of Lent, called Ember Days, were marked by an increase in the number of readings and prayers in the liturgy. Parenthetically, it may be noted that Ember Days occurred not only in Lent, but at three other times in the year. Despite the fact that the season of Lent has undergone some major adjustments in theology and piety, it is clear that today's liturgy has aspects which are directly derived from the Ember Days tradition. The entrance antiphon and opening prayer for today are taken from the Mass formula in use until the present reform, thus indicating perduring elements from the Ember Wednesday tradition. The responsorial psalm (Psalm 51) is the same as Ash Wednesday's, except that verses 18–19 are used today instead of verses 14 and 17, used last week.

The first reading from the prophet Jonah (3:1–10), with its reference to "ashes and sackcloth," adds to the serious and penitential tone of the liturgy today. In the perspective of what has already been celebrated this week, today's liturgy is in continuity because Jesus is portrayed in the gospel as referring to the "sign of Jonah," and calling "the crowds" to repentance (Luke 11:29–32).

Liturgy of the Eucharist
The entrance antiphon (Psalm 25:6,3,22) sets a confident note with which to begin the liturgy, praying that the Lord will continue to make his mercy known, as in the past.

The opening prayer, taken from the second collect for the Ember Day Mass in the Roman Missal, is traditional for this day. The present translation, "help us to discipline our bodies and to be renewed in spirit," is adequate, yet the sense of the Latin original gives greater emphasis to the discipline of bodily abstinence that will bear fruit and renew us in spirit. Formerly, church law imposed fasting and abstinence, especially in Lent. Today the requirements are more lenient, but the liturgy still emphasizes that works of penance have an important spiritual effect.

The texts of Jonah 3:1–10 and Luke 11:29–32 are newly chosen for this day and obviously complement each other. The statement about "the word of the Lord" coming to Jonah (vs. 1) is a common introduction to prophetic pronouncements. The prophet's proclamation: "Forty days more and Nineveh shall be destroyed," reflects the forty days of the deluge and the forty years of Israel's wandering in the desert leading to the promised land. We can apply the forty-days theme to the church's celebration of the forty days of Lent. Just as the forty days were a time for conversion and repentance by the Ninevites, Lent is our forty days for conversion and repentance, leading to our celebration of Christ's resurrection and our salvation in him at Easter.

Jonah's call to the Ninevites can be applied to today's liturgical assembly, which gathers to hear and ponder this same prophetic warning. Lent is the time for deep conversion and serious repentance. Otherwise we, too, can run the risk of being "destroyed."

The familiar Psalm 51 with the response, "A broken, humbled heart, O God, you will not scorn," fittingly accompanies the text from Jonah. It invites our internal and free response to the Lord, whose mercy is remembered and relied on.

Today's gospel is the single exception to the use of the Matthean text this week. Luke uses the Jonah story as background to emphasize the importance of the preaching of Jesus: "at the preaching of Jonah they reformed, but you have a greater than Jonah here" (vs. 32). It is the word that disposes and changes hearts as Christians celebrate the liturgy and sacraments of the church. The eucharist and the liturgy of the hours, especially in Lent, guide and inform our penitential practices; these are the means offered to inspire and ground our conversion and repentance.

The prayer over the gifts points to the bread and wine that through Christ's words will become the "sacrament of our salvation" in the eucharist. Hence it can be understood as a bridge between the proclamation of the word and the sacrament as a "visible word" bringing us salvation.

The communion antiphon asks the Lord to give joy to those who trust in him, "and to make them happy forever" (Ps 5:12). Repentance need not mean morbidity. In fact, when properly understood, repentance means joy, peace, and tranquility of spirit because through it we come to experience the very presence of God with us.

The prayer after communion is more eschatological in its Latin original as it speaks of our being led to eternal life rather than simply "to salvation" as in the translation. Jesus in the eucharist is our "food of life" who renews our strength and leads us to life eternal.

Celebration of the Eucharist

Today's entrance rite could include a simple introduction to the powerful scripture readings, followed by the second form (B) of the penitential rite in which we acknowledge our need for forgiveness and mercy: "Lord, we have sinned against you: Lord have mercy. . . ."

Another option that might provide variety and a form of instruction would be to introduce the two readings after the opening prayer and before the proclamation of the first reading itself. This way the assembled community can be helped to focus clearly on the importance of the words of the prophet and the challenging words of Jesus.

Since the text of today's responsorial psalm has now become familiar in Lent, it might be good to offer a variation on how it is recited or sung today. The psalm can be read by a leader with the congregation joining in reciting the antiphon after each strophe, or the community may recite the whole psalm together, or they may respond with the antiphon only at the end of the first and the end of the last strophe.

The use of number 9 (Lectionary 224) of the verses before the gospel ("Repent, says the Lord, the kingdom of heaven is at hand") would be a suitable introduction to the gospel text proclaimed today.

In composing the general intercessions, the community might want to be particularly attentive to modern problems such as food distribution, the arms race, or the like. All too often even general intercessions can come to focus especially on the local community's needs; these prayers ought to extend beyond the domestic church to the needs of the people of God and of all peoples in the world.

The third preface for Lent speaks of our "self-denial" and our responsibility "to master our sinfulness and conquer our pride" and reiterates the concrete forms that repentance must take, especially our conversion and turning to the Lord.

One way of concluding the liturgy today (perhaps on every Wednesday and Friday) would be to choose one of the prayers over the people provided in the Sacramentary. These prayers, which have been used to conclude the eucharist from the sixth century, have a special place in the Lenten liturgy since they have traditionally been used to dismiss the community. Today, number 6, asking for "a complete change of heart," would stress the meaning and intent of the readings.

Liturgy of the Hours

At the office of readings, the first reading, from the book of Exodus (10:21–11:10), continues with the story of the plague on Egypt—darkness over the country for three days and the death of the firstborn. The intent of such texts is to illustrate the Lord's ever-faithful care for Israel.

The second reading is a text from Aphraates, subtitled "Circumcision of the Heart." It concerns the covenants forged by God with Adam, Noah, Moses, and Abraham, and finally the sign of the acceptance of that covenant—circumcision. Since Jesus came, the "mark and seal" of his covenant with his people is baptism. Our Savior does not demand the rite of circumcision. He asks for the circumcision of the heart—conversion. Lent helps us to renew our baptismal commitments to Christ, the sign of our conversion, and prepares the catechumens to accept their new responsibilities as covenanted believers.

The short scripture readings at morning and evening prayer are the same as those used last week. They will be used each Wednesday until the fifth week of Lent.

The antiphon to Zechariah's canticle is based on the gospel reading at today's eucharist; no sign will be given except that of Jonah. This antiphon is an apt introduction to the canticle which speaks about the Lord's promises "through his holy prophets," his promised "mercy to our fathers," and his remembrance of "his holy covenant."

At evening prayer, the antiphon to Mary's canticle is based on Matthew 12:40, and acts as an extension of the Lukan gospel proclaimed today. It sees Jonah as a figure of Jesus and likens the "three days" that Jonah spent in the belly of the whale to the "three days" the Son of Man will spend in the earth.

Celebration of the Hours

Since another invitatory psalm may be substituted for the traditional Psalm 95, Psalm 100 might well be used today with the second antiphon, about hearing the Lord's voice. This text establishes many elements which mark the Lenten liturgy:

"Know that he the Lord is God;
    he made us, his we are;
    his people, the flock he tends.
Enter his gates with thanksgiving,
    his courts with praise;
Give thanks to him; bless his name,
    for he is good:
    the Lord, whose kindness endures forever,
    and his faithfulness, to all generations" (Ps 100:3–4).

Wednesdays in Lent are often days on which parishes have special Lenten meetings, educational programs, or days of spiritual enrichment, and so it might be helpful to use either morning or evening prayer as part of such a gathering. When these hours are celebrated with a larger group than usual, it would be helpful to practice with leaders, readers, cantors, and others so that the liturgy can run smoothly.

Carefully composed intercessions can help focus the attention of the group on the needs of all peoples, including those involved in parish Lenten activities. The option of preaching a homily at the hours, especially when there is an extended reading from scripture, should perhaps be activated at such gatherings as noted above.

Reflection—"Twice Told Tales"

We are people who like the news. Whether it is a local story or a national or international event, we like to find out what happened. We pick up the daily paper (sometimes one in the morning and another at night), switch on television for the evening news, or turn on a car radio for the hourly coverage or the "all-news" stations.

But it is equally true that we quickly turn the page for something newer if we have already heard about the lead story. We switch channels if the hourly newscast is a mere repetition of the one an hour before. We like to get information, but once gotten we yearn for something really new. We are usually less than comfortable with twice told tales.

Unfortunately we may feel the same way about the scripture readings in the liturgy that are repeated over the years. But unlike the daily news we read and hear, the good news is meant to be told again and again. Unlike the news we hear every day, the good news is not for our information so much as it is for our formation and reformation in the faith. What can seem to be a barrage of words in the liturgy of the word is meant to serve our being caught up again and again in the story of God's revelation to us as his people. The repeated telling of the good news is meant to penetrate to the very depths of our lives so that we can experience the truth that will truly set us free and the light that will shatter our self-deceptions and personal delusions.

The liturgy proclaims God's revealed word in a succession of twice and thrice told tales. We must understand that what is preached and proclaimed is not just an informative news story. It is the good news that is meant for our conversion. These stories are told again and again to give us opportunities for reflection and renewal. We are privileged to gather at the eucharist to hear the good news again and again and to draw ever closer to Christ who is himself the Good News of eternal life.

THURSDAY OF THE FIRST WEEK OF LENT

Liturgical Context

As mentioned before, Thursday was the last weekday to be provided with its own liturgical prayers and readings. Thus this Thursday (like other Thursdays in Lent), the liturgy has none of the special liturgical characteristics of such days as Wednesday, Friday, and even Saturday.

Today's liturgy continues some of the major themes already developed this week, such as dependence on God (first reading at eucharist), treating others as you would want to be treated (gospel reading), and the promised passover of Israel (first reading, office of readings). While this day is less "special," it nevertheless spurs us on to continued reflection on treating others "the way you would have them treat you" (Mt 7:12).

Liturgy of the Eucharist

Today's entrance antiphon, Psalm 5:2–3, is a good introduction to the first reading from the book of Esther, about reliance on God, for it prays: "Let my words reach your ears, Lord" and "listen to my groaning."

The opening prayer, stating "without you [God] we can do nothing," sharpens the notion of total reliance on God. Calling on God as the source or our very being reminds us, especially in Lent, that all we have comes from God, and that all we do is accomplished through and in him. The prayer, like the entrance antiphon, opens our hearts and minds to the first reading.

This section of the book of Esther is a confession of faith, a declaration of dependence and acknowledgment of trust in God. In fact, it is this characteristic of Jewish piety and prayer that is reflected in Jesus' teaching on prayer in Tuesday's gospel.

The petition, "be mindful of us, O Lord" (vs. 23), is not a request that God merely think about his people, somewhat the way we "think about" someone's plight and offer no help. Rather, as stated a bit later, it is a petition that the Lord "manifest" himself, come actively to the aid of his people "in the time of their distress" (vs. 23). The meaning of remembrance and memorial in Jewish piety is disclosed in this reading. Such an understanding of memory lies at the base of Christian worship. Remembrance implies active presence and favorable intervention of God on our behalf. In asking God to "remember," we call upon him who has acted in history and who continues to act in our time and situation. Such an understanding of memorial lies, for example, at the heart of the prayer, "Remember, Lord, your people. . . . Remember all of us gathered here before you . . . ," and, "Remember, Lord, those who have died . . . ," in eucharistic prayer I.

Psalm 138, a psalm not used elsewhere in Lent, is a most fitting responsorial to the reading from Esther. The response, "Lord, on the day I called for help, you answered me," is based on the fact that the Lord does "answer" his people's prayers and builds up "strength within them" (vs. 3). Again, this reflects the pattern of Jewish piety and Christian liturgical prayer. God's intervention in the past establishes the confidence on which the prayer of petition is made in the present. The psalm is a thanksgiving (vs. 1) to God and a request that he will complete his work in us (vss. 7-8).

Today's gospel from Matthew 7:7-12 is itself a confession, that is, an acknowledgment of our dependence on God, the God who promised that if we but ask, seek, and knock he will answer us. If even a human father will try to give his children good things, "how much more will your heavenly Father give good things to anyone who asks him" (vs. 11). But, as this week's gospel readings have emphasized, God requires that we treat others the way we would have them treat us.

In the prayer over the gifts, "let us turn to you with all our hearts" reflects a common, but significant, Lenten theme.

The communion antiphon is a verse from today's gospels, "whoever asks will receive. . . ."

That the sacred mysteries of the eucharist provide for our spiritual renewal and nourishment in the present and will lead to future salvation is noted in the prayer after communion.

Celebration of the Eucharist

The liturgy might well begin on a prayerful, meditative tone, with a short introduction followed by period of silence. The verse before the gospel (Lectionary 224, no. 8), from the prophet Joel, "With all your heart turn to me for I am tender and compassionate," would fit in well with the Matthean text.

Since the gospel speaks of prayer and petition, today might be a good time to evaluate how well the intercessions reflect the needs of the whole church as well as those of the celebrating community. People could also write out their intentions and give them to the lector, who could edit them if need be and who could then read them. The names of the sick or deceased could be given to the lector or to the priest. These could be mentioned in the intercessions or in the commemoration of the living or the commemoration of the dead in the Roman Canon. According to liturgical custom and longstanding tradition, the last petition in the general intercessions is for the deceased. Guidance for planning the petitions during Lent may be found in Appendix I to the Sacramentary, nos. 5 and 6, entitled Lent I and Lent II.

The fourth preface for Lent, containing the phrase, "you correct our faults," "raise our minds to you," and "you help us grow in holiness" would be a suitable choice.

Because today's liturgy focuses on our heavenly Father who hears our prayers, a special introduction to the Lord's Prayer, based on the second sample invitation, "Jesus taught us to call God our Father . . . ," would be suitable.

Liturgy of the Hours

Today's first reading at the office of readings is again from Exodus, 12:1–20, and concerns the feast of Passover and unleavened bread. Secions of this reading will be proclaimed as the first scripture reading of the triduum on Holy Thursday night at the evening Mass of the Lord's Supper.

The use of unleavened bread signified the haste with which the Hebrews prepared for the journey to the promised land. They had no time to wait for dough to rise before they could bake their bread. Later, the Jewish celebration of Passover was a time for cleaning out the old leaven and making ready for the new leaven. This last meaning has associations with the liturgy and theology of Lent. For us, this is the time of year when we purge our lives of our old ways so that the fullness of the new leaven, Christ, may infuse our lives and make us truly new and holy at Easter.

The patristic text from Asterius of Amasea exhorts us to be like Christ, for just as he sought and searched after the lost sheep, so we ought be kind and helpful to our erring brothers and sisters. We are to act with gentleness and compassion toward each other, for we ourselves know how often we have erred and strayed like lost sheep.

The readings at morning and evening prayer repeat those used last Thursday and will continue to be used until the fifth week of Lent.

The antiphons for the canticle of Zechariah at morning prayer and for the canticle of Mary at evening prayer are both taken from the gospel proclaimed at today's eucharist. Both of these are positive statements inspiring hope and confidence in the Lord.

Celebration of the Hours

As already mentioned, texts may be substituted for those presently given for the invitatory, extended readings at morning and evening prayer, and for the intercessions at the hours. So today it might be well to review the actual celebration itself and determine specifically how the psalms are prayed. Like the responsorial psalm at the eucharist, there are a number of ways the psalms can be sung or recited. The most common practice would seem to be antiphonal. An option at the hours might be to follow the responsorial style generally used at Mass. Or the community could recite the whole psalm in unison. When one psalm is divided into parts for common recitation as, for example, Psalm 18:31–51 in the office of readings today, a "Glory be to the Father" can conclude each section, or sections may be followed by a period of silence, or the section breaks can be ignored and the whole psalm recited straight through.

Preparation should take place before the celebration of the hours to select options for texts and ways of praying.

Reflection—"Prayer: For and with Each Other"

From Jesus' assurance in Matthew's gospel (15:20) that he is present with his followers "where two or three are gathered" in his name, to the primitive Christian community that "devoted themselves to . . . the breaking of bread and the prayers" (Acts 2:42), to the church's liturgical worship today, there is the constant emphasis on communal prayer in God's presence with and for each other. The relationship forged with each other as brothers and sisters at baptism is experienced and expressed in and through the liturgy. We pray the Lord's Prayer to *"Our* Father," and we offer each other the sign of peace as a reconciling and unity-building gesture before sacramental communion. The prayer of the faithful and the tradition of naming those who are sick and deceased attest to our concern for each other.

During the season of Lent, those who are already baptized into Christ's life offer a welcoming hand to the catechumens who seek admission to full membership in the church.

Each time we join in prayer for and with each other our shared responsibility is manifest. For all those who are fellow pilgrims on the way to the kingdom, the church provides solidarity with God and with each other. The season of Lent is a time for deepened awareness of this solidarity and for deeper prayer—for and with each other.

FRIDAY OF THE FIRST WEEK OF LENT

Liturgical Context

Today's liturgy is interesting because of its traditional status in Lent and because of the new readings selected in accordance with the reform of the liturgy. As noted above, this day was formerly designated as Ember Friday in Lent; hence the Lenten fast and abstinence were given special emphasis.

Today's scripture readings, especially the gospel, reaffirm the message that has been proclaimed all this week—that the Lenten penance and conversion lead to living in peace and reconciliation with all people. We recall that the first reading last Friday considered fasting in its relationship for others—sharing food with those in need. Today's gospel, also on a Friday in Lent, considers our Lenten observances in the light of our readiness to reconcile our differences with others.

Liturgy of the Eucharist

The eucharist today begins with the traditional entrance antiphon (Psalm 25:17–18) invoking God's forgiveness of our sins.

The opening prayer connects the season of Lent with the sacred triduum to come in Holy Week when we participate most fully in the paschal mystery of Jesus. The Latin text speaks of the discipline of the body that is part of the ascetical tradition of Lent.

The first reading from the prophet Ezekiel (18:21–28) is the traditional text assigned to this day. Portions of this same chapter (vss. 21–23,30–32) are offered as an option for proclamation at Masses for the forgiveness of sins (Lectionary 886, no. 2), while verses 21–28 are suggested for the Rite of Penance (no. 124). The conversion required is literally a turning from wicked ways and sins to leading life according to the Lord's statutes. The promised result of the conversion choice is true life with God.

The main point of this reading is reflected in the first reading assigned to Thursday after Ash Wednesday (Deuteronomy 30:15–20). The fact that these same sentiments are repeated within eight days and this theme is developed throughout Lent reminds us that the required conversion takes a long time to effect.

The response to the Ezekiel text from Psalm 130 speaks of our iniquities and God's forgiveness, of our guilt and the kindness of the Lord. (This same responsorial psalm will be used after the reading of Ezekiel 37 on the Fifth Sunday of Lent, "A" cycle.)

The gospel, Matthew 5:20–26, shows that the end and goal of repentance and penance is reconciliation. The criterion for offering your gift at the altar is whether or not "your brother has anything against you" (vs. 23). In some churches of the sixth century, the celebrant refused to accept the gifts of those whose enmity toward others was a scandal.

This text has been used in liturgical tradition as a rationale for placing the sign of peace before offering the bread and wine at eucharist. The practice of extending the sign of peace before the offertory still exists in some liturgies, but it is not done in the Roman Rite until just before the rites preceding communion.

Just as last week's first reading from Isaiah interpreted fasting as a practice that involved others, so today's gospel speaks about the intrinsic connection between fidelity to liturgical worship and fidelity to the gospel command to live reconciled lives.

The prayer over the gifts indicates that through the celebration of the eucharist, we receive the "saving power" of God.

The communion antiphon is not taken from the gospel (as has been customary at many Lenten liturgies), but is from another part of the book of Ezekiel (33:11) that reiterates the message of the first reading: "By my life, I do not wish the sinner to die, says the Lord, but to turn to me and live."

In the prayer after communion, we ask God to "free us from our sinful ways" and to "bring us new life" so that the gift of Christ's reconciling love may "lead us to salvation."

Celebration of the Eucharist

Today's introductory rites might well reflect the depth and seriousness of the liturgy by a pause for silence after the introduction, followed by the "Lord, have mercy" in a meditative musical setting.

For the verse before the gospel, the use of the phrase from 2 Corinthians 6:2 (no. 16), "This is the favorable time, this is the day of salvation," points to the urgency of the gospel's message. Appropriate intentions in the prayer of the faithful could reflect the needs of the catechumens preparing for initiation, those weighed down by a sense of their sin and guilt before God, and those factions needing reconciling within a given liturgical community. The use of the second eucharistic prayer for Masses of reconciliation would be especially appropriate today, most notably the section that states:

"God our Father,
we had wandered far from you,

but through your Son you have brought us back.
You gave him up to death
so that we might turn again to you
and find our way to one another.

Therefore we celebrate the reconciliation
Christ has gained for us."

Once again, because the rites before communion emphasize reconciliation, perhaps a variation on the third invitation to the Lord's
Prayer could be worded to proclaim God's forgiveness of our sins
as we forgive the sins of others. There could also be a special
introduction to the sign of peace to stress the true meaning of
offering Christ's peace to others.

One way to recapitulate today's readings would be to conclude
the eucharist with number 2 of the prayers over the people, which
asks for "perfect love for one another."

The three forms of the dismissal in the Sacramentary instruct us
to "go in peace." It is this peace, which is established by Christ
through the eucharist, that the community has celebrated.

This is the same gift of peace that we are to share with one
another that leads to reconciliation through and in him.

Liturgy of the Hours

The first reading from Exodus in the office of readings (12:21–36)
deals with the plague inflicted on the firstborn of Egypt as well as
with pharaoh's order that Israel leave Egypt. Once again we find
the mention of events in Jewish history that have significant meanings for Christians. The blood of lambs was placed on the dwell-
ings of those to be saved; we are saved by the shedding of the
blood of Christ, the true Lamb of God. The Lord "passed over" the
houses of the Israelites in Egypt; the redemption won for us is
often called our passover in the blood of Christ.

The second reading, from the Mirror of Love by St. Aelred, is a
reflection on today's gospel. The model of all love is Christ who
submitted to hostile treatment and accepted crucifixion for our
salvation. The "serene patience" with which our "beloved Lord and
Savior" accepted his passion and death is a model for our own
attitude toward those who are hostile and inimical to us. To mirror

divine love in our relationships with others is what reconciliation really entails.

As is customary, the readings at morning and evening prayer today repeat those used last week, while the antiphons for the canticles at morning and evening prayer are taken from today's gospel. The most challenging aspects of Matthew's text are thus reiterated in morning prayer ("If your virtue does not surpass that of the scribes and Pharisees . . .") and evening prayer ("If you are bringing your gift to the altar . . .").

Celebration of the Hours

The first invitatory antiphon and Psalm 95 would be a fitting way to begin the liturgy of the hours today.

A review of our response to the voice of the Lord in this psalm would be particularly appropriate today because of the references both at eucharist and at the hours to listening and responding to the Lord.

Since Fridays have an obvious association with the passion and death of Jesus, a passion-oriented hymn at morning and evening prayer would be suitable. But once again, it is important to point out that the liturgy involves our participation in the paschal mystery of Jesus.

The intercessions at morning prayer are introduced by reference to the cross of Christ, and one intention speaks of our self-denial. This is an example of the subtle way in which these intentions bring out some of the richness inherent in celebrating the liturgy on a Friday in Lent. At evening prayer, the next to last intention emphasizes the same theme: "Teach the faithful to see your passion in their sufferings. . . ."

Because the antiphon to Mary's canticle stresses reconciliation, the Lord's Prayer could be given a special introduction at evening prayer.

Reflection—"Virtue and Holiness"

"Unless your holiness surpasses that of the scribes and Pharisees you shall not enter the kingdom of God" (Mt 5:20). With these words, Jesus instructs us that holiness is not a commodity to be selfishly cherished; it is a gift that enables us to give [our] strength to all in distress." Lent is an annual opportunity for us to realize in our lives a total and free response to the God who calls and saves not only us believers, but also those who do not yet know him.

During these weeks, the liturgy focuses on our relationship to our brothers and sisters in the faith. Lent is also a time when we welcome into our hearts the brothers and sisters who are preparing to be initiated into God's family. Unfortunately, we sometimes find that it is hard to bear with the weaknesses of our own brothers and sisters in the Lord. When such is the case, our recourse must be to Christ in the eucharist, asking him to give us the "serene patience" he manifested in his sufferings and death for us. It may well be that we need a lifetime of Lents to make us into a people of total virtue and holiness. In fact, that may not ever be accomplished. But not to make the effort would be to stagnate and ultimately reject the grace we have been given by God. Lent is the season, and the liturgy is the daily occasion for us to grow in the love Jesus poured out for those who hurt him.

SATURDAY OF THE FIRST WEEK OF LENT

Liturgical Context

Saturday of the first week of Lent was the last of the Lenten Ember Days. On that day the liturgy of the word comprised four Old Testament readings (with a collect after each), one epistle reading, and a gospel. With the elimination of Ember Day observances in the revised liturgy, today's eucharist resembles all other weekdays in Lent in terms of structure and ritual. However, some elements of the former Ember Day observance still perdure: the first reading today is one of those formerly proclaimed, and both the prayer over the gifts and the prayer after communion come from the church's traditional prayers for this day (although neither of them appeared in the former Roman Missal).

In addition to these Ember Day traces, today's texts give a finishing touch to the theme of reconciliation that has been so prominent in the liturgy this week.

Liturgy of the Eucharist

The entrance antiphon, from Psalm 19, "the law of the Lord is perfect . . . his commandments are the wisdom of the simple" (vs. 8), expresses the keynote of today's liturgy. Remembering that in the Old Testament the laws and commandments of God are radicated in his very being, we can begin this liturgy by acknowledging our submission to his will as revealed in scripture.

The first reading today from Deuteronomy (26:16–19) points out that God's covenant with Israel assumed that the people would observe "his statutes, commandments and decrees, and to hearken to his voice" (vs. 17).

The responsorial psalm (119) echoes this same theme, with its meditative reflection on the law of the Lord. The response couples commitment to the Lord's decrees with true joy: "Happy are they who follow the law of the Lord."

The gospel proclaimed today (Matthew 5:43–48) helps bring out the differences between a superficial and a full response to God's word. The Matthean gospel demands nothing less than the love of one's enemies.

The last sentence of the gospel reading shows what a full response to God's word means: "You must be perfected as your heavenly Father is perfect" (vs. 48).

To be "perfected as your heavenly Father is perfect" means that we are to identify as fully as we can with Jesus, the revelation to us of the perfection of the Father. He is the unique reflection of God's perfection, and in growing more and more fully into the life of God through Christ, we become ever closer to perfection.

Perfection is not a moral category in the sense that we amass more and more good deeds; it is an evangelical disposition whereby we become more and more like God. Such a process is only possible in and through the life of grace we receive from God.

The God revealed in the scriptures who calls us to such a gospel ethic is the same God who is present to us through liturgical rites and sacramental symbols so that we can become more and more perfected—more and more like God through Christ.

Today's prayer over the gifts asks that we may "be renewed by this eucharist" and may "become more like Christ your Son."

Today's communion antiphon, as is often the case, quotes part of the gospel reading—"Be perfect. . . ."

The prayer after communion is a traditional text of Ember Saturday in Lent. The Latin original lays emphasis on the precepts of the Lord, whereas the present text offers a parallel between word and sacrament. The word asks for peace in the kingdom; the eucharist is Christ's reply: he strengthens us with God's ever faithful love.

Celebration of the Eucharist

In light of the solemnity of the eucharist that will be celebrated tomorrow, today's celebration should be more restrained. A brief introduction to the liturgy, pointing to our openness to the word of God, and the use of the second form of the penitential rite would simplify the introductory rites and focus the assembly's attention on the scripture readings.

The use of no. 6 of the verses before the gospel (Lectionary 224), "This is the favorable time, this is the day of salvation" (2 Cor 6:2), would prepare the assembly to accept the challenge offered in the gospel.

The intentions for the prayer of the faithful might include some that would ask for the deepening of our commitment to the Lenten discipline that leads to forgiveness of and reconciliation with others.

The first eucharistic prayer for Masses of Reconciliation would be an appropriate choice today with a section reflective of today's gospel:

"Now is the time
for your people to turn back to you
and to be renewed in Christ your Son,
a time of grace and reconciliation."

The Our Father could be introduced by a special invitation to forgive others—so that there may be reconciliation in Christ. The work of reconciliation that the eucharist implies and demands could be underscored by using the third form of dismissal today: "Go in peace to love and serve the Lord."

Liturgy of the Hours

The verse between the psalmody and readings in the office of readings draws on the light/darkness theme, so apparent in the celebration of the hours of morning and evening prayer. It is this same light/darkness theme that will dominate much of the liturgy toward the end of Lent as the catechumenate culminates in initiation at the Easter Vigil (also called the Night Watch of the Resurrection).

The first reading at the office of readings (Ex 12:37–49; 13:11–16) tells of "the night of vigil" when the Lord led Israel out of Egypt. Their bondage in this foreign land had ended (after 460 years, according to vs. 40), and forever more this night was to be commemorated (remembered and reactualized in worship) by observing the passover regulations described here. The summary statement in 13:11–16 forms a brief reminder of what the Lord did for this chosen people and what he has promised to Abraham's posterity.

The second reading in the office of readings is a section of the Pastoral Constitution on the Church in the Modern World from Vatican II (nos. 9–10). This text speaks about the fundamental problems that necessarily must be faced as we live by faith, and it outlines God's demands that his people "walk in his ways." If the people hearken to his voice, he promised that he would raise them "high . . . above all nations he has made." God demands of us that we too walk in his ways today. This leads us to ask ourselves some serious questions about our religious practices and the quality of life we are living in our modern world. As the Constitution points out, we suffer from "conflicts within [ourselves], and this in turn gives rise to many great tensions in society." If we are to overcome our own "conflicts," we must walk in God's ways. Then we can help our brothers and sisters throughout society to become "sacred to the Lord."

This concept is reiterated in the reading from Isaiah (1:16–18) at morning prayer.

The antiphon to the Canticle of Zechariah reflects the gospel: "pray for those who persecute you" (Mt 5:44).

Celebration of the Hours

Today's celebration of the hours should not emulate the solemnity of the Sunday eucharist, and so the hours today should be celebrated with simplicity. The use of Psalm 24 as the invitatory with the first antiphon about Christ enduring temptation and suffering would be an appropriate choice today.

At the office of readings, Psalm 105 is split into three sections, with the antiphon and the doxology at the end of each section. As an option, a pause may take place between each section with the antiphon used at the beginning and the antiphon and doxology repeated at the end.

Similarly, since the responsory after the scripture reading at morning prayer is optional, today might be a good day to omit it.

Reflection—"This is the Day"

"This is the day the Lord has made, let us rejoice and be glad in it," will be proclaimed on Easter. Indeed, a new day and the dawn of a new creation has occurred in the resurrection of Jesus. But for Easter to be the new day, there must be the days of a preceding Lent during which we prepare to allow the risen Christ to take over our lives. We must seize this day, not tomorrow or yesterday, but this day and determine to what extent we choose God's ways and not our own and determine to live according to his word, not according to our own inclinations.

Morton Kelsey uses the image (in *The Other Side of Silence*) of "breaking the husk." Sometimes, he argues, we live life in the same way day in and day out. We do not, or cannot, stop to evaluate our real lives and to ask the really important questions. We cover over hurts, wounds, and sins so that there is built up a hardened husk that we grow accustomed to. What happens when we allow God's grace and life to penetrate to the level of our real need is "breaking the husk." Only when we allow the husk to break do we allow God to become the healer, forgiver, and reconciler. But once we experience God's healing of our hurts, his forgiveness of our sins, and his reconciling of our relationships we can develop attitudes of healing, forgiveness, and reconciliation that constitute gospel living.

Today's eucharist and liturgical prayer strengthen us to "break the husk" of our lives and to experience the light of Christ. What we must do *today* is to accept the Lord who comes to challenge and to heal us. For the *day* of Easter to bring its expected and astounding joy, we need these *days* of Lent, especially this day in Lent to allow our hardened husks to break and the Lord to rule our lives.

Chapter Three

Second Week of Lent

SECOND SUNDAY OF LENT

Liturgical Context

The structure, prayer texts, and scripture readings for this Second Sunday of Lent were late in being established when compared with the traditional themes for the other Lenten Sundays (about the temptation of Jesus and obvious initiation themes). This was due to the fact that Ember Saturday had taken priority as a day for a special morning liturgy (sometimes of ordinations) or for the elaborate Saturday evening vigil liturgy ending early Sunday morning (sometimes with the reading of the resurrection gospel and a simple eucharist). This extended Saturday evening vigil was the customary way to look forward to the Lord's day on any Sunday; its emphasis on this Saturday in Lent was due to a combination of penitential and renunciation themes characteristic of Lent.

This historical fact helps to explain why the transfiguration of Jesus, the event proclaimed in the gospel in all three cycles today, dominates the liturgy even though this would seem to be more resurrectional in theme than penitential. When proclaimed this Sunday, the transfiguration gives us a glimpse of what we share fully through the resurrection of Christ. Yet the gospel accounts themselves combine the promise of future glory with the reality of having to accept suffering in this life. To those preparing for initiation, as well as to the already baptized, the message of today's liturgy is that following Christ requires that we accept suffering for the sake of living the gospel as freely as we accept participation in his risen glory.

The transfiguration of Jesus reminds us of the suffering he will endure before the glory of his resurrection. We share in the glory of Christ by sharing in both his humiliation and triumph through the works of sacrifice and prayer during Lent. We live in the tension between the kingdom that is here and now and the fullness of what will be realized in the world to come. The liturgy this Sunday gives us the hope of eternal life that should mark the Christian church as it moves onward to the kingdom.

Cycle "A"

The first reading today, taken from the book of Genesis, introduces a common theme running through the first reading in each Lectionary cycle for this Sunday: the call and response of Abraham. Today's passage about the call of Abraham (Gn 12:1–4) is followed in the "B" cycle by the text about Abraham's sacrifice of Isaac (Gn 22:1–2,9,10–13,15–18), and in the "C" cycle by the text about Abraham's faith in the Lord (Gn 15:5–12,17–18). God called Abraham to leave "the land of [his] kinsfolk" and "[his] father's house." Abraham's obedient response to the Lord is a model for all believers. The obedience that faith requires should mark catechumens on their way to initiation, penitents who are returning to the eucharistic community this Lent, and all who are renewing their lives and turning again to the Lord.

Today's responsory in cycle A reflects Abraham's and our trust in God: "Lord, let your mercy be on us, as we place our trust in you" (Ps 33:22). In the responsorial psalm itself (33:4–5,18–19,20,22), the Lord is acclaimed as "trustworthy" (vs. 4); his eyes are on "those who fear him" (vs. 18), and it is to this Lord that we look for his "kindness," for we "have put our hope in [him]" (vs. 22).

Today's second reading from 2 Tm 1:8–10 is deceptively short, but it contains great wisdom and insight. The author speaks of the unmerited salvation we have received in Christ, for it is God who has saved us (vs. 8) and whose grace is "now made manifest through the appearance of our Savior" (vs. 10). It is Christ the Savior whom we experience in the liturgy and whom we acknowledge in the event of transfiguration. Through his humiliation, Christ "robbed death of its power and has brought life and immortality into clear light through the gospel" (vs. 10). The power of the resurrection shines through the sufferings of this world as they, like Christ's sufferings, lead to eternal glory.

The transfiguration gospel today discloses how important it is to sustain this vision through life. Just before the transfiguration narrative in Matthew's gospel, the evangelist tells how Peter confesses his faith in Jesus as the Messiah (see Mt 16:16, as well as Mk 8:29, and Lk 9:20). Then follows Jesus' first prediction of his passion: "Jesus started to indicate to his disciples that he must go to Jerusalem and greatly suffer there . . . and be put to death. . . " (Mt 16:21). All of this, along with the transfiguration story itself, is meant to show that Jesus would indeed be revealed in glory as the Messiah. Moses and Elijah appear with Jesus symbolizing the fact that the "law and the prophets," which they represent, were to make ready the way for the coming of the Messiah.

Each of the synoptics tells of the voice from the cloud identifying Jesus as the Son of God, and the command to "listen to him" (Mt 17:5; Mk 9:7; Lk 9:15). The voice from the cloud reminds us of the scene of Jesus' baptism where a voice from the heavens said, "this is my beloved Son, my favor rests on him" (Mt 3:17). It is through this favored Son, because of his ministry inaugurated at his baptism and his resurrected life after his passion, that we experience God's grace, peace, and favor.

Each evangelist repeats Peter's proposal to erect three booths on the mountain to memorialize this event. The reference to "booths" recalls the dwelling of God with his people in tents in the desert, the annual Jewish festival of Tabernacles that looked toward the fulfillment of messianic hopes, and the new Jerusalem.

In addition to the stylistic and theological motifs that are shared by all the synoptics, there are specifically Matthean understandings operative here. Matthew sets the scene of the transfiguration on a "high mountain" (Mt 17:1). In addition to the obvious Old Testament reference to the mountain of Sinai, where the law was first given to Israel, there are other meanings that Matthew attaches to a "mountain." The third temptation of Jesus, mentioned in last week's reading from Matthew's gospel, takes place on a "very high mountain" (Mt 4:8). The giving of the beatitudes takes place "on the mountainside" (Mt 5:1ff.). After Jesus went "up onto the mountainside," he cured the crippled, the deformed, the blind, and the mute (Mt 15:29). The eleven "went to the mountain to which Jesus had summoned them" (Mt 28:16) to be sent forth to make disciples. By situating the transfiguration on the mountain, Matthew places it in the realm of most significant revelations, on a par with the giving of the law and the beatitudes.

Another stylistic trait shared with the other synoptics, but that has greater significance in Matthew, is the association between the saying, "this is my beloved Son . . ." (Mt 17:5), and the attestation of the centurion at Jesus' crucifixion, "clearly this was the Son of God" (Mt 27:54). (While this text is also found in Mark, it is not in Luke.) Hence the affirmation from the cloud of Jesus' identity invites other affirmations, the centurion's and ours as well. For Jesus to be recognized as God's son requires an act of faith. The revelation of Jesus' identity by the Father invites us to recognize in the transfigured Jesus the presence of the fullness of God's revelation to us.

Both Matthew and Mark note that Peter, James, and John were overcome with fear (Mt 17:6; see Mk 9:6) at the sight of the transfigured Jesus and at the announcement of his identity. This fear is calmed when Jesus takes the initiative in the next verse and tells them "get up! Do not be afraid." In Matthew's narrative, this parallels the fear of the disciples in the boat when the storm rose up (Mt 8:23–27). The disciples cry out, "Lord, save us! We are lost" (vs. 25). Jesus reproves them with the words, "how little faith you have" (vs. 26), and then he calms the storm. As the psalmist says:

"He hushed the storm to a gentle breeze,
and the billows of the sea were stilled" (Ps 107:29).

At the postresurrection scene of commissioning the eleven to go forth to teach and baptize, the evangelist states that "at the sight of [Jesus], those who had entertained doubts fell down in homage" (Mt 28:17). We are very much like the disciples at the transfiguration and like those on the storm-tossed sea. We often cry out for help and healing from Jesus. We acclaim him as "Lord" but we still half-doubt, half-believe that he will be with us in our need. The event of the transfiguration proclaimed on this Lenten Sunday is a reassurance that indeed the Lord is with us and sustains us through this life, especially when we have "little faith." Lent is a season to grow in and deepen the faith we profess in Christ as the transfigured and now risen Lord.

Among the many themes that emerge from reflection on the meaning of the transfiguration in Matthew's gospel, the other readings in today's liturgy also shed light on the meaning of the faith we have in the transfigured Christ. In Jesus, God has robbed death

of its power (second reading) and through Christ his lifegiving
strength is given to us all.

Cycle "B"

The first reading at today's eucharist is taken from the story of
Abraham in the book of Genesis (as are the first readings in the A
and C cycles for this Sunday). This text from Genesis 22 (1–2,9,10–
13,15–18) has been a traditional reading at the Easter Vigil, and the
reformed Lectionary assigns verses 22:1–18, that is, the shorter
form used today, as the second reading at that celebration.

God asked Abraham to sacrifice his only son, the one born to
Sarah in her and Abraham's old age. Abraham is an Old Testament
example of one who was willing to give all, even his only son, to
God. Thus, Abraham is revered as a "type" of Christ in that his
obedience presaged Jesus' own. It is by identifying with Jesus'
obedience, leading even to suffering and death, that we can share
in the fullness of his risen life.

As the responsorial psalm states: "Precious in the eyes of the
Lord is the death of his faithful ones" (Ps 116:15). "I am your
servant; you have loosed my bonds" (vs. 16). With confidence and
hope, we respond to the text of this psalm with the refrain: "I will
walk in the presence of the Lord in the land of the living" (vs. 9).

The second reading states that God "did not spare his own but
handed him over for the sake of us all" (Rom 8:32). This summary
of the paschal mystery reflects not only the Old Testament examples of faith and obedience as in the case of Abraham, but also
helps us appreciate that, through Christ's obedience to the Father,
the liturgy helps us to grow in loving obedience to the divine will.

The gospel of the transfiguration is proclaimed today from Mark
9:2–10. (See above, "A" cycle, on the elements common to the
synoptic authors as they recount this scene.) Many exegetes point
out that verses 2–8 of this reading contain the story of the transfiguration, while verses 9–10 reflect such events as Moses descent
from Mount Sinai, where as he conversed with the Lord, "the skin
of his face had become radiant" (Ex 34:29).

Jesus strictly admonishes Peter, James, and John "not to tell
anyone what they had seen, before the Son of Man had risen from
the dead" (vs. 9). He wants to be sure that the disciples do not
think that from now on they would share his glory on earth.

But the disciples do not understand: "they continued to discuss what 'to rise from the dead' meant." A few short verses later Mark describes Jesus as again predicting his passion (Mk 9:30–32) and again Mark tells us that "they failed to understand his words" (vs. 32).

They fail to see that suffering, renunciation, and even death are required for one to share in the risen life of Christ.

Is it really any different in our lives? When suffering enters our lives what is our response? If we realize that to profess Christianity means to care for the oppressed and not to continue oppressing them, and that the Christian life involves sharing with the hungry and the homeless, not just being sympathetic toward them, then we will be ready to share in Christ's own suffering and death, and to share in his glory with those whose sufferings we have alleviated here on earth.

Cycle "C"

The first reading today, from Genesis (15:5–12,17–18), continues the theme of the faith of Abraham, this time dealing with the covenant that the Lord made with him affirming that he would be the father of many descendants.

As St. Paul notes, it was Abraham's faith that made him great in the sight of God (see Rom 4:1–25 and Gal 3:6–9). "Certainly the promise made to Abraham and his descendants that they would inherit the world . . . was made in view of the justice that comes from faith" (Rom 4:13).

The liturgy again offers us Abraham as an example and model for our lives. Our new covenant relationship with God demands our surrender, a total giving of ourselves as did Abraham. Then do our acts of worship and piety signify our dedication to and dependence upon God alone.

The responsorial psalm (Ps 27) speaks of what should be our attitude before God: waiting and hoping that we shall share in his bounty forever in the land of the living (vs. 13). The response expresses our faith in "the Lord . . . [our] light and [my] salvation" and affirms our faith in imitation of Abraham, "our father in faith."

Today's second reading from Philippians (3:17–4:1) challenges contemporary congregations to look upon things of this world in the light of our destiny as citizens of heaven (vs. 20). By baptism we are "citizens of heaven," and as such we are members of his body and await the coming of Christ, who will remake our bodies "according to the pattern of his glorified body."

Insofar as we believe this, we will grow more and more detached from the allurements of this world, such as money, power, and status. Lent offers us a special opportunity to experience what detachment means. But we can practice it only if, as Paul admonishes us, we "stand firm in the Lord" (4:1).

Today's gospel gives the Lukan version of Jesus' transfiguration. This version has its own significant variations from that of the other synoptics.

The first verses of the pericope (Lk 9:28–36) recount that "Jesus took Peter, John and James, and went up onto a mountain to pray" (vs. 28). While he was praying, the transfiguration occurred.

Throughout his gospel, Luke stresses the part that prayer played in Jesus' life. At his baptism and at the agony in the garden (Lk 3:21 and 22:40) Jesus is at prayer. In the latter text, he instructs his disciples to "pray that you may not be put to the test." In 11:5–13, Luke gives two parables interpreting the Lord's Prayer. And it is Luke alone who provides the parable on the necessity of praying always and not losing heart (18:1–8).

At the scene of the transfiguration, Luke has the disciples falling into a deep sleep (vs. 32) just as they were to do on the Mount of Olives (22:45–46). At the transfiguration, the disciples wake up and see the change in Jesus and have a glimpse of his glory; at the agony in the garden they awake and find that he is being arrested. One can awake to experience the glory of Christ only if one awakes to share in his humiliation and death.

Luke tells how Peter, John, and James heard the voice from the cloud: "This is my Son, my Chosen One. Listen to him" (vs. 35). The "Chosen One" mentioned here is the same chosen one foretold in Isaiah 42:1 and is the same chosen one who is taunted by the crowd at his crucifixion: "He saved others; let him save himself if he is the Messiah of God, the chosen one" (Lk 23:35). Luke is the only evangelist to use the term "chosen one" at the crucifixion scene. This same Jesus, the chosen of God, who is servant, transfigured Lord, and who dies on the cross is the one through whom we have access to the Father. In Lukan theology, Jesus is the pivotal center of history. He fulfills the hopes of Israel and brings salvation; he inaugurates the mission of the church to the ends of the earth.

The liturgy this Sunday speaks about our covenant relationship with God (first reading). Today might well be an opportune time for us to reflect on the quality of our prayer and our response to the covenant we share in and through Christ.

Just as Abraham's faith was a response to God and a submission to God's will, so our prayer ought be a regular response we offer to the Father and a ready submission to his will for us. Our prayer can help us perceive the work of God active in all aspects of our lives, especially when the glory of transfiguration seems distant and the reality of suffering and humiliation is so clear.

Sacramentary Texts

Either one of the two entrance antiphons would be a good choice to introduce today's liturgy. The first one is the traditional text (Psalm 25) from the former Roman Missal and asks God to remember his mercy "from ages past." Once again in the liturgy we ask God to remember his people and in remembering to save them from present misfortune. (See comments on Exodus texts from the office of readings for the first week in Lent.) The second option, from Psalm 27, by speaking of seeking God's face, reflects the transfiguration theme: "his face changed in appearance. . . ." The glimpse of God's glory that we experience through the liturgy sustains us in our journey toward sharing his Son's glory in heaven.

The opening prayer today is taken from the Mozarabic (Spanish) liturgical tradition. It asks that the God who reveals himself through his Son may "enlighten us" and help us find our "way to [his] glory." This prayer, as well as the alternative opening prayer, reflects the transfiguration, although the alternative prayer speaks of such general Lenten themes as "repentance and a change of heart."

The prayer over the gifts expresses the traditional belief that the eucharist takes away our sins. The Latin original asks that we may be prepared to celebrate the paschal mysteries (not just the "resurrection," as appears in the English).

Today's preface is newly composed from traditional sources and reflects the gospel. It notes that through the "Law and the Prophets" Jesus' disciples are prepared for his approaching death.

The wording of the communion antiphon appears in the gospel of the "A" cycle: "this is my Son . . . listen to him" (Mt 17:5), as well as in the verse before the gospel in all three cycles of this Sunday's liturgy.

The prayer after communion is taken from one of the oldest sacramentaries. It calls the eucharist the "holy mysteries" for which we give thanks.

Celebration of the Eucharist

Last Sunday, the rite of election was celebrated, and on the Third, Fourth, and Fifth Sundays of Lent, the scrutinies prior to initiation will take place. In comparison, today's eucharist is familiar in structure. However, this does not mean that the candidates for initiation should be neglected in the intercessions or in the homily. Nor should emphasis on the glory of the transfiguration eliminate any reference to the Lenten penances that continue until Easter. A balance between penance and exaltation should be evident in today's celebration.

The introduction to the liturgy, even in this time of penance, could incorporate some mention of the transfiguration because Sunday is our weekly commemeration of the resurrection of the Lord.

A definite pause before praying the opening prayer could make the congregation aware of being silent before the glory of God.

The intercessions today should include the community's Lenten projects and programs, those who are preparing for the sacraments of initiation (adult baptism and confirmation for those already initiated), as well as those whose sufferings in union with the sufferings of Christ will ultimately lead them to the glory of heaven. It might be well to use the special preface for the Second Sunday of Lent, with either the second or third eucharistic prayer.

If the Lamb of God is extended to cover the breaking of bread and the filling of the cups for communion, it might be well to add some strophes about the risen and the transfigured Christ.

The Mass formula in the Sacramentary assigns a prayer over the people for today's celebration but another prayer may be selected in its stead. If the solemn blessing of the Passion of the Lord was used last Sunday, it might well be used for this and all the Lenten Sundays to establish a continuity throughout the season.

Liturgy of the Hours

Evening prayer I on Saturday provides antiphons to the psalms that speak of Peter, James, and John (first), the face of Jesus becoming radiant as the sun (second), and the witness of Moses and Elijah to this event (third), all emphasizing the transfiguration theme of Sunday's liturgy. The scripture reading is the same as the one used last Saturday, 2 Corinthians 6:1–4a (the first two verses of which were part of the second reading on Ash Wednesday).

The antiphon to Mary's canticle significantly points to Jesus, Mary's son, as the Son of God, and as the one to whom we must listen.

The first text in the office of readings, Exodus 13:17–14:9, concerns the journey of Israel toward the Red Sea. It is interesting to note that in this text there is a reference to a cloud: "the Lord preceded them, in the daytime by means of a column of cloud to show them the way . . ." (vs. 21). "Cloud" here, as well as in Sunday's gospel, denotes divine intervention and sustaining care; it takes on messianic meanings at the scene of the transfiguration.

The second reading from St. Leo the Great explores the meaning of the transfiguration. It contrasts the old law (Moses and Elijah) with the grace and truth of the new law (Jesus). As is typical in patristic literature, woven into this text are a number of scripture passages, among them St. Paul's statement that the sufferings of the present being nothing as compared with future glory. Our response to the transfiguration is to continue steadfast in faith and love, obeying the word of the revealer, Jesus Christ.

The antiphons and psalms at morning and evening prayer today refer in general terms to Lenten themes and theology. As is customary, the antiphons for the canticles reflect the gospel of the day, and thus they should be emphasized.

Interestingly, the canticle used as part of the psalmody at Evening Prayer II is taken from 1 Peter 2:21–24 (used also last week and to be used on Sundays throughout Lent) and emphasizes the suffering of Jesus.

On this Sunday, when the transfiguration could tend to eclipse the appropriate place of suffering and the passion in accomplishing redemption, this canticle might well be emphasized in the celebration of Lenten evening prayer, especially today.

Celebration of the Hours

Since the antiphons for Evening Prayer I are about the transfiguration, they could be sung at the beginning and end of the psalms to help to introduce this theme today.

If the psalm prayers are said at evening prayer, they might well take some phrases from the texts of these antiphons.

Since the second antiphon at the invitatory is so significant in terms of reiterating the seasonal nature of the liturgy and the importance of hearing the Lord's voice, it should be emphasized by singing as a response by the community throughout Psalm 95. For the psalmody at this hour, since Psalm 104 is divided into three sections, it might be helpful to use the first antiphon at the beginning and the end of the psalm to eliminate the doxologies between each section, and to allow for a significant pause before the readings.

Should a community want to emphasize evening prayer during Lent, for example, establishing one format for the prayer with singing (both responsorial and antiphonal), silence, proclamation, and appropriate gestures (incense at the Canticle of Mary) would help make the liturgy of the hours a celebration in rite and word instead of the usually wordy prayer form.

Reflection—"Glory-sharing and Cross-carrying"

In the gloom and doom with which so many Catholics have surrounded Lent, today's liturgy stands out as a contradiction. The important event of the transfiguration of Jesus offers us not an escape from suffering and humiliation, but a way of viewing these human realities in order to transform them into means of sharing in the mission and person of Jesus. In Christianity it is not a question of experiencing suffering *or* glory, but of experiencing both.

Sharing in Christ's suffering by our penitential exercises, especially during Lent, should force us to put an end to false notions of self. We find out that we must eliminate from our lives whatever hinders us from loving God above all and loving each other in him.

We come to this Lenten liturgy today to be confronted with a glory story. We are indeed "confronted" but not immediately consoled because the glory of the transfiguration also pointed to the humiliation and suffering Jesus was to undergo. Yet we must also remember that the glory of the transfiguration was a sign of what was yet to be revealed in Christ's resurrection from the dead.

Today's liturgy reminds us of the transfigured glory of Jesus who, now in eternal glory in heaven, sustains us and helps us to face the humiliations, the sufferings, and the trials of this life that lead to life forever with him in the kingdom.

MONDAY OF THE SECOND WEEK OF LENT

Liturgical Context

While the liturgy of the eucharist for the days after Ash Wednesday deals with the interior renewal that is brought about by the discipline of Lent, and the liturgy for the first full Lenten week deals with forgiveness and love of neighbor, this week's liturgy is based on no one particular theme, but its structure shows the imprint of traditional usages and contemporary reform. The scriptures at Mass on Monday, Tuesday, and Saturday deal with forgiveness and reconciliation (with the proclamation of the traditional gospels for Tuesday and Saturday). On Wednesday and Friday, the texts are also traditional and deal with the dissension caused by Jesus' preaching and the events that lead to his crucifixion. The texts for Thursday are the traditional ones used on this day and concern the choices one must make in order to reach eternal life.

The office of readings at the liturgy of the hours continues the proclamation of the book of Exodus: crossing the Red Sea, the feeding with manna, water from the rock, judges appointed by Moses as leaders, the law to be given at Sinai, and the giving of the decalogue. This week, some familiar Lenten themes, such as penance and conversion reemerge in the liturgy and are intensified.

Liturgy of the Eucharist

The entrance antiphon from Psalm 26:11–12 is traditional; it emphasizes our need for redemption: "Redeem me, Lord, and have mercy on me."

The opening prayer, from the earliest collection of collects available, speaks about our spiritual renewal as a result of penitential practices, and prays that we be kept from sin.

Both scripture readings are newly selected for proclamation today and are closely related to each other. The first, from the book of Daniel (9:4–10), begins by emphasizing the covenant relationship enjoyed by Israel with God, who keeps his merciful covenant toward those who love him and keep his commandments (vs. 4). The text acknowledges the sin of both rulers and people (vs. 5), even though they have heard the words of the prophets. This acknowledgment of sins is accompanied by the prayer that the Lord who is compassionate and forgiving (vs. 9) will extend his mercy to the repentant believers. The covenant love of God is similarly invoked at liturgy when Christians gather to hear the word of the Lord and to pledge their adherence to the new covenant.

The responsorial psalm (Ps 79) reiterates the compassion and love of God; its refrain states: "Lord, do not deal with us as our sins deserve" (Ps 103:10).

The gospel brings out a characteristic New Testament theme: forgive and you will be forgiven (Luke 6:36–38). The text forbids us to judge others, but encourages us to appreciate God's mercy toward us, so that we will extend our loving forgiveness to others.

The prayer over the gifts asks that the Lord prevent us from becoming absorbed in material things. That is to say that we use the things of this world not merely for the pleasure they give us, but as gifts of God that can focus our minds on spiritual things. Sharing in the sacred mysteries of the eucharist helps us to see material things in God's light.

The communion antiphon is taken from the first verse of today's gospel: "Be merciful as your Father is merciful"—a particularly poignant reminder that as we approach the eucharist we also are to approach others with mercy and love.

The prayer after communion, from a traditional text, asks that by receiving God's pardon in the eucharist he may lead us to "the joy of heaven."

Celebration of the Eucharist

In planning the Lenten liturgy, especially for weekdays, a careful choice of options can subtly underscore Lenten themes or the scripture readings without indulging in wordy comments.

To begin today's liturgy with greeting A, about the grace of the

Lord Jesus, the love of God, and the fellowship of the Spirit, would indicate that the love we share in Christ is to be extended to others in the fellowship of the Spirit, thus giving a foretaste of the message of today's gospel.

The second form (B) of the penitential rite: "Lord, we have sinned against you," and "Lord, show us your mercy and love," looks forward to the first reading from the prophet Daniel.

For the verse before the gospel (Lectionary 224), number 7, about seeking good, not evil, would adequately introduce the gospel text.

Those who compose the general intercessions might well consult the set of sample intercessions for Lent (Lent I) in Appendix I of the Sacramentary, noting especially petitions C and D, about reconciliation and repentance.

The use of the second eucharistic prayer for Masses of Reconciliation would coincide well with the gospel today, as would a brief introduction to the communal praying of the Lord's Prayer that would speak of reconciliation as the response of those who receive God's reconciling love. Form C of the dismissal, "Go in peace to love and serve the Lord," would be a subtle reminder that the effects of the liturgy are meant to be seen in life.

Liturgy of the Hours

Today's office of readings contains the account of Israel's crossing the Red Sea (Ex 14:10–31). The people grumble angrily at Moses' leadership, but he assures them that "the Lord will fight for you" and allow his people to pass through the sea unharmed, thus saving them from the Egyptians. Significantly, this text is followed by a responsory taken from the same section of the book of Exodus, the "song of Miriam" (Ex 15:1–3ff.). The invitation, "Let us sing to the Lord, glorious in his triumph, horse and rider he has thrown into the sea," indicates a pattern often found in Judaeo-Christian piety: a declaration of praise is offered.

This particular responsory forms part of the canticle used at morning prayer (on Saturday, Week I) and the pattern is seen in many of the psalms and blessing prayers of the liturgy (see for example the eucharistic prayers).

The second text for this hour, from John Chrysostom, is significant in that it is from a series of instructions for catechumens and is typical of patristic typology. Chrysostom sees the Israelite's passage of the Red Sea as a type of baptism, and Moses as a type of the new Moses, Christ. Patristic typology is often used when applying the scriptures in Lent to the rites of initiation, as will be seen more clearly in the liturgy after the Third Sunday of Lent.

The antiphons for the New Testament canticles at morning and evening prayer are taken from today's gospel reading about being compassionate (morning) and not judging (evening).

Celebration of the Hours

The verse before the readings in the office of readings today, "Turn away from sin and be faithful to the gospel—the kingdom of God is at hand," is the one assigned for the Mondays of Lent up to Holy Week. It could be used as the invitatory to the hours today, appropriately joined to Psalm 95.

The psalmody for the office of readings is taken from Psalm 31, thus allowing the option of praying it in three sections with antiphons and doxologies, or in three sections with pauses in between the sections.

At the conclusion of the hours, a blessing or a prayer over the people from the Sacramentary could be used; for example, number 5, "Lord, bless and strengthen your people. May they remain faithful to you and always rejoice in your mercy. . . ."

Reflection—"Words of Comfort, Some Uncomfortable Words"

The dynamic of biblical revelation includes God's continual call to us and our response in faith to him. This covenant relationship is foundational for understanding the scriptures, for appreciating the place of liturgy in our lives, and for evaluating how Lent fits into our spiritual journey. Lent is our annual time to begin anew to pay greater attention to the Lord's call to us and to our response to him.

The comforting thing about today's liturgy is that it emphasizes the ever-faithful covenant love that God has for us as his chosen ones. We are the sheep of the good shepherd's pasture; we are the faithful who respond to the constant fidelity of the God we worship. We can and do rely on the covenant love of God for comfort and strength.

But there is another side of today's liturgy that challenges us to forgo our comfortable way of life in order to live up to the covenant with God. To do so means that we will give our support and love to those in need.

Today's readings assure us that God is always present to sustain us despite our lapses into infidelity. But these words of comfort require our response to God's love in ways that may be uncomfortable to us; to show compassion to others, especially during Lent, is a sign of our sharing in Jesus' passion and death.

TUESDAY OF THE SECOND WEEK OF LENT

Liturgical Context

Today's office of readings, continuing the account of Israel's journey to the promised land, deals with his feeding his people with manna from heaven. The first reading at the eucharist once again assures us of God's forgiveness, "if you are willing and obey him." The gospel offers a particularly severe denunciation of those who fail to practice what they preach. The liturgy of the word thus focuses both on God's loving care, and its corollary, our need to respond to him by willing obedience.

Liturgy of the Eucharist

The entrance antiphon speaks about "light" for our eyes as opposed to the sleep of death, thus expressing faith in the God who is light shining in our darkness.

The opening prayer asks God to guide the church with his "unfailing love." The reliance on God, spoken of in the entrance antiphon, finds an echo in this prayer as we ask God to "protect us from what could harm us" and "lead us to what will save us." In this sense, both texts introduce the message of Isaiah in the first reading about right conduct and God's forgiving love.

The prophet begins by calling us to "Listen to the instruction of our God" (Is 1:10,16–20). We are to "hear" the word of the Lord and obey it as our rule of life. This is the very message that the liturgy of the word brings us at each eucharistic celebration.

God's command to "put away misdeeds," to "make justice your aim" (vs. 16), is clearly stated. But, as if this were not enough, the prophet specifies how the Lord wants this command carried out: by redressing the wrongs of the marginal and fringe people, the "orphans" and "widows." These challenging prophetic words call upon us to "set things right," and the Lord will forgive and support us, his people. Though our sins be scarlet, they will become white as snow, though they be crimson red, they will become white as wool, says the prophet (vs. 18). This same text is used on Saturday as the short reading at morning prayer, thus making it an important text in the Lectionary cycle in Lent.

The responsorial psalm, Psalm 50, is used to complement the reading from Isaiah with the refrain: "to the upright I will show the saving power of God" (vs. 23). The text of the psalm emphasizes the gospel message that the Lord demands good deeds, not just fine words: "Why do you recite my statutes/and profess my covenant with your mouth,/though you hate discipline/and cast my words behind you?" (vs. 21).

Today's gospel, the traditional text for this Lenten weekday, contains a particularly harsh criticism of the "scribes and Pharisees," the leaders of Jewish religion at the time of Jesus (Mt 23:1–12). The integrity that God calls for, as mentioned in the first reading and responsorial psalm, is reflected in this text, which indicts religious works that are done only "to be seen." The next part of the gospel deals with those who set themselves up as teachers, but who are themselves proud and hypocritical. Jesus affirms that there is really only one teacher, rabbi, and father (vss. 8–9) and he is in heaven. Just as the words of Isaiah call for justice for the poor, the orphans, and widows, so Jesus' words in the gospel declare that the only real authority is exercised by those who serve, not dominate, others. The fact that the liturgy offers such critical statements today reminds us that our religious practices, especially during Lent, should reflect inward dispositions and not merely be an outward show of piety.

The prayer over the gifts today is well attested in liturgical tradition and asks that this celebration may bring us closer to God, "cleanse us from our faults," and lead us to the gift of eternal life in heaven.

The prayer after communion reiterates these sentiments by asking that "we may live better lives" through God's "constant assistance."

Celebration of the Eucharist

Today's liturgy could appropriately begin with the first greeting (the same as was used yesterday), with its reference to the "fellowship of the Holy Spirit," to remind us that we are called as a community to share in God's love and forgiveness, a theme of today's liturgy.

The use of the "I confess" formula for the penitential rite can also make each of us realize where we have failed to make our deeds accord with our belief in Christ. Again, number 7 of the verses before the gospel (used yesterday) would appropriately introduce today's gospel.

In the general intercessions today, prayer for the marginal or the outcast in our local communities (orphans, battered children and wives, widows) as well as for a true and deep change of heart to live, not just speak, the word of God, would be appropriate, along with others of a general Lenten theme.

The use of the Lenten preface III, with the text, "We are to show to those in need your goodness to ourselves," reflects the main theme of the readings—to practice what we preach.

Introducing the Lord's Prayer with a variation on the third (C) invitation to pray, "Let us ask our Father to forgive our sins and to bring us to forgive those who sin against us," would be fitting.

The invitation to offer the sign of peace could also be phrased so as to affirm our intention to make the sign meaningful by living in love and peace with others.

Number 23 of the prayers over the people, asking God to give us "a true love for one another," would epitomize the theme of today's liturgy.

Liturgy of the Hours

The text of Exodus 16:1–18,35, about the manna from heaven, narrates that once again the chosen people are "grumbling" (vs. 2) against their leaders. In their hunger they yearn for the fleshpots of Egypt, symbolic of their former "good life." Once again, however, it is the Lord who responds to their cry and through Moses promises to feed them with quail in the evening and, in the morning, "bread from heaven"—manna. God's gift of manna to the Israelites in the desert was one of the ways he showed both his power and his presence among them. The gift of his food from heaven prompted the people to respond. They did so by obeying the Lord's command about gathering the manna and by faith in him that he would continue to feed them. Like the Israelites in the desert, we too are pilgrims on the way to the promised land of heaven. We are fed with bread from heaven, Jesus Christ in the eucharist. As our response to this great gift we obey Christ's loving commands and we live by faith in him.

The responsory to the reading contains references to Wisdom 16:20, which text is used as the versicle and response during benediction of the blessed sacrament. It is followed by the text of John 6:32 referring to the gift of manna and to the present gift of sustenance through Jesus: "It was not Moses who gave you bread. . . . It is my Father who gives you true bread from heaven."

St. Augustine's commentary on Psalm 141 likens the passion of the Lord to the evening sacrifice, and his resurrection to the morning sacrifice that took place in the Temple according to the Old Law. Jesus is the victim "that brings salvation; the holocaust acceptable to God." Our prayers offered during the celebration of the eucharist "rise like incense from a holy altar," for prayer is in its way a sacrifice, fragrant to the Lord.

Celebration of the Hours

Today's verse before the readings (used on all Tuesdays in Lent) is the familiar Lenten theme: "This is the favorable time.—This is the day of salvation," and is a suitable invitatory to Psalm 95, with its references to the Exodus story that, in turn, is so central to the Lenten liturgy at the office of readings. To evoke the connotations of the responsory after today's first reading, the community might recite each of the three sections into which Psalm 37 is divided at the office of reading with a short period of silence after each one. Then the responsory mentioned above could be used at the end of the entire psalm to make its presence there especially striking.

Reflection—"Do As I Say, Not As I Do"

We have all experienced, at one time or another, being hurt by someone who said one thing and did another. Whether in business, families, or friendships there is scarcely anything more disappointing than being victimized by a two-faced person. And once we have been made the victim, we tend to expect that person to victimize us again.

Today's gospel relates to these very human situations by reminding us that we are all fallible, we are all likely to be less than totally honest all the time, and we are all not yet perfect in God's sight—even those we honor with the prestigious title of "father" or "teacher."

The gospel by no means tells us to spend our time looking for faults in others and criticizing them for lack of integrity. In fact, in another section of this same gospel Matthew is at pains to tell us to look to ourselves and our imperfections rather than those of others. In today's gospel, we are not given license to treat others harshly; rather we are to accept what is good about them and to obey God above all.

In fact, what the scriptures reveal today is that we ourselves may well be among those who avidly seek titles, power, and social status. After all, Jesus says that it is in serving, not lording, that we perform the works of God. It is the essence of biblical revelation that the despised are exalted, the lowly are raised high, and the outcast are made the center of attention. The canticle we pray daily puts it this way:

"He has cast down the mighty from their thrones,
and has lifted up the lowly.
He has filled the hungry with good things,
and the rich he has sent away empty" (Lk 1:52–53).

Today's Lenten liturgy reminds us that the poor and the lowly are welcomed into the embrace of God. This side of the kingdom we are *all* imperfect. But in the family of the church we can become less so by turning to Christ in the Eucharist, who asks us "to set things right" in a world that has so often lost compassion for the poor. Only one is our teacher, and that is Jesus Christ the Messiah.

WEDNESDAY OF THE SECOND WEEK OF LENT

Liturgical Context

It has been noted that liturgical tradition prescribed for the Wednesdays and Fridays of Lent special penitential practices that, in their turn, affected the choice of liturgical texts. Just as the readings and prayers of the liturgy of Ash Wednesday spoke about the seriousness with which one should begin Lent, and last Wednesday's texts at the eucharist urged ever greater fidelity to the word of God, so today's eucharistic liturgy contains a significant pair of readings and liturgical texts. The gospel is traditional for this day. In the reformed liturgy, however, the former Old Testament reading has given place to a reading that reflects the message of the gospel, which speaks of the death that Jesus will undergo, as well as of the humility required of those who follow him.

Liturgy of the Eucharist

The entrance antiphon is traditional; it is the prayer of one who urgently calls for God's help. We pray that the Lord will not abandon us (Ps 38:22–23), lest we fail to continue our penitential practices as we journey through Lent.

The Latin version of the opening prayer asks that the Lord preserve his family, the church, which has always known how to perform good works, so that, with his present support and encouragement, he may lead it to its fulfillment in the kingdom. The "works" referred to could be the Lenten penances undertaken to sanctify our lives during this season.

The first reading from Jeremiah (18:18–20) was chosen to reflect the gospel text of the day. In it the enemies of Jeremiah speak about a plot against the prophet (vs. 18) that will use his own words against him. A Christian might apply this passage to Jesus' enemies, who twisted his words into blasphemy in order to achieve his condemnation and death. Today's responsorial psalm, based on Psalm 31:17, expresses the hope of the believer: "Save me, O Lord, in your steadfast love." The text of Psalm 31 acknowledges that the choices made in faith by believers sometimes lead to misunderstanding and even persecution by unbelievers. Hence such an appeal to God is essential for guidance, strength, and perseverance.

The third passion prediction from the gospel of Matthew introduces today's gospel reading (20:17–28), the major portion of which concerns the request by the mother of James and John that they receive places of honor and glory in the kingdom. This woman says to Jesus, "Promise me that these sons of mine will sit, one at your right hand and the other at your left, in your kingdom" (vs. 21).

In reply Jesus assures her that they must drink from his cup of suffering (vs. 22) and that assigning places of honor is not his to do (vs. 23). Service to others, as noted in yesterday's gospel (Mt 23:1–12) is reiterated forcefully today with the words, "anyone among you who aspires to greatness must serve the rest. . . " (vs. 27). The example of Jesus who gave his life as a ransom for all people should be sufficient to prove to all believers that their lives must be spent in similar service.

The essential place of suffering in the Christian life is brought out forcefully today, whereas last Sunday the emphasis was on the glory revealed in Jesus' transfiguration. Fittingly the Lenten liturgy emphasizes both aspects of the dying/rising pattern established in Jesus. The evangelist uses the misunderstanding of the disciples to remind us that we too may well misunderstand the cost of being a disciple of Jesus. The liturgy today provides an occasion for us to realize once again the place of suffering and humiliation in the Christian life. Today's eucharist invites us to share more and more deeply in Christ's victory over death.

Today's prayer over the gifts, a traditional text, asks that we be freed from the sins that ensnare us through this exchange of gifts. That is, we offer the gifts of bread and wine that will be changed into Christ's body and blood, which is his saving gift to us.

The communion antiphon is from the gospel of the day (Mt 20:28) and reiterates that the Son of Man came to serve and give his very life for the many. The Latin text of the prayer after communion asks that what we share now in the eucharist as a pledge of salvation may be fulfilled in heaven.

Celebration of the Eucharist

The introduction to today's liturgy could well point out that today's gospel message is about serving others rather than being served.

The invocations in IV of the third form of the penitential rite may be used as a prelude to the gospel message, which deals with divisions that arise when people seek dominance over others. Of the verses before the gospel, Lectionary 224, number 9, about repentance, would be an appropriate choice.

The fourth Lenten preface (Lent IV) would be a suitable choice today since it mentions Lent as a season for correcting our faults and for growing in holiness.

The second (B) memorial acclamation ("dying you destroyed our death . . .") combines our thanksgiving for Christ's saving death with our loving anticipation of his second coming in glory.

The introduction to the Lord's Prayer could be reworded to refer to our doing the will of the Father, especially when it entails our renouncing self for the sake of his glory.

The Lamb of God could be expanded today to include strophes referring to Christ's passion and death, again a subtle reflection of the gospel.

To conclude the liturgy, the presider might use number 17 of the prayers over the people, which speaks about the love that Jesus showed "when he delivered himself to evil men and suffered the agony of the cross," thus showing that we too must follow him in suffering and death as a sign of our love.

Liturgy of the Hours

The reading from Exodus (17:1–16) in today's office of readings continues the story of Israel's journey through the desert. The unfailing love of God for his people is shown by his giving them water from the rock to slake their thirst (vs. 6). Significantly, the place where this occurred is memorialized in Psalm 95, the classic invitatory psalm of the liturgy of the hours:

"Do not grow stubborn, as your fathers did in the wilderness, when at Meriba and Massah they challenged me and provoked me, Although they had seen all of my works" (vss. 8–9).

Today's reading also recounts the battle between Amalek and the Israelites led by Joshua. When Moses did as the Lord commanded and held his hands upraised, "Israel had the better of the fight" (vs. 11). This gesture has been utilized in scripture and patristic teaching to refer to Jesus lifting up his arms on the cross, an action that brought eternal salvation and victory to all. This story, and others like it, helped to develop Israel as God's chosen people. By recounting these stories, Israel made present, at times and places far removed from the original events, God's loving concern for their welfare. The Christian scriptures and the church fathers see in these stories a prefiguring of Jesus the Messiah. Thus, when Moses raises his hands and the Israelites get the better of the fight, Christians liken this gesture to the extension of Jesus' arms on the cross, an action symbolic of his giving his life for our salvation.

Today's responsory to the Exodus story about water from the rock quotes Isaiah, about "drawing water from the springs of salvation" (Is 12:3). Then the liturgy mentions John's account of Jesus' promise to the Samaritan woman, about giving water that will become a fountain to those who drink it. The liturgy thus presents three separate texts from the scriptures and weaves them together to remind us that Jesus is living water from whom we all receive life.

The reading from Irenaeus is a superb example of the kind of theology and spirituality which the Church fathers derived from their interpretation of the scriptures. Here Irenaeus reviews the salient points of salvation history from creation, through the patriarchs, the Exodus and the prophets, and finally to Christ. Parts of this reading are particularly relevant to the catechumens approaching baptism and to those of the initiated who will renew their baptismal commitment at Easter. There are, for example, the references to water, likening the rock from which Israel drank to Christ. Thus there are the remarks about God's law as "a school of instruction for them and a prophecy of what was to come" in Christ.

The responsory takes up this theme by quoting Galatians (3:24–25,23), which refers to the old law as the people's guardian until the coming of Christ, but now because Christ has come we no longer need that law, for we have access in faith to the Father through Christ.

Christ's coming did not destroy the law and the prophets. We saw this last Sunday as Christ spoke with Moses and Elijah at his transfiguration. What Christ did do, however, was to fulfill the law. He did this by his passion, death, and resurrection in which we share every time we celebrate the eucharist.

The reading at morning prayer (which is used on all Wednesdays in Lent) is particularly significant today for it summarizes much of the sense of the Exodus texts from the office of readings these past days. The chosenness enjoyed by Israel is fulfilled in us as the chosen of Christ: "The Lord, your God, has chosen you from all the nations . . . to be a people peculiarly his own" (Dt 7:6). The antiphons for the New Testament canticles at morning and evening prayer repeat the message of today's gospel, that the Son of Man came to serve (morning prayer) and to be handed over to be mocked, scourged, crucified, and raised on the third day (evening prayer).

Celebration of the Hours

The seasonal invitatory for Lent and Psalm 95 deserve special attention in celebration today because of the connection between the events at Meribah and Massah recounted in the Exodus reading and in the psalm itself. In addition, the responsory to the Exodus reading at the office of readings could well be emphasized today because it links the water from the rock with other moments of salvation history.

At morning prayer, the reading from Deuteronomy could be lengthened by the addition of verses reiterating the election and chosenness of Israel. This notion could also be reflected in the intercessory prayers at morning prayer by referring to Israel, to the baptized, to those preparing for baptism, and to all God's people, and asking that they may witness to their vocation in service and love.

At evening prayer today, in the reading from Philippians (2:12b–15a), Paul admonishes his hearers to "act without grumbling or arguing" (vs. 14); hence to conduct themselves contrary to the example of Israel in the desert. This text could easily be extended to include verses 12–18.

Reflection—The Way Some Mothers Are

She did what she thought best. She wanted her sons not to be forgotten in the new Jesus movement that surely would become a successful enterprise. And so she let her maternal instinct take over and she tried to get Jesus to give her boys good positions in his entourage. She wanted to see her sons secure and protected, she wanted their lives to be all set. And that is quite understandable.

However, Jesus explains to her, and to her sons, and to the other disciples that following him requires suffering. Jesus tells them that they would indeed drink of his cup of suffering, but whether they would sit at his side in glory was not his to give.

Is it really any different with us? Do we expect from religion the same thing we expect from a job or position in society? Do we expect accolades and recognition for what we do? Do we expect to be spared sadness and trial because we have paid our dues at the Sunday liturgy? If we do, perhaps we ought to put ourselves in the places of James, John, and their mother. Perhaps we ought not to chide them, but rather chide ourselves for seeking a reward just because of our faithful attendance, especially the extra time we put in during Lent. The way to sanctification lies in humbly accepting whatever God has in store for us and by living according to his word. This is the road to glory, Jesus assures us; this is the way to salvation. There are no front seats in the kingdom, or special certificates of merit in heaven. There is the eternal presence of the God for whom we have longed throughout this life.

THURSDAY OF THE SECOND WEEK OF LENT

Liturgical Context

Today's liturgy of the eucharist has more in common with the Thursday after Ash Wednesday than it has with the other liturgies of this second Lenten week. It points out that the choices we make in this life must be in accord with true Christian values, and then shows the differences between those who profess faith fully and those who do not. As the responsorial psalm states: "Happy the man . . . who . . . delights in the law of the Lord and meditates on his law day and night" (Ps 1:3). Meditating on the will of God and living in accord with his will are marks of the true Christian, especially during Lent.

Liturgy of the Eucharist

The use of Psalm 139:23–24 as the entrance antiphon indicates the intimate bond that exists between God and his chosen people. We pray that God will guide us "along the everlasting way" (vs. 24).

The Latin text of the opening prayer addresses God as one who both loves and restores innocence. We ask him to turn our hearts toward him in this holy season and to strengthen the faith we profess.

The readings today are traditional for this Lenten weekday and offer a study in contrasts. Jeremiah, speaking in the name of the

Lord, says that "cursed" are those who trust in "human beings" (17:5), and "blessed" are those who trust in the Lord (vs. 7). Scripture describes the life of those who trust in human beings as barren, dry, and empty, and the life of those who trust in God as fresh, green, and bearing fruit. The real test comes at the end when the Lord, who "alone probe(s) the mind and test(s) the heart" (vs. 10) rewards "everyone according to his ways, according to the merit of his deeds" (vs. 10).

The responsorial psalm reiterates this study in contrasts and declares as "happy" those "who hope in the Lord." This same response and the same verses of Psalm 1 are used on Thursday after Ash Wednesday, thus establishing a certain relationship between these two liturgies. The responsorial psalm, like the first reading, refers to trees that grow and bear fruit when it states that the faith-filled man:

". . . is like a tree
   planted near running water,
That yields its fruit in due season,
   and whose leaves never fade" (vs. 3).

The rather deliberate though gentle study in contrasts found in the first reading is sharpened and made very direct in the gospel's comparison of the rich man with Lazarus (Lk 16:19–31). This text, also found in the Lectionary for Masses for those suffering from famine and hunger, penetrates to the heart of the issue of riches and poverty in Luke's gospel. Jesus tells the story of a rich man, well off in his lifetime, who eventually dies and goes to "the abode of the dead," where he undergoes torment, while poor Lazarus, destitute throughout life, dies and is welcomed into a state of bliss with Abraham. But that is not all. The rich man requests that Lazarus be sent to warn his family that their fate will be like his if they continue to enjoy the good life and to exploit others. In Jesus' story, Abraham replies that there is no need for such special revelations: "If they do not listen to Moses and the prophets, they will not be convinced even if one should rise from the dead" (vs. 31). Just as there was a greater than Jonah in the person and preaching of Jesus (see gospel for Wednesday of the first week of Lent), so the preaching of Jesus and the tradition of prophetic teachings about living a good life should be enough to convince us.

The message of the text is clear: we are to obey and be faithful to the word of the Lord, and that concern for the poor is central to the Christian revelation.

The prayer over the gifts is traditional, but where the original Latin speaks of the "fasting" dedicated to the Lord, the new Latin version speaks of our "observance" of Lent, thus indicating that fasting is not the only way of "keeping Lent."

The communion antiphon, from Psalm 119, speaks of the law of the Lord, which is also mentioned in the responsorial psalm. Those of "blameless life" follow the law of the Lord and will be rewarded "according to the merit of his deeds" (Jer 17:10). The prayer after communion asks that we might experience the effect of the liturgy in our daily lives, and come to deeper love for one another.

Celebration of the Eucharist

The introduction to today's liturgy could focus on making choices that will strengthen our love for God and neighbor.

The third penitential rite (C) with the fifth set of sample invocations, about raising the dead to life in the Spirit, bringing pardon and peace to the sinner and light to those in darkness, could be an appropriate choice. A brief comment before the readings may show their relevance to the celebration if this has not already been done in the introduction to the liturgy.

For the verse before the gospel, Lectionary 224, number 12 (from Jn 3:15), about all who believe in Christ having eternal life, would be suitable.

Today's intercessions could mention the powerless of this world, those seeking for liberation from oppressive structures, and those in need of food and shelter.

The preface of Lent II, with its text: "You teach us how to live in this passing world with our heart set on the world that will never end," would be an appropriate choice to coincide with the readings.

To introduce the Lord's Prayer, the presider might use the fourth sample invitation or his own variation on it, mentioning prayer "for the coming of the kingdom."

The invitation to communion, "This is the Lamb of God . . . ," is especially significant at today's celebration, for it refers not only to communion under the sacred species but also to the eschatological banquet in the kingdom of heaven, thus offering us the peace that Lazarus is depicted as enjoying after his life of suffering.

Liturgy of the Hours

The reading from Exodus (18:13–27) recounts the appointment of judges under Moses to help in rendering decisions for the people of Israel. Interestingly, the responsory to this text, from Numbers 11:25, refers to the "spirit" the Lord had given Moses being shared with the "seventy elders." Spirit here is seen as a divine power that is given to the seventy elders to help them cooperate with God in his work of liberating the people.

The text from Hilary concerning the fear of the Lord points out that this fear is not to be confused with the anxiety we feel when we are faced with something we do not want to have happen to us. Fear of God is rooted in our love for God, which in turn begets respect for his laws and trust in his promises. By learning God's ways, we grow in this reverential fear and respect for his holiness.

The antiphons for the canticles of Zechariah and of Mary are taken from the gospel of today's eucharist and act as a study in contrasts: ". . . remember the good things you received in your lifetime and the bad things Lazarus received in his" (morning prayer, see Lk 16:25), and "The rich man . . . pleaded for a drop of water."

Celebration of the Hours

The verse before the readings in the office of readings and the responsorial psalm at the eucharist are both based on Psalm 40. Those planning the liturgy might well want to provide a special musical setting for each text. The first text used as the invitatory to the hours may be recited responsorially (as is the custom), and at the liturgy of the eucharist the other text can be sung by all, or the responsory can be sung by all at the beginning and the end of the psalm, with the text of the psalm sung by a cantor or schola.

The intercessions at morning and evening prayer could well refer to the contrasts found in the antiphons to the canticles and in the scripture readings at Mass. A series of intentions for the poor and the oppressed could serve to emphasize these texts. In addition, some reference to sharing our goods would also relate the liturgy to the ascetical practices of this Lenten season.

Reflection—"Shades of Gray"

It all seems simple. We make the choices, stick by them, and live happily ever after. What believing person would willfully choose wrongdoing when justice and peace are found in God alone? What believing person would choose to despise the poor when they are specially befriended by the Lord? It all seems so simple. We make the right choices, align ourselves with God, and live happily ever after. Or do we?

Do we always choose God's ways over man's ways? Do we believers always choose those things that reflect faith over what we can see, hear, and touch in this world? Do we forsake extra comforts so that the poor can have a greater share in the bounty of this world? Are we so content with our choices that we can say that we truly live happily now, and for the hereafter?

Today's liturgy calls us to deeper reflection on what our choices have been and ought to be as we seek to live the Christian life. For most of us there are probably few completely black or white issues. There are probably more shades of gray in our lives and in the decisions we have made in leading the Christian life than we would like to admit. The fact is, we on earth are still this side of the kingdom of God in its fullness. It is for this reason that we need Lent, this whole forty-day season, to turn again a bit more resolutely, a bit more convincingly, a bit more firmly to the Lord's ways, not ours.

For us to remove the insipid shades of gray in our lives, we need the challenge, guidance, and strength from the Lord that comes from the liturgy of this season.

No one else can answer the questions for us that today's liturgy poses. But answer them we must. What are the firm and committed principles according to which we live and move on this earth? Do they really lead us to God? Have we forgotten that baptismal allegiance must be renewed and ratified again and again? What will our answers be at Easter when we are asked:

"Do you reject sin, so as to live in the freedom of God's children? Do you reject the glamor of evil, and refuse to be mastered by sin? Do you reject Satan, father of sin and prince of darkness?"

May the Lord keep us faithful to the promises we have made and to the faith we share in the liturgy today.

Liturgical Context

The readings at today's liturgy of the eucharist, about Joseph being sold into slavery by his brothers, together with the parable of the tenants who killed the son of the man who owned the vineyard, offer us a foretaste of Good Friday that recalls the humiliation of Jesus that has brought eternal life for all peoples.

Liturgy of the Eucharist

The entrance antiphon calls on the Lord as our "refuge" from the snares set for us by wicked people (Ps 31:2,5). The opening prayer, which is traditional for this day, asks our heavenly Father to prepare us for the coming celebration of the passion, death, and resurrection of his Son.

The first reading from Genesis (37:3–4,12–13,17–28) concerns Joseph, the beloved son of Jacob. As such, he incurred the jealousy of his brothers, who determined to kill him. Instead of actually killing him, they decided finally to sell him for twenty pieces of silver to some passing slave traders. This boy, who became a slave in Egypt, was finally to become a ruler in that land and make Israel great among the Egyptians.

This text can be seen as a prefiguration of Christ, who himself was sold for a price, was betrayed by Judas, and who finally brought his people salvation by his sufferings and death.

The responsorial psalm, from Psalm 105, is also used on Thursday of the fifth week of Lent and refers to Joseph (vs. 17). The text can be applied to the sufferings Christ endured for us and his subsequent glorification by the Father.

The gospel from Matthew (21:33–43,45–46) is the parable that Jesus tells about the owner of a vineyard who sent his son (vs. 37) to collect his father's share of the grapes from his tenants. These tenants killed the son when he came to them. The gospel writer tells us that on this occasion Jesus quoted from Psalm 118:22: "The stone which the builders rejected has become the keystone of the structure." This text is used at various times in the liturgy of the Easter season, and it serves as the responsorial psalm on Easter itself and on the Second Sunday of Easter.

Both this reading as well as the Old Testament reading have a common theme: the killing, or at least the intention to kill, a person who is doing his father's will. Joseph's father sends him to his brothers; Jesus comes to teach us to do his Father's will. We know the result: Joseph is sold into slavery; Jesus is crucified. But Joseph saves his people and Jesus saves us. It all goes to show God's plan; out of adversity comes triumph, out of defeat comes victory.

The communion antiphon from 1 John 4:10 refers to Jesus who came "to take away our sins."

The prayer after communion is traditional for this day. It speaks of the eucharist ("the pledge of eternal salvation" in the Latin text) as the sacrament that helps us to properly direct our course to Christ.

Celebration of the Eucharist

The introduction to today's liturgy could mention some of the paradoxes in salvation history where apparent defeat leads to victory, where suffering leads to glory, where death leads to new life. That the pattern established in the Joseph story and in Jesus' life applies to us can be indicated by using the third form of the penitential rite with invocations composed about Christ's humiliation, enduring the cross, and offering us new life in his resurrection.

A fitting way to introduce the gospel today would be to use number 12 of the verses before the gospel (Lectionary 224), God who loved the world so much that he gave his only Son for our salvation.

In composing general intercessions for today, it would be good to mention the needs of the suffering and of those tempted to deny their faith.

The prayer after the intercessions could state that humiliation and triumph end in glory for those who follow Christ. The preface of Lent I could help underscore this season as a time to prepare for the paschal triduum (already referred to in the opening prayer) as it states:

". . . you give us this . . . season
when we prepare to celebrate the paschal mystery
with mind and heart renewed."

The second eucharistic prayer with its reference to Jesus' free acceptance of death ("Before he was given up to death, a death he

"makes his word known to Jacob,
to Israel his laws and decrees.
He has not dealt thus with other nations,
he has not taught them his decrees" (vss. 19–20).

Given the significance of these psalms, in celebration they might well be accompanied with corresponding psalm prayers composed by the leader, or they may be recited or sung prayerfully and with silences between them so that their meaning is emphasized and not obscured by wordy commentary.

At evening prayer, the psalms could be prayed in the above-mentioned fashion. The first psalm (116:1–9) is a hymn of thanksgiving, the second expresses confident trust in God (Ps 121), and the last is the canticle from Revelation (15:3–4) in praise of God for his ways and for the holiness we receive from him who alone is holy (vs. 4).

Reflection—"The Price, Not the Prestige, of Election"
The Lenten liturgy never tires of reaffirming the chosenness of Israel and the election of the followers of Christ as the new people of God. As the new people of God, we must not only acknowledge this status in faith but submit to the obligations that it imposes on us.

Joseph is an example of one whose lot in life seemed to be estrangement from his family, from home and hearth. But through divine providence he becomes the instrument through which his family and all Israel are saved.

The story of Joseph's enslavement points to the price that election, that is, being among the chosen of God, exacts. To accept enslavement and humiliation in our lives requires the firmness of faith and trust in God that marked the lives of both Joseph and Jesus. The question for us is to what extent we truly trust in the Lord's will for us and thereby accept the crosses in our lives.

Our life lived in faith is our response to God's choosing us to be his special possession, even when that chosenness means suffering and enduring humiliation for his sake. When we feel least favored, do we react and manipulate situations to remove the burden it places on us, or do we try to comprehend the hand of God at work

in our lives as it was in Joseph's? When we see that living according to the gospel will require some humiliation or embarrassment,
do we look to Jesus as an example of acceptance, or do we hedge
on the issue and carry around a portable fence so we can fall on
the expedient side no matter what the Christian principle involved?

Although we cannot make immediate decisions on these matters,
we can be assured that although election carries with it a price, one
that needs to be paid continually in good times and in bad, we can
rely on the strength and support that comes from God through the
liturgy we celebrate this day.

Election carries with it a price, not just prestige. It was that way
for Joseph. Should it be any other way for us?

SATURDAY OF THE SECOND WEEK OF LENT

Liturgical Context

Today's liturgy of the eucharist concludes the treatment begun
early in the week on forgiveness. The gospel recounts the parable
of the prodigal son, showing how sorrow for sin must precede
reconciliation.

Liturgy of the Eucharist

Today's entrance antiphon, by calling on the Lord who "is
loving and merciful," sets the theme of confidence and trust in God
that is developed in the readings.

The opening prayer speaks of the gifts that, through the liturgy,
enable us now to share in God's life. We pray that "in all we do,"
God will lead us to the light of the kingdom, our final end and
destiny.

In the reformed liturgy, the first reading from Micah (7:14–
15,18–20) acts as a prelude to the gospel, which is the dominant
text today. Portions of this reading from Micah, stressing God's
compassion, are proposed as an optional reading for use at the
celebration of reconciliation (see Rite of Penance, Chapter IV,
no. 131).

The prophet speaks of God as the one who "removes guilt . . .
[and] pardons sin" (vs. 18), "who does not persist in anger forever
but delights rather in clemency" (vs. 18) and who "will again have
compassion on us" (vs. 19). The Son of God who showed his

faithfulness to Israel (vs. 20) is made incarnate in Jesus who "welcomes sinners and eats with them" (Lk 15:2).

The God we worship at the liturgy, especially in the liturgy of baptism, penance, and the eucharist, is the God who continually offers us the forgiveness of our sins and the removal of all our guilt.

The responsorial psalm (Ps 103) with the refrain, "The Lord is kind and merciful" (which is also used on the Third Sunday of Lent "C" cycle), contains many of these same notions about God: "he pardons all your iniquities, he heals all your ills" (vs. 3), he "crowns you with kindness and compassion" (vs. 4), and he does not deal with us as our sins deserve (vs. 10).

The parable of the prodigal son, or better, of the forgiving father (Lk 15:1–3,11–32), is also used on the Fourth Sunday of Lent "C" cycle, and it is offered as an option for Masses for the forgiveness of sins, for the Sacred Heart, and in the Rite of Penance. In fact, in the Rite of Penance it is used as the gospel text and dominant motif in the sample penitential service in the Appendix: "the Son returns to the Father."

The parable narrates how the son broke his relationship with his father. But the father never ceased to love his wayward child. On the son's return, the father "ran out to meet him." The penitent son admits that he has offended both God and his own father. This change of heart wins his father's forgiveness. As a sign of this restored relationship, the father prepares a banquet for the son. Unhappily, the elder son is disturbed at his father's liberality. This faithful son had stayed home, worked hard, and never squandered any money on dissolute living. And yet here was this fool, not only forgiven and tolerated, but welcomed home by friends, relatives, and neighbors at a festive meal.

The parable makes us think of our own attitudes toward those we look down upon from our lofty position as sound, solid church-goers. God, our Father, reaches out to all of us in the sacrament of reconciliation. He has prepared for us the banquet of his Son as our spiritual food and drink. At that banquet, we must eat and drink without judging others as to race, status in life, or the state of their soul. Each of us, after all, is a child who at one time or another has strayed from our Father.

Celebration of the Eucharist

The introduction to the eucharist today could begin with a reference to the significant gospel story that so dominates the liturgy.

The use of the third penitential rite with either the fourth or fifth set of sample invocations, about reconciliation and Christ healing the wounds of sin (IV) and his raising the dead to life, granting pardon and peace, and giving light to those in darkness (V), would be appropriate.

Since one of the main functions of the verse before the gospel is to prepare for the proclamation to come, the use of number 11 of the options (Lectionary 224), taken from Lk 15:18, would be most fitting: "I will rise and go to my father and tell him: Father, I have sinned against heaven and against you."

Among the intercessions today, prayers for the end of hostility among nations, a lessening of tensions among family members, and an end to social sins that continue to oppress classes of people would be appropriate.

Of the eucharistic prayers and prefaces, the first prayer for Masses of Reconciliation would be most suitable today, especially with the text:

"God of love and mercy,
you are always ready to forgive;
we are sinners,
and you invite us
to trust in your mercy."

An introduction to the Lord's Prayer that refers to God's forgiveness and the hope that this inspires would be fitting, as would a special introduction to the sign of peace that would refer to reconciliation with our brothers and sisters as an essential part of reconciliation in the Christian community.

Liturgy of the Hours

With such emphasis given to the gospel reading today, it should be remembered that the liturgy of the hours has its own readings and emphases. For example, today's first reading stresses the giving of the law at Sinai. In this reading, the decalogue is given as it appears in Exodus 20:1–17. Yesterday, it will be recalled, the first reading ended with a portion of Exodus 20:18–21. Thus today's reading precedes the account of how frightened the people were *after* the Lord had delivered the ten commandments. The responsory adds a dimension that should not be overlooked or forgotten; that is, the law and word come and are "of the Lord." Hence, the "law" for Israel is by no means a detached set of prescriptions; they embody the revelation of a personal God to his people. In effect, they personify the Lord. For an observant Jew to abide by the law is to come to know God intimately. The psalmist says "the Law is my delight" because through the law Israel came to know God. It is also worthy of note that the praise of the law is followed by Paul's observation that "the whole law is summed up in love."

The text from Ambrose, used as the second reading at the office of readings, counsels Christians to "hold fast" to God who is "the good that permeates creation." Without wishing to force analogies, it can be said that the God who is at the center of the decalogue and of biblical revelation is the God who, Ambrose tells us, permeates creation and is the source of all good.

At morning prayer, the scriptural reading from Is 1:16–18 reiterates what is found in a longer form on Tuesday this week at the eucharist, and which summarizes much of what is enshrined in today's gospel text about the prodigal son. The theory expressed here is made incarnate in and through Christ.

The antiphon to the Canticle of Zechariah contains the important acknowledgment by the son that he ought no longer be called a son but a servant.

Celebration of the Hours

In place of Psalm 95 as the invitatory, it may be well to substitute Psalm 100, which speaks about God's merciful love. Psalm 106, contrasting the goodness of God with the faithlessness of his people, is assigned to today's office of readings, and thus acts as a prelude to the reading from Saint Ambrose, about God as the source of all good things.

At morning prayer, an opening hymn referring to the Lenten season in general would be a fitting introduction so that the context of the season is recalled in a subtle but significant way.

Reflection—"The Loving Father and His Two Sons"

This parable is about a loving father who showed his love for his two sons—but in different ways. We might well call the younger son the "selfish son" because he wanted to go it alone, he wanted to "take the money and run," he wanted to do things *his* way. What was prodigal about his behavior was that he spent all he had quickly and cared nothing about planning for the next day. He was foolish and selfish indeed. Yet by the story's end he realized his need for forgiveness, his need for reconciliation with his father, his need to be made one again with family and friends.

As for the "elder son," we might call him the "logical son." He was the solid stock, the day-by-day good, industrious, and reliable worker, who carried the burden of the chores at home while his brother was living the good life (or what he thought was the good life). The logical son no doubt reasoned that his share of the inheritance was now to be divided with his brother. He had paid his dues and now balked at his father's show of liberality and love to the foolish son.

Interestingly, the gospel does not tell us what happened to the logical son. In fact, it gives us no clue that "they lived happily ever after" except to say that the father asked the logical son to celebrate and rejoice: "This brother of yours was dead, and has come back to life. He was lost and is found" (vs. 32).

What about us? Would we have gone to the banquet to toast the return of the spendthrift? Do we share in God's showing mercy and love to those whom the world counts as "sinners"? Would we understand if a child of ours wanted to come back after doing what the younger son did? How many times do we enjoy the first part of the story and praise the father for his love, precisely because we ourselves need to rely on that same love? Yet do we secretly side with the logical son when it comes to forgiving others? Are we not aware that forgiveness from God without forgiving others is hypocrisy? Are we really our brothers' and sisters' keeper?

Chapter Four

Third Week of Lent

THIRD SUNDAY OF LENT

Liturgical Context

By design, the liturgical texts and rites for the Sundays of Lent have a definite shape and pattern. For the first two Sundays, all three cycles of the Lectionary explore two events in the life of Jesus, namely the temptation (First Sunday) and the transfiguration (Second Sunday). Beginning with this Sunday, and for the next two Sundays, the gospel readings for the "A" cycle will deal with initiation; the "B" cycle with identification with Christ; and the "C" cycle with reconciliation.

On the Third, Fourth, and Fifth Sundays of Lent, the "scrutinies" of the candidates for initiation were held in the early church. These scrutinies are once again celebrated after the liturgy of the word and they depend on the readings (of the "A" cycle) for much of their content and inspiration. The notion of "scrutiny" is best understood as prayer interceding for the elect and communal support for them rather than an examination of preparedness or moral fitness. It will become clear in the commentaries that follow that the dominant gospel texts from John 4, 9, and 11, dealing with the Samaritan woman, the man born blind, and the raising of Lazarus, offer much rich material for reflection, including the emphases placed on the symbolism of water, light, and life. The scrutinies lead to the celebration of initiation at the Easter vigil. The baptismal bath (water) takes place at night in the presence of the community holding lighted candles (light) and brings the newly baptized into the community of those who now experience the life of God in them through Christ (life).

In addition to the scrutinies, these Sundays were also occasions when the catechumens received the essentials of the faith into which they would be baptized: the creed, the Lord's Prayer, and the gospels. The ceremony of "handing over" these central elements of the Christian life symbolizes the doctrines to be believed, the prayers to be prayed, and the word to be pondered and lived. In the present reform of adult initiation, the rites of handing over and receiving back the creed, the Our Father, and the gospels may take place either during the week following these scrutinies or during the catechumenate, which may be begun well before Lent.

In order to emphasize the initiation character of these Sundays, the Lectionary directs that the readings assigned to the "A" cycle on the third, fourth, and fifth Sundays may be used even on Sundays of the "B" or "C" cycles. The rite of adult initiation states:

"The scrutinies ought to take place during the Masses for the Scrutinies held on the Third, Fourth, and Fifth Sundays of Lent; the readings from Year A with their chants are used, as given in the Lectionary. If for pastoral reasons this cannot be done on the proper Sundays, other Lenten Sundays or even suitable weekdays may be chosen" (no. 159).

The rite of adult initiation asserts that:

"The purpose of the scrutinies is mainly spiritual; they are concluded by exorcisms. The scrutinies are intended to purify the catechumens' minds and hearts, to strengthen them against temptation, to purify their intentions, and to make firm their decision, so that they may become more closely united with Christ and make progress in their efforts to love God more deeply" (no. 154).

While it is true that the notion of an exorcism can carry with it many negative connotations (not to mention "possession"), it should be noted that the scrutiny prayers rely on scriptural imagery and liturgical tradition for their formulation. These same sources illumine our understanding of them. The readings for the first Sunday of Lent about the temptation of Jesus serve to emphasize the biblical understanding of doing battle with Satan and of the setting for that battle. The fact that Jesus was so tempted serves as a model and inspiration for facing evil and sin in our lives, aided by the same Spirit who strengthened him in the desert. The scrutinies are meant to aid the candidate to engage in the lifelong struggle to "put aside the deeds of darkness" and to "put on the armor of light" (Rom 13:11–12). Their purpose is twofold:

". . . to teach the catechumens gradually about the mystery of sin, from which the whole world and every person longs to be delivered and thus saved from its present and future consequences; to fill their spirit with an understanding of Christ the Redeemer, the living water (see the gospel about the Samaritan woman), the light of the world (see the gospel about the man born blind), the resurrection and the life (see the gospel about the raising of Lazarus). From the first to the final scrutiny there should be progress in the recognition of sin and the desire for salvation" (no. 157).

In the present reform, the scripture readings for these Sundays in the "C" cycle refer to another sacramental process in Lent—penance and reconciliation. Even though the public reconciliation of penitents no longer takes place at a special liturgy during Holy Week, liturgical tradition looked upon initiation and penance in Lent as leading to the paschal celebrations.

While today's Sunday liturgies need not refer to sacramental penance and reconciliation, nevertheless the theology underlying the Rite of Penance and the major thrust of these Sunday liturgies in Lent make an examination of some of the parallels worthwhile.

The first paragraph of the introduction to the Rite of Penance states:

"The Father has shown forth his mercy by reconciling the world to himself in Christ and by making peace for all things on earth and in heaven by the blood of Christ on the cross. The Son of God made man lived among us in order to free us from the slavery of sin and to call us out of darkness into his wonderful light. He therefore began his work on earth by preaching repentance and saying: 'Repent and believe the Gospel' (Mk 1:15).

"Jesus, however, not only exhorted people to repentance so that they would abandon their sins and turn wholeheartedly to the Lord, but welcoming sinners, he actually reconciled them with the Father. Moreover, he healed the sick in order to offer a sign of his power to forgive sin. Finally, he himself died for our sins and rose again for our justification. Therefore, on the night he was betrayed and began his saving passion he instituted the sacrifice of the New Covenant in his blood for the forgiveness of sins. After his resurrection he sent the Holy Spirit upon the apostles, empowering them to forgive or retain sins and sending them forth to all peoples to preach repentance and the forgiveness of sins in his name" (no. 1).

This same introduction states that penance is the concern of the whole church and that it is not limited to sacramental penance:

"The people of God accomplish and perfect this continual repentance in many different ways. They share in the sufferings of Christ by enduring their own difficulties, carry out works of mercy and charity, and adopt ever more fully the outlook of the Gospel message. Thus the people of God become in the world a sign of conversion to God. All this the Church expresses in its life and celebrates in its liturgy when the faithful confess that they are sinners and ask pardon of God and of their brothers and sisters. This happens in penitential services, in the proclamation of the word of God, in pra; er, and in the penitential parts of the eucharistic celebration.

"In the sacrament of penance the faithful 'obtain from God's mercy pardon for having offended him and at the same time reconciliation with the Church, which they wounded by their sins and which by charity, example, and prayer seeks their conversion' " (quotation from *Lumen Gentium*, no. 11) (no. 4).

The relationship between penance and Lent is stated in the introduction:

"Lent is the season most appropriate for celebrating the sacrament of penance. Already on Ash Wednesday the people of God hear the solemn invitation, 'Turn away from sin and be faithful to the Gospel.' It is therefore fitting to have several penitential services during Lent, so that all the faithful may have an opportunity to be reconciled with God and their neighbor and so be able to celebrate the paschal mystery in the Easter triduum with renewed hearts" (no. 13).

Unlike the readings chosen for the "A" cycle that come from the church's tradition concerning initiation, the texts chosen for these Sundays to reflect reconciliation are newly chosen. On the Third Sunday the gospel is about the parable of the fig tree and the need for reform and conversion (Lk 13:19). On the Fourth Sunday the gospel is from Luke 15 (vs. 1–3,11–32), about the prodigal son welcomed home and reconciled with family and friends. On the Fifth Sunday the gospel is from John 8 (vs. 1–11) on the woman caught in adultery and who was forgiven her sin.

Clearly these texts add a significant dimension to the Lenten liturgy by emphasizing the need for repentance (Third Sunday), the welcome of our Father in heaven who assures reconciliation (Fourth Sunday), and the forgiveness of God enabling us to live less sinful lives (Fifth Sunday).

Pastoral planning for these three Sundays would determine which set of readings to use, the place of the scrutinies at a main parish liturgy each week, and the place that the initiation readings have in the Lenten liturgy in years when the "B" and "C" cycle readings are used as options. What should be borne in mind when preparing the liturgy for these three Sundays is that while there is an emphasis on initiation and reconciliation (as well as on central Lenten themes), these themes should not become so dominant that they negate the other readings and prayers at the eucharist and at the hours. To insist that all texts refer to one single important theme, for example, initiation or reconciliation, would be to miss the various nuances that emerge from the other liturgical and scripture texts.

Cycle "A"

Today's gospel (Jn 4:5–42) was used in the Roman tradition when the Second Sunday of Lent evolved and had a Mass formula of its own. The gospel for this Third Sunday, from John 8:12–59, speaks of Jesus as the light of the world who existed before Abraham and who thus had priority in time and in significance for salvation history.

The dialogue between Jesus and the Samaritan woman described in John 4:5–42 has elements that can be applied to the sacraments of initiation, to the renewal of the baptismal promises by the already initiated, and to an understanding of Jesus as the one who is the living water for all who have faith. The verse before today's gospel summarizes much of its content: "Lord, truly you are the Savior of the world; give me living water, that I may never thirst again."

It is significant that Jesus meets the Samaritan woman at "Jacob's" well, for in the Old Testament, wells were prominent as meeting places where important events took place. For example, in Genesis 29:1ff., Jacob meets Rachel at a well, an event that was to have great consequences for Israel. The "Jacob's well" mentioned in John 4, is called "the well of Shechem" in the Old Testament. The woman was a Samaritan, and the Jews despised the Samaritans. So Jesus' speaking with her was a sign that he was breaking down the barriers of prejudice. At the beginning of the dialogue Jesus makes a distinction between the water of everyday life and "living water" that will become a "fountain . . . to provide eternal life" within the person who drinks it (vs. 14).

The natural and customary use of water should not be forgotten when interpreting this passage, especially because the creative and life-giving properties of water are emphasized in the liturgy (see blessing prayer for baptismal water at the Easter vigil).

In the dialogue with Jesus, the woman's immoral life (five husbands) comes into focus through Jesus' questioning. Aware that this man is someone special, the woman digs deeper into the Samaritan-Jew split by stating that this mountain is special to Samaritans, whereas Jerusalem is for the Jews. Jesus responds that authentic worship will be "in spirit and truth," and not limited to specific geographical locations (vs. 23). Then Jesus astounds her by stating that the Messiah she knows is coming (vs. 25) is present in Jesus (vs. 26). The text "I am he" refers back to Moses receiving the revelation of the name of God in Exodus 3:14–15 (read at the office of readings, Saturday after Ash Wednesday).

After the woman goes into town to tell others about the Messiah, Jesus' disciples come and urge him to eat. He, however, turns attention to his mission and ministry in Samaria (vss. 39–42), and it is this ministry that is the will of his Father (vs. 33). Many of the Samaritans came to believe "on the strength of the woman's testimony" (vs. 39); they affirmed that he was "the savior of the world" (vs. 42).

Among the many meanings of this scripture passage an obvious one concerns initiation. The woman's coming to faith, her turning from her immoral life, her telling others of Jesus, and their believing in him because of her all are symbolic of the process of conversion and initiation into the church at baptism. The thirst for God that the catechumen experiences is slaked only through Jesus.

The first reading from Exodus (17:3–7) recounts Israel's sojourn in the desert and their need for water. (Since it was read at the office of readings on Wednesday of the second week of Lent, see that commentary.) The reason this text is used today is to establish a connection with the gospel of the day.

The responsorial psalm is also a text commonly used in the liturgy of the hours. The continual call to the chosen to "hear his voice" and to "harden not your hearts" is part of Psalm 95, the classic invitatory psalm to the hours.

This same responsorial psalm will be used on Thursday of the third week of Lent at the eucharist, thus reiterating its special Lenten significance.

The second reading, from Romans (5:1–2,5–8), deals with our justification through faith (vs. 1). God's love and grace are operative in us and are in our hearts through the Holy Spirit (vs. 5). What made all this possible, however, was the death of Christ (vs. 6); "while we were still sinners Christ died for us" (vs. 8). This significant theological statement provides a frame of reference within which to view the message of the other two readings. All that was accomplished through Jesus' life, death, and resurrection is now operative in us through faith. We appropriate the paschal mystery through rites and liturgies that draw us into the life of God. Today's readings offer much to ponder in this Lenten season regarding initiation, conversion, faith, justification, Jesus as Messiah and Savior, and our longing to be firmly and more fully one with Christ.

Cycle "B"

Unlike the scripture readings in the "A" and "C" cycles, those assigned to "B" do not refer to any specific liturgical rite or particular theme of the Lenten liturgy. Today's readings focus on our identification with Christ in his passion and in his exaltation.

The gospel from John 2 (vs. 13–25) is the incident of the cleansing of the temple, and Jesus' foretelling of his death and resurrection. In all of this John sees the end of temple worship and the newness of Christian worship through the person of Jesus. Jesus transcends and fulfills all that is represented by the temple and its cultic prescriptions. It is he who not only cleanses the temple area, it is he who becomes the new temple, the means of worship in spirit and truth. As he cleanses the temple area of things required for offering sacrifice (vs. 14–16), he also indicates that worship through him would no longer need such elements as oxen, sheep, and doves. The use (in vs. 17) of Psalm 69 (vs. 10) with the text "zeal for your house consumes me" is a reference to a psalm that has been used elsewhere in the New Testament because of its Christological overtones (Ps 69:29 in Acts 1:20; Ps 69:10 in Rom 15:3). While the Jews ask for a "sign" (missing the sign and action already performed right before their eyes) Jesus refuses to perform another sign. The final and definitive sign will not be the destruction of the temple so much as it will be Jesus' dying and rising that will replace the destroyed temple. The "three days" reference is to his death and resurrection and the temple of his own body (vs. 19).

The first reading from Exodus (20:1–17), about the law given through Moses, was used yesterday in the office of readings. Verses 1–21 are also used in the revised Rite of Penance.

The responsorial psalm (Psalm 19) and its accompanying response from John's gospel (6:69), "Lord, you have the words of everlasting life," show the relationship of the commandments of the old law to Christ, who has "the words of everlasting life."

The second reading from 1 Corinthians (1:22–25) speaks of Jesus as the sign of the Father's love. Without wanting to overplay parallels between texts of different genres and from different historical times, nevertheless we can legitimately say that this is another way of reinforcing the message of the gospel, that Jesus transcends the temple as the sign of God's presence to his people. The crucifixion of Jesus is a stumbling block to those Jews who expected a royal Messiah. It is also an absurdity to Gentiles who look for another Lord. Yet to those who believe, both Jews and Gentiles alike, Christ becomes the source of life, of wisdom, and of grace. He is "the power of God and the wisdom of God" (vs. 24).

The new covenant and its paradoxes might well offer ample reflection for Lenten congregations who hear these words today.

Cycle "C"

This Sunday, which begins the penance and reconciliation themes of this Lectionary cycle, takes its lead from the gospel of Luke (13:1–9). The two sections of this text deal with the requirement that Jesus' hearers admit their sin and need for repentance (vss. 1–5) and the parable of the fig tree (vss. 6–9) illustrating this teaching.

The first section concerns the massacre of Galileans by Pilate as they were offering temple sacrifices: "whose blood Pilate had mixed with their sacrifices" (vs. 1) and the incident of the falling tower that killed eighteen (vs. 4). These two disasters are used by Jesus to refer to the need for all to reform. His hearers will come to the same end, death, unless they reform (vs. 5).

The parable of the fig tree that was to be cut down if it did not bear fruit in a year can be interpreted as showing that God, in giving us sinners a time to reform our lives, does not mean that we should put off doing so indefinitely.

This gospel can be applied to all of us today who stand in need of reform and reconciliation. To reform means to live according to the preaching and teaching of Jesus, whatever the cost. In addition to emphasizing penance on this Sunday, these readings prepare us for what is to come during the next Sundays in the "C" cycle.

The first reading from Exodus (3:1–8,13–15) is also used at the office of readings on the Saturday after Ash Wednesday (see the commentary for that day about the revelation of God in the burning but unconsumed bush). Verse 8 indicates God's initiative for Israel: "Therefore I have come down to rescue them [Israel] from the hands of the Egyptians and lead them out of that land. . . ." God asserts that his name is "I am who am." Moses is to tell the Israelites that "I Am sent me to you" (vs. 14). This somewhat enigmatic title reveals that God simply is. He is the Creator of all that is. He is true to his word, and ever faithful to his promises. He is "the God of Abraham, the God of Isaac, and the God of Jacob"; hence he is a God of relationship and relatedness to Israel. It is this God who continues to take initiative with the new people of God, the people of Christ. It is this same notion of God on which we rely when we worship and pray at liturgy.

The responsorial psalm, Psalm 103 (1–2,3–4,6–7,8,11), emphasizes the pardon of the Lord to all (vs. 3) and that he is a God "slow to anger and abounding in kindness" (vs. 8). The refrain, "The Lord is kind and merciful," was also used yesterday at the responsorial psalm.

The second reading from 1 Corinthians (10:1–6,10–12) points out that the chosen people of God were not without fault and guilt.

They, too, needed to repent and follow the Lord more closely. The same is true for us who worship the Lord on this Lenten Sunday. We, the baptized and those to be baptized, need to be reminded that we must turn again and again to the Lord in penance to receive his reconciling and merciful love.

Sacramentary Texts

There are two options offered for today's entrance antiphon. The first is traditional for this day, Psalm 25:15–16. It acknowledges the wretchedness and loneliness of the believer who trusts firmly in the Lord. The other option is from Ezekiel (36:23–26). If the Mass is that at which the scrutinies take place, the text from Ezekiel is to be preferred. The initiative of God on behalf of his people to sprinkle them with clean water, to wash away their sins, and to give them a new spirit is emphasized here. These same verses form part of the seventh reading at the Easter vigil about Old Testament types and figures that foreshadow Christ's work of salvation. These same verses are also offered as one option for the antiphon to be sung at the introductory rite of sprinkling with holy water at the Sunday eucharist, as noted in the Appendix to Latin edition of the Missal. The association of forgiveness of sins and being given a new spirit with the water symbolism in this brief text lends emphasis to today's liturgy of the word.

The opening prayer, taken from the oldest collection of Sacramentary prayers, speaks of God as the source of all mercy and goodness who leads us in Lent to deepen our conversion by fasting, prayer, and works of mercy. The alternative opening prayer states the same themes in greater detail as it reminds us that Lent leads "to the beauty of Easter joy."

The prayer over the gifts refers to a dominant theme of the Lenten liturgy in general and to the "C" readings in particular. It prays to the Lord that we who ask forgiveness for our sins be ready to forgive others.

Two communion antiphons are offered. The first is taken from the gospel about the Samaritan woman and is to be used when that gospel is read at the eucharist. The second, taken from Psalm 84:4–5, is to be used when other gospels are read.

The prayer after communion asks that through this sacrament in which we implore God's forgiveness we may also be "joined in unity and peace."

First Scrutiny

What marks this Sunday liturgy is the inclusion of the first scrutiny from the rite of adult initiation. This communal, liturgical event, while brief and to the point, serves as a reminder that Christians are initiated into the faith of a community, which faith is expressed in a special way at Sunday eucharist. The format of the scrutiny includes a homily drawn from the liturgy of the word (thus making the choice of the "A" readings a natural selection today). Following this there is prayer in silence (see Rite of Christian Initiation of Adults, no. 162) and then the "prayer for the elect" (no. 163), filled with invocations that follow the style of the general intercessions (which are eliminated when the scrutiny takes place). The needs expressed concern initiation, the importance of the word of God in conversion, the need for forgiveness, salvation in Christ, the power of the Spirit in conversion, and general needs of the community. While these may be adapted, along with the introduction, such adaptation should follow the genre of intercessory prayers at the liturgy. The following exorcism prayer (no. 164) may be replaced by another of the options noted. However, its imagery centers on the gospel story read from John in the "A" cycle and therefore deserves emphasis today:

"God our Father,
you sent your Son to be our Savior:
these men and women preparing for baptism
thirst for living water as did the Samaritan woman.
May the word of the Lord change their lives too,
and help them to acknowledge the sins and weaknesses that burden them.
Keep them from relying too much on themselves
and never let the powers of evil deceive them.
Keep them from the spirit of falsehood
and help them recognize any evil within themselves,
that with hearts cleansed from sin
they may advance on the way to salvation.
We ask this through Christ our Lord.
℞. Amen.

Then the celebrant lays his hand on each of the elect (in silence) and extending his hands over all the elect he continues to pray:

Lord Jesus,
you are the fountain we thirst for;
you are the teacher we seek;
you alone are the Holy One.
These chosen ones open their hearts honestly
to confess their failures
and be forgiven.
In your love, free them from evil,
restore their health, satisfy their thirst, and give them peace.
By the power of your name,
which we call upon in faith,
stay with them and save them.
Command the spirit of evil to leave them,
for you have conquered that spirit by rising to life.
Show your chosen people the way of life in the Holy Spirit
that they may grow closer to the Father and worship him,
for you are Lord forever and ever.
R̟. Amen."

The celebrant dismisses the elect with the words: "Go in peace until we meet at the next scrutiny. May the Lord be with you always." To this the elect respond: "Amen."

The prayers and gestures that mark this scrutiny are clearly scripturally oriented and traditionally founded. Any overly negative connotations of exorcism and combat with evil are nuanced and presented here in imagery derived from the readings of the day. These prayers at the scrutiny in particular serve to emphasize the evangelical nature of formation given to the elect as they prepare for initiation at Easter.

Celebration of the Eucharist

"A" Cycle

Today's entrance antiphon from the prophet Ezekiel (the second option), emphasizing cleansing and being freed from sins, would be a good introduction to the liturgy today.

The third option of the penitential rite, with invocations about Christ as the one who raises the dead to life and who brings pardon and peace, would be appropriate.

The alternative opening prayer could be used today because it concludes with a reference to the joy of Easter. The Sacramentary also notes that the Mass formula for Masses at which the scrutinies take place (see Ritual Masses for Christian Initiation, no. 2) can be used instead of that for the Third Sunday of Lent.

The gospel about the Samaritan woman could be proclaimed in the format used for the reading of the passion, using readers to assist the priest or deacon in a dialogue. This would help alleviate distraction caused by its length. Whatever is planned, it should be remembered that special preparation is required to sustain interest and attention during a gospel of this length.

The presider should be attentive to the silences, gestures, and the rhythm of the prayers used at the scrutinies. This rite can gain much in significance when planned beforehand with the elect, their sponsors, and liturgical ministers so they know what to do and where to stand during the rite. Should the prayer for the elect be adapted, the reader should have these adapted invocations in hand well before the celebration in order to prepare for this important ministry.

The preface of the Third Sunday of Lent, about the Samaritan woman, is especially designated for use this day.

If a scrutiny has taken place, the Roman Canon could be used with the inserted prayers from the rite of adult initiation:

"[at the "Remember, Lord, your people . . .]
Remember, Lord, these godparents
who will present your chosen men and women for baptism
(the names of the godparents are mentioned)
Lord remember all of us . . .

[at the "Father, accept this offering . . .]
Father,
accept this offering
from your whole family.
We offer it especially for the men and women
you call to share your life
through the living waters of baptism" (no. 377).

During the rites of communion today, additional invocations about Christ as the Lamb of God might well be derived from or inspired by the gospel reading for today.

The solemn blessing (no. 5) for the Passion of the Lord, could be used today and on the rest of the Lenten Sundays.

"B" Cycle

If a scrutiny is celebrated on this Third Sunday of Lent, the scripture texts from the "A" cycle should be proclaimed because of the close association in theme and theology between them and the gospel.

On a Sunday when the "B" texts are used, the introduction to the liturgy could be followed by the third penitential rite with the seventh set of sample invocations. These acclaim Christ as the one who has shown us the "way to the Father," as the one who has given us "the consolation of the truth," and who is the "Good Shepherd." While these titles refer to the risen Christ, their use today could help establish the close association between the community and Christ at liturgy.

In today's general intercessions, intentions could be announced for Israel and those of Jewish faith. Petitions that we might know Jesus and abide by his word would be appropriate as would reference to initiation and penance, perennial Lenten themes.

The use of Lenten preface I (*not* that assigned for the Third Sunday) would be appropriate because it stresses the spiritual meaning of Lent.

The second memorial acclamation ("dying you destroyed our death . . .") recalls *the* event that as the preface says, "gave us new life in Christ."

The use of the second invitation to the Lord's Prayer ("Jesus taught us to call God our Father . . .") would be helpful as a way of showing our dependence on God as Father.

The use of the solemn blessing of the Passion of the Lord (no. 5) would be a fitting conclusion to the liturgy:

"He humbled himself for our sakes.
May you follow his example
and share in his resurrection."

"C" Cycle

The introduction to the liturgy could prepare the worshippers for the readings by speaking about the Lord's call that we repent and turn to him in penance during Lent. The use of the "I confess" with the words "that I have sinned" in thought, word, and deed would be an initial introduction to the major thrust of the readings today. This could be suitably followed by a sung "Lord, have mercy."

The alternative version of the opening prayer with the words, "We acknowledge our sinfulness, our guilt is ever before us" (see Psalm 51:5), would be a good choice today. Among the intentions in the general intercessions, it might be well to mention Lent as a time for penance, the lack of harmony among nations, society, and even family members.

The forgiveness motif of the readings could be carried through in the liturgy of the eucharist by using the preface of Lent II, about purifying our hearts, controlling our desires, and serving the Lord in freedom. A special introduction to the Lord's Prayer as well as extra invocations for the Lamb of God, emphasizing the Lord's gift of reconciliation and peace, could be prepared.

The gesture of the sign of peace as a significant communal action could be introduced in such a way that its force would be made especially apparent today.

Today's eucharistic prayer could be the first of the eucharistic prayers for reconciliation, especially because of the text:

"Now is the time
for your people to turn back to you
and to be renewed in Christ your Son,
a time of grace and reconciliation."

Liturgy of the Hours

Although this Sunday's eucharist emphasizes the ritual of first scrutiny and proclaims the gospel of the Samaritan woman and may help us to appreciate today's liturgy of the hours, it should also be remembered that the cycle of the hours is independent of the eucharist and refers to general Lenten themes.

At Evening Prayer I the first antiphon reiterates the formula for imposition of ashes, "Turn away from sin and open your hearts to the gospel." The second refers to offering a sacrifice of praise to the Lord. The third refers to Christ who freely laid down his life for us. The psalms and canticle speak of praising the name of the Lord (Ps 113), of trusting in him despite affliction (Ps 116:10–19), and of the humiliation of Christ leading to his ultimate glorification (Phil 2:6–11).

The short scripture reading from 2 Corinthians 6:1–4a repeats the text used at Saturday evening prayer in Lent.

The antiphon to the Canticle of Mary is taken from the second reading of the "A" cycle, Romans 5:1, about our being justified by faith and at peace through Jesus Christ. Essentially, then, we are presented with a liturgy that reflects general Lenten images and themes.

The verse before the readings in the office of readings introduces the water symbolism of the gospel about the Samaritan woman.

The psalmody for the office of readings is taken from Psalm 145 (divided into three sections), praising God for his glory and majesty: the "Lord is faithful in all his words/and loving in all his deeds."

The scripture reading from Exodus (22:20–23:9) is from the section dealing with the law for aliens and the poor.

The reading from St. Augustine (on the gospel of John) is rich in its symbolism of water. Augustine sees in Jesus' words about the living water a promise of "the Holy Spirit in satisfying abundance." This relationship of Spirit and water is found in baptism, when the Father by water and the Holy Spirit frees the candidate from sin (see RCIA, no. 269).

The antiphon to the canticle of Zechariah at morning prayer is taken from John 2 (the gospel assigned to the "B" cycle) about the temple of Jesus' body. The antiphons to the psalms refer to the decrees of the Lord (first), to "springs of water" (second), and to the praise of God (third). The psalmody itself reflects general praise themes and hence complements the Lenten motifs.

The antiphons for the psalmody of Evening Prayer II concern our turning from sin, the precious blood of Christ the lamb, and his bearing our sufferings.

The canticle from 1 Peter 2:21–24, about Jesus' acceptance of the cross and his suffering for us, points to this central Lenten theme on a Sunday when other aspects of the liturgy (rightly) stress initiation and reconciliation.

The antiphon to the Canticle of Mary refers to the gospel of the Samaritan woman; "whoever drinks the water . . . will never be thirsty again."

Celebration of the Hours

At evening prayer on Saturday, a general Lenten hymn to begin the hour and psalm prayers of a similar theme could help to stress the Lenten character of the liturgy. In addition, invocations about the humiliation of Christ and our self-emptying through him, our thirsting for the good things that will lead us to eternal life, and initiation and reconciliation in the community could highlight some of the themes in the Sunday eucharist that are present in the liturgy this evening.

In conjunction with the seasonal invitatory at the office of readings, the use of a psalm other than Psalm 95, which will be used as the responsorial psalm in year "A" at eucharist, would be appropriate. One possibility would be Psalm 100.

Morning prayer could begin with a Lenten hymn along with psalm prayers of praise.

Instead of the short reading from Nehemiah that has been used on the previous Lenten Sundays, an appropriate text from one of the cycles of the Lectionary, other than the one in current use, could be proclaimed. This same principle applies to the reading at evening prayer.

At evening prayer the canticle from 1 Peter deserves special emphasis in celebration because it reflects the central reality of this season. This could be accomplished by singing or by varying the method of psalm recitation. For example, the cantor could sing each strophe and the community could sing the antiphon as a refrain.

The intercessions this evening could well cover the traditional and contemporary emphases of this liturgy by praying for those to be initiated and their sponsors, for reconciliation in the world and in this community, for forgiveness of sins, and for the attitude of self-effacement that marked Jesus as he willingly gave himself up for our redemption.

Reflection—"Thirsting for God"

Do we truly hunger and thirst for God? What are the things that we really hunger and thirst for? At Easter we will be asked: Do you renounce Satan? Do you believe in God? Such soul-searching and spirit-wrenching questions are asked of us all as we gather this Sunday to reflect on a gospel that requires our self-scrutiny—do we thirst for God?

The notion of thirsting for water may well be a less than poignant one for our culture. We have faucets in at least two rooms of our homes, and we have water on tap for cooking and washing. But such was not the case with Jesus' listeners who had to draw water daily (sometimes twice) from a clean fountain, and who had to wash clothes at the river's edge. The supply of water was sometimes scarce (the closest we come is an "alert" or a "short-age") and the repeated imagery of the psalms about thirsting for God draws on the real experience of being thirsty (like Israel) in the desert. The elect obviously thirst for God. Do we?

Even if we affirm that we do, are we willing to thirst not only for God, but for the realization of his justice in this world, even when that will mean a change in our lifestyles? Are we willing to thirst for God when that means thirsting for reconciliation and harmony with family members with whom we have disagreed, or with neighbors whom we feel have offended us? Are we willing to thirst for Christian moral values and to put ourselves on the line to live them when cultural convention often supports other systems that lead to "success," even when that means deception and less than total honesty in business? These are some of the questions implied in the incident of the woman at the well.

Today we celebrate a scrutiny of the candidates for baptism. May we pray for those whom we have elected and for ourselves that, like the Samaritan woman, we may come to recognize Jesus as prophet and Messiah. May we surrender to him all that holds us from conforming totally to his will and his gospel. As we hunger and thirst for many goals in this life—happiness, success, and security—may we realize that in thirsting for God alone we will receive the fulfillment of all life's longings.

Liturgical Context

The context for today's liturgy was set by yesterday's gospel reading from John 4, about the symbol of water and its meaning in the scrutiny prayer for the elect, who will be initiated by water and the Spirit on Holy Saturday. The season of Lent reaches its culmination in the communal renewal of baptismal vows and the initiation of new members—all symbolized in and accomplished through the use of water. The heritage of Israel as the chosen of God is transcended; now all who submit to the Lord in faith and who obey his word are counted among the chosen of the Lord.

Liturgy of the Eucharist

The entrance antiphon has been newly chosen to reflect the message of the scriptures today. In Lent (and throughout our lives on earth) we "long" and "pine" for the "courts of the Lord" and for the joy of the "living God" (Ps 84:3).

The opening prayer (as seen more clearly in its Latin text) asks the Lord to preserve his church from evil, because without his governance it cannot endure.

The scripture readings from 2 Kings 5:1–15 reflect the use of water as a means of curing and cleansing, both from physical infirmity and from spiritual lassitude. The text from 2 Kings is also used at the celebration of christian initiation outside the Easter vigil. Naaman the leper (vs. 1) went to the king of Israel to be cleansed (vss. 5–7) but the king told him that he could not cure him. Instead, the king sent him to the prophet Elisha. When Naaman stopped at Elisha's house, the prophet told him to wash seven times in the Jordan (vs. 10, the same place where Jesus was baptized by John). At first Naaman resisted, but eventually did as he had been commanded. When he obeyed and performed the required washings (vss. 13–14) he was cured of his leprosy. Naaman finally affirms: "Now I know that there is no God in all the earth, except in Israel" (vs. 15).

This text has been used in the church's traditional catechumenal liturgy to demonstrate the necessity of water baptism for entrance into the church. The process of coming to faith and of growing in obedience to the Lord is central to the catechumenate. This Old

Testament text is, as it were, a preparation for today's gospel and together these readings offer instruction about the attitude of believers and what is required of those coming to faith.

The responsorial psalm (Ps 42), also used at the Easter vigil after the reading from Ezekiel (36:16–28) about "clean water," refers to "my soul" thirsting "for the living God" (vs. 3). The believer knows that God is experienced in the liturgy and in life, and yet, like the psalmist, we still cry out: "When shall I go and behold the face of God?" (vs. 5). Even the initiated long for the second coming and the unveiled presence of the Lord.

Today's gospel reading (Lk 4:24–30) should be seen in relationship to the preceding verses 16–23, which tell of Jesus' coming to Nazareth and preaching in the synagogue. They asked him to "do here . . . the things we have heard you have done in Capernaum" (vs. 23). They are looking for him to perform "signs and wonders." But he is aware of their hard hearts when he states: "No prophet gains acceptance in his native place" (vs. 24). The congregation rejects Jesus' implication that other peoples besides themselves are also to be called God's people. All nations are invited to the community of the faithful. All, however, are required to submit to the Lord in faith, to be schooled in his word, and to live as his witnesses. Such are among the primary requirements of the elect and the catechumens.

The prayer over the gifts asks God to bless those we offer that they may bring us salvation. What occurs in liturgy is an exchange: we present gifts and they become God's gifts to us.

The communion antiphon emphasizes the universality of salvation by quoting Psalm 117 (vss. 1–2), "All you nations, praise the Lord, for steadfast is his kindly mercy to us."

The Latin text of the prayer after communion brings out the purifying and unifying aspects of the eucharist we celebrate.

Celebration of the Eucharist

The introduction to the liturgy could speak of our need for redemption and the generosity of God to all who call upon him. The third penitential rite, with the fifth set of sample invocations about the dead being raised to life, sinners receiving pardon and peace, and those in the dark receiving the light, implies the effects baptism will have on today's catechumens, and the eucharist will have on the faithful.

As the verse before the gospel, the first option from Psalm 51 (Lectionary 224), "Create a clean heart in me, O God," could remind the assembly that they come to the liturgy to be cleansed and purified spiritually.

Among the intercessions today, invocations asking that all nations and all classes in society may experience the love of God, that the elect may successfully journey toward initiation, that all of us may live more Christian lives would be in order.

Lenten preface II would be an appropriate choice today.

Liturgy of the Hours

The verse before the readings in the office of readings today is the familiar one used on Mondays in Lent: "Turn away from sin and be faithful to the Gospel.—The kingdom of God is at hand." It is an appropriate reminder that the catechumenate is intensified in these weeks immediately before Easter.

The reading from Exodus at the office of readings (24:1–18) is about the ratification of the covenant. The willing response of the people, "We will do everything that the Lord has told us" (vs. 3), is a sign of submission to the Lord's commands. There are liturgical elements here, such as the building of the altar, Moses' reading from the book of the covenant, and the blood rite (vss. 4,7,8). The Lord invites Moses to come up the "mountain" (vs. 12), where he will receive the commandments written in stone. Symbolically the mountain, the cloud, the glory of the Lord, seen as a consuming fire on the mountaintop, all point to the transfiguration of Jesus and his crucifixion, all of which take place on "mountains." Moses remained there "forty days and forty nights" (vs. 18), a period symbolic of Israel's wandering in the desert and the church's annual celebration of Lent. The glory of God revealed to Moses is incarnate in Jesus and shared by the church through the signs and symbols of the liturgy.

The text from St. Basil the Great, about boasting only in the Lord, is a lesson in Christian humility. We are to take pride, not in our own goodness, but in the fact that we have "been made righteous only by faith in Christ." This lesson must be learned not only by the elect on their way to baptism, but must also be

130 *Monday of the Third Week of Lent*

continually relearned by one already baptized; especially now as Lent brings us closer to the great event of Easter.

At morning prayer today the scripture text, about the chosenness of Israel (Ex 19:4–6a), is that used on Lenten Mondays.

The antiphon to the Canticle of Zechariah contains the quotation from the gospel at the eucharist, "No prophet is accepted in his own country."

The references to baptism in the first intercession and to the forgiveness of sins in the fourth reflect the emphasis on initiation and penance begun in yesterday's scripture readings in the "A" and "C" cycles.

At evening prayer the scripture reading from Romans 12:1–2 reiterates a prophetic theme (that will occur again later this week) where Paul insists that we offer our bodies as living sacrifices to God, not just cultic sacrifices alone.

The antiphon to the Canticle of Mary is also from the gospel: "Jesus walked through the crowd and went away," and recalls his escape from those who wanted to "hurl him over the edge" of the hill because he had challenged their mistaken beliefs.

The themes enunciated in the intercessions today: forgiveness of sins (introduction), being washed clean by water and the word (first petition), about baptism (fourth petition), and prayer for the dead (fifth petition) show how the liturgy can subtly reflect the theology and spirituality of a liturgical season and offer insights into the scriptures read that day.

While the psalms assigned for morning prayer were not chosen to coincide with today's eucharist, still some implications are too important to ignore: "My soul is longing and yearning for the courts of the Lord" (Ps 84), the mountain of the Lord as the highest mountain and all nations streaming toward it (Is 2:2–3).

At evening prayer we state that we rely on the mercy of the Lord (Ps 123), that "our help is in the name of the Lord, who made heaven and earth" (Ps 124), and that "God chose us in his Son to be his adopted children" (Eph 1:3–11).

Celebration of the Hours

Today's verse before the readings, in conjunction with Psalm 95 and its references to Exodus, is a fitting invitatory to the hours today.

At the office of readings, each of the three sections of Psalm 50 can be followed by doxologies and antiphons, or with silences between the sections of the psalm. This latter arrangement would be preferable since this hour can tend to be unusually wordy.

At morning prayer the third psalm prayer offers a good example of the way these prayers can be used to bring out the meaning of the psalms for present-day congregations.

An intercession for the elect, who were prayed for yesterday, could be added at both morning and evening prayer today.

Since the scriptures assigned to morning and evening prayer have already been used for two weeks, today might well be a day to read other scripture texts suitable for the season. They might be taken from the Lectionary readings for initiation since this emphasis will become stronger from now until Easter.

Reflection—"Are We Still Sinners?"

To Christians, the story of Naaman and the cure of his leprosy has long been a symbol of how Christ works through the sacrament of baptism. Naaman was cured of his loathsome disease by obeying the word of the prophet Elisha, who told him to wash in the waters of the Jordan River.

At the word of Christ, we the baptized have been released from the power of sin by the waters of baptism. This is not to say that we are no longer sinners, however, for we can and do often refuse to obey the Father's will. Such being the case, we are always in need of renewal and conversion. Lent is a special time for undergoing such a period of renewal. It is a time when we the baptized join our brothers and sisters who are preparing for baptism at Easter.

So for both the baptized and for those about to be baptized, this is a time for prayer and special Lenten observances that will make us ready to live the new life of the resurrected Lord at Easter.

TUESDAY OF THE THIRD WEEK OF LENT

Liturgical Context

The liturgy of today's eucharist returns to a theme that has already been emphasized in Lent (yesterday in cycle "C" of the Lectionary and during most of last week)—forgiveness and recon-

ciliation. The gospel reading at the eucharist recounts one of Jesus'
parables that, as usual, teaches a lesson by reversing the way
people have been accustomed to think. Today's parable teaches the
lesson that God's forgiveness of our sins depends on how we
forgive those who have hurt us.

Liturgy of the Eucharist

The liturgy begins on a note of dependence and trust in the
Lord. We proclaim that the Lord "will answer me" and we ask him
to "guard me" and "hide me"—indications of the close union with
God we experience in faith (Ps 17:6,8).

In the opening prayer God's "saving work among us" refers to
Christ's redemptive passion, death, and resurrection in which we
share at the liturgy.

The first reading is from the prophet Daniel (3:25,34–43) and
beseeches the Lord not to deliver up his people or to "make void
your covenant" (vs. 34). This is a plea for God's mercy, a mercy
based on the covenant relationship initiated through Abraham,
Isaac, and Israel (vs. 35: "Do not take away your mercy from us,
for the sake of Abraham, your beloved, Isaac your servant, and
Israel your holy one").

All who believe in God should do so with contrite heart and
humble spirit (vs. 39). This text is a communal acknowledgment of
sin and of dependence on the Lord for mercy and forgiveness. The
covenant is recalled as the basis of Israel's "claim" on the Lord.

The responsorial psalm (Ps 25), in familiar biblical language,
refers to God's forgiveness: "remember your mercies" and teach me
"your paths . . ." (vs. 4). The Lord has compassion, goodness, and
kindness (vss. 6–7); he leads the humble to justice (vs. 9).

The gospel text (Mt 18:21–35) is the traditional reading for this
day. It is also found cited as one of the optional readings for the
Rite of Penance (no. 184). The parable points out the necessity of
forgiving those who have hurt us. The introduction to the parable
has Peter asking Jesus: "When my brother wrongs me, how often
must I forgive him? Seven times?" Peter is really asking whether
there is not a definite number of times beyond which one need not
forgive another's offenses against oneself. Jesus answers that there
is no limit to the number of times one forgives one's neighbor.

To clarify the matter, Jesus tells the parable about the servant whose master forgave him a great debt. And yet the same servant refused to forgive a fellow servant who owed him but a small debt. When the master heard what the heartless servant had done, he demanded retribution of that servant's entire debt. The typically Matthean punchline states: "My heavenly Father will treat you in exactly the same way unless each of you forgives his brother from his heart" (vs. 35). The forgiveness must come from the "heart" and such forgiveness of others is essential to Christian reconciliation. The limitless forgiveness of God to us is the foundation for this demand to forgive others. Being loved by God requires that we show his love to each other and especially to the hungry, thirsty, naked, and infirm as is stated so clearly in Matthew's account of the final judgement (Mt 25:31–46).

This teaching of Jesus is reflected in the prayer over the gifts as it speaks of the cleansing (forgiving) effect of the liturgy. We pray: "Lord may the saving sacrifice we offer bring us your forgiveness, so that freed from sin, we may always please you."

The communion antiphon reminds us that those who "walk without blame" will one day live with God, whose dwelling place is the "high mountain" of heaven (Ps 15:1–2).

The prayer after communion asks that this eucharist will bring us "protection, forgiveness and life" and, as sharers in the holy mystery, strengthen us to forgive others.

Celebration of the Eucharist

The introduction to the liturgy could well speak about God's forgiving us and our response in forgiving others. The use of the "I confess" form of the penitential rite with its reference to "in what I have done and in what I have failed to do," would be suitable.

A meditative setting to a sung "Lord, have mercy" would help to emphasize the Lord who is filled with mercy and forgiveness and on whom we rely at this eucharist.

For the verse before the gospel, number 11 (Lectionary 224), from the parable of the prodigal son who acknowledges his sin, would be a helpful way to introduce the gospel.

Among the intercessions today, invocations about the need for reconciliation among nations and classes, the ending of violence in our cities and putting aside long-held grudges against others would emphasize the teaching of the gospel parable.

The use of the first preface for Lent (Lent I), with the statement: "You give us a spirit of loving reverence for you, our Father, and of willing service to our neighbor," would be fitting today.

The second eucharistic prayer for Masses for Reconciliation, with the statements in its preface about the work of the Spirit in reconciling enemies, would be a good choice.

The Lord's Prayer and the sign of peace could be introduced with statements about how peace and reconciliation come from Christ, through whom we pray to the Father for forgiveness and from whom comes our ability to forgive others.

To conclude the liturgy the presider could use the prayer over the people, number 23, about receiving grace, remaining close to God in prayer, and about having "true love for one another."

Liturgy of the Hours

The verse before the readings in the office of readings to the liturgy of the hours today is usual for Lenten Tuesdays and is an appropriate reminder: "This is the favorable time.—This is the day of salvation."

The section from Exodus (32:1–20) read at the office of readings recounts the incident of Israel forsaking the worship of the one true God for the worship of the golden calf. The people forget the God of the covenant and shamelessly offer homage to a "molten calf" fashioned from their "golden earrings." They acclaim this idol as the "God . . . who brought you out of the land of Egypt" (vs. 4). At this turn of events, the Lord says to Moses: "They have soon turned aside from the way I pointed out to them . . ." (vs. 7). The Lord is described as being ready to "consume them" in his "blazing wrath." Moses, however, by recalling the covenant (vss. 12–13) and the people's special relationship with God, implores the Lord on their behalf, at which God relents. Moses then returns to the people, bearing in his hand the tablets on which God had inscribed the words of the law. But when he sees his people, his "wrath flared up . . . at seeing the calf and their dancing in revelry" (vss. 18–19).

The God of fidelity is here faced with a fickle and unfaithful people. Yet the Lord relents and forgives them. These people "forgot the God who had saved them" (Ps 106:20–22, used as the responsory to this reading), yet their Lord was true to his promises and did not forsake them.

The text from Peter Chrysologus returns to a theme already explored in Lent: the unity of prayer, fasting, and works of mercy. All of these together comprise the ascetical aspect of Lent, not one or two in isolation. The author states that the person who prays knocks at the door of the Lord, the person who fasts obtains what he asks of the Lord, and the person who does works of mercy receives mercy from the Lord. The responsory to this reading from the book of Tobit (12:8,9) states: "Prayer accompanied by fasting and giving to the poor is good, since giving to the poor expiates every sin."

It is interesting to note how the readings at the eucharist and this one from the office of readings reiterate our active involvement in extending God's kingdom by works of charity and by forgiving others as God forgives us. The antiphon to the canticle of Zechariah repeats the reply of Jesus to Peter about forgiving seventy times seven; at evening prayer the antiphon to the canticle of Mary repeats the gospel's urgent warning that unless we forgive others from our heart God will not deal with us mercifully. This antiphon captures the sense of the day's gospel and at the same time reiterates a classical theme of evening prayer—repentance for misdeeds done during the day and prayer for God's forgiveness.

Celebration of the Hours
The invitatory (using the seasonal text or preferably the verse before the readings) and Psalm 95 today would be a fitting introduction to the office. The fact that Israel bowed down and danced before the molten image of a calf is countered in the psalm by the text:

"Come, then, let us bow down and worship,
    bending the knee before the Lord, our maker
For he is our God and we are his people,
    the flock he shepherds" (vss. 6–7).

This would be an especially fitting option if the office of readings follows immediately.

During the office of readings, the single psalm (68) can be sung or recited as printed, with doxologies and antiphons, or with a single antiphon at the beginning and end, with pauses between sections.

The assigned psalm prayer would be better reworked since it refers more to the eucharist than to this hour of prayer.

At both morning and evening prayer a general Lenten hymn chosen for each hour would be appropriate, as would the use of psalm prayers that are designed to reflect the text of the psalms and the needs of the community.

The intercessions at morning prayer (especially) could be reworked to include invocations relative to the community's Lenten programs. The assigned texts reflect a eucharistic theme by referring to "bread from heaven" and to "eucharist."

At evening prayer the antiphon to the Canticle of Mary and the nature of the hour would warrant considering the use of a sung Lord's Prayer at the end of the intercessions and/or a special introduction that speaks about our forgiving others and being reconciled in Christ.

Reflection—"Forgive As You Are Forgiven"

It is something of a psychological truism that we find it hardest to forgive others when they have touched on sensitivities that we like to nurture and use for self-pity. This kind of attitude results in our setting up defense mechanisms against those we consider to be our enemies.

Jesus' assurance of forgiveness to those who call upon him in trust and humility can make us realize that we are not abandoned, that God can break through our pitiful defense mechanisms against him and our neighbor. This process then leads to true and real charity in loving and forgiving others.

Because of our continual need for forgiveness from God and because we are continually called upon to forgive others, we come to the liturgy to be reassured of the Lord's forgiving love. It is a love that is not cheap, however. It is a love that seeks extension in loving others as God loves us.

WEDNESDAY OF THE THIRD WEEK OF LENT

Liturgical Context

From today through Friday the readings at the eucharist have been arranged to focus on the restored catechumenate. Hence, the liturgy on these three days contains much valuable material for reflection both for catechumens and the faithful.

Liturgy of the Eucharist

Today's entrance antiphon, from Psalm 119 (vs. 133), replaces the antiphon from Psalm 31, formerly used in the Roman Missal. This new antiphon is taken from the lengthy psalm in praise of God's law that is still used at the minor hours.

The opening prayer has been inspired by a text from Leo the Great and is found in the earliest collection of Sacramentary prayers. It speaks of our being nourished by the word of God during Lent and asks that we may all be made "one in love and prayer." In the first reading, from Deuteronomy 4:1,5–9, Moses speaks to the people and tells them to "hear the statutes and decrees . . . which the Lord, the God of your fathers, is giving you" (vss. 1–2). We Christians today are also called to obey God's statutes and decrees as revealed by his Son Jesus Christ. Hence the appropriateness of the entrance antiphon.

The responsorial psalm praises the Lord who "sends forth his command to the earth; swiftly runs his word" (Ps 147:15). It also reiterates the covenant relationship established by God through deed and word:

"He has proclaimed his word to Jacob,
    his statutes and his ordinances to Israel.
He has not done thus for any other nation;
    his ordinances he has not made known to them" (vss. 19–20).

The gospel reading, Matthew 5:17–19, relates the old law to the community of Jesus' followers by stating that Jesus came "not to abolish the law and the prophets but to fulfill them" (vs. 17).

The morality that Jesus taught is more demanding and rigorous than the ethics of the old covenant. It is only through the person of Jesus himself that we are enabled to live according to his moral teaching. Here the intimate relationship between the very being of God and his law is reaffirmed in Jesus; he is no mere legislator, he is the Lord who remains with and sustains his people as they live on in his love.

The prayer over the gifts asks that those who celebrate this eucharist may be protected by God "in time of danger."

The communion antiphon, from the former Roman Missal, speaks of the "path of life" and of being filled with joy in the presence of the Lord (Ps 16:11).

The prayer after communion, from the former Roman Missal, asks that the heavenly banquet that has nourished us may be an atonement for our sins and prepare us for the eternal life that has been promised us. The Word incarnate, present in word and sacrament, will draw us to himself in his kingdom if we observe his statutes and live according to his commands.

Celebration of the Eucharist

The major theme of the liturgy of the eucharist is the same for the next three days, thus giving a continuity to these celebrations.

The introduction to today's liturgy could speak about the liturgy of the word as the occasion when God addresses us and the liturgy of the eucharist as the "heavenly banquet" at which God feeds us.

The use of the third penitential rite with invocations such as the following would be appropriate: ". . . you are the Word made flesh and the splendor of the Father's glory."

The importance of the liturgy of the word over the next three days could be expressed by having the lector proclaim the first reading from the Lectionary and then having the deacon or priest proclaim the gospel from the gospel book that has been carried in a simple procession to the ambo. This procedure is in accordance with the instructions in the Sacramentary suggesting that one book be used in proclaiming the first and second reading (if there is one) and another book from which the gospel is proclaimed, thus enhancing the importance of the readings.

The use of number 8 (Lectionary 224) of the verses before the gospel ("Man does not live on bread alone . . .") would be a reminder of the important place that the word plays in the Lenten liturgy.

The intercessions could include references to the Jews, the first to receive the word of God, and to those who inspire us to witness to the word by the example of their lives.

Lenten preface II mentions controlling our desires and living in this passing world with our hearts set on the world that will never end, attitudes that are sharpened and focused as we reflect on the Lord's word.

To introduce the Lord's Prayer the presider might use the formula from the former Roman Missal that speaks of God's word: "taught by our Savior's command and formed by the Word of God, we dare to say. . . ." In the Lamb of God an additional strophe that acclaims the Lord as "Word made flesh" would be appropriate today.

Liturgy of the Hours

The first reading in the office of readings, from Exodus 33:7–11,18–23; 34:5–9,29–35, emphasizes Moses' mediating function and the revelation of the glory of God. Moses meets God in the "meeting tent" (vss. 7–11). The Lord, however, cannot be seen by any merely human person, "for no man sees me and still lives" (vs. 20) says the Lord. The glory of God is here clouded in mystery; Moses' response is reverence and awe.

As Moses spoke with the Lord his face had become radiant—a reflection of God's glory. It is most significant, therefore, that Moses (along with Elijah) appear at the scene of the transfiguration. They personify the revelation of God through the law and the prophets, revelations that have come to fulfillment in Jesus, the mediator of the new covenant.

The responsory to the reading from Exodus is based on 2 Corinthians 3:13,18,15: "Moses veiled his face to hide it from the people of Israel.—But we reflect the glory of the Lord with unveiled faces and grow ever more radiant as we are transformed into his likeness by the Lord who is Spirit." In this passage Paul is pointing out that the people of the new dispensation, the gospel, have a "clear" view of God's love and glory. The people of the Old Testament saw that love and glory through a "veil," as it were, of the old law.

The text from Theophilus of Antioch contrasts darkness and light, showing how we are in darkness "because of evil deeds." The soul should be a mirror that reflects the light, but should this not be possible because of sin, then the Lord, who heals through his word, through his wisdom, and through his acts of creation, will heal as does a doctor. What ought to take first place in our hearts is faith and the fear of God.

Psalm 89, used at the office of readings (vss. 2–38), speaks of God's favors to the lineage of David, which favors are shared with all who believe. We rely on the Lord who states, "I will never violate my covenant nor go back on the work I have spoken" (vs. 35).

The antiphon to the Canticle of Zechariah at morning prayer repeats the statement from the gospel at today's eucharist: "Do not think that I have come to abolish the law and the prophets; I have come not to abolish but to fulfill them."

The usual Wednesday scripture reading, from Deuteronomy 7:6–9, is about Israel's status as an elected nation.

At evening prayer the reading from Philippians 2:12b–15a is about God having accomplished salvation for us, which salvation is experienced in those who believe.

The antiphon to the Canticle of the Blessed Virgin is from the gospel of the day: "The one who obeys God's law and teaches others to do so will be great in the kingdom of heaven."

Celebration of the Hours

For the invitatory today it would be preferable to use Psalm 100 instead of Psalm 95 since this text reflects the chosenness of Israel and, by extension, those who have been baptized in Christ.

The psalmody at the office of readings today is from Psalm 89 (vss. 2–38), which extols God's favors to the house of Israel. The covenant established with David and his descendants and the glory of all created life are used as examples of the Lord's faithful love. This same Lord affirms the continuation of his covenant love for Israel: "I will never violate my covenant/nor go back on the word I have spoken." The fact that the text is presented in three sections offers the possibility of praying it in three parts with silences between or with doxologies and antiphons in between. The use of psalm prayers, or one psalm prayer at the conclusion of the three sections, would be a useful way of drawing out the meaning of the psalm text.

Since the responsory to the first reading juxtaposes two texts, one from the Old Testament and the other a Pauline interpretation of it, the responsory should be introduced and followed by silence or enhanced by being sung.

At morning and evening prayer, a general Lenten hymn would appropriately begin these hours of prayer. At morning prayer the psalm prayer after the first psalm is a good example of how these prayers can expand the meaning of a psalm:

"God of mercy and goodness, when Christ called out to you in torment, you heard him and gave him victory over death because of his love for you. We already know your affection for us; fill us with a greater love of your name, and we will proclaim you more boldly before men and happily lead them to celebrate your glory."

The Canticle of Zechariah, with its emphasis on fulfilling the "law and the prophets," would almost demand some special treatment of the canticle itself, such as having it sung.

At morning and evening prayer the scripture text suggested might be extended or replaced by another since it has already been used for three weeks. The intercessions given provide a good example of what is possible at Lenten evening prayer. An appropriate addition would be mention of the elect who are in their final stages of preparation for initiation and who, along with the already initiated, are specially attuned to the word of God during this season.

Reflection—"Living Word: Dead Letter?"

Sometimes physical impairment may hinder some people from hearing God's word, but often the real obstacle is that we sometimes hear only what we want to hear. The word is addressed to each of us to challenge and disturb as much as to comfort and console. To hear the word, to truly heed its message, means that we are willing to accept the challenge along with the comfort it offers.

This is one of the reasons why scripture is such a major part of the liturgy, especially during Lent. To accept the challenge often means to give up some of our selfish comforts before we experience the lasting comfort of doing God's will.

Lent is a time when we should pray not only for ears to hear with but for a willing spirit to heed and live by God's word. Is the Word of God a "living word" or a "dead letter" for us?

Liturgical Context

Today's liturgy of the eucharist continues to reflect the importance of heeding the word of God. The process of initiation continues during these weeks of Lent.

Liturgy of the Eucharist

Today's entrance antiphon is not, as is usually the case, based on one of the psalms, but is adapted from a type of prayer common to the Old Testament. The statement that the Lord is "savior of all people," that he "will answer their cry," and that he "will always be their God" is a summary of basic teachings found in the Old Testament and reiterated in the New.

The opening prayer asks that this Lenten celebration prepare us to celebrate "the great paschal mystery" at Easter, as we grow in love each day.

The first reading, from Jeremiah (7:23–28), reiterates the Lord's command that his people "listen to my voice" (vs. 23). But, says the prophet, "they obeyed not, nor did they pay heed" (vs. 24 and repeated in vs. 26). Even though God has sent his "servants the prophets" (vs. 25), the people refuse to listen to them (vs. 27), a fact that is all the more disturbing since it was these same people who were first called by God and who entered into a covenant relationship with him (as described in the readings from Exodus in the office of readings).

The responsorial psalm (95) is also traditionally used as the invitation to the liturgy of the hours. It is a forceful reminder that each day the believer must turn again to God, to hear and to obey his voice: "Harden not your hearts."

The gospel from Luke (11:14–23) tells of Jesus casting out a devil from a dumb man. Among the crowds witnessing this sign of Jesus' power, there were some who thought that Jesus was in league with "the prince of devils." Jesus disabuses the people of such notions by distinguishing himself and his mission from the devil and his works of deception and division. Jesus then makes another distinction: "The man who is not with me is against me, and he who does not gather with me scatters" (vs. 23). For one to be a true follower of Jesus requires obedience to him and to the Father.

The prayer over the gifts makes its own subtle distinction between the gifts God promises and the "false joys" in which, unfortunately, we can become lost. We pray that God will help us choose his gifts.

The communion antiphon, from Psalm 119 (vss. 4–5) reasserts the importance of God's law and his commands, which are to be fully and faithfully kept.

The prayer after communion asks that the celebration of this sacrament may "bring us the gift of salvation and make our lives pleasing to [God]." The celebration of the eucharist strengthens the faithful to live more faithfully and inspires the elect to come before the Lord in humility.

Celebration of the Eucharist

The basic theme of yesterday's eucharist is present in today's celebration. By way of offering some appropriate variety within this theme, the presider might select number 13 of the verses before the gospel (Lectionary 224): "Your words, Lord, are spirit and life; you have the message of eternal life."

The intercessions could include an intention on behalf of those who hear the revealed word, especially the elect preparing for initiation, that they may be obedient to it. This notion of obedience in the believer is predicated on the example of the obedient life of Jesus, a life that led to his death, "a death he freely accepted." This phrase, taken from the second eucharistic prayer, makes this prayer a clear option for celebration today.

Should the celebration conclude with a prayer over the people, number 11, about being "ready to do your will" would be appropriate.

Liturgy of the Hours

The text from Exodus (34:10–28) read at the office of readings today offers another account of the giving of the Law on Sinai. The promise of the Lord is reiterated (vs. 10) and the requirement that the community keep the commandments is reaffirmed (vs. 11). The "forty days and forty nights" (vs. 28) during which "Moses stayed with the Lord" is a special period of time that is mentioned often in the scriptures. Our forty days of Lent mark a special period of time for us Christians.

The responsory offers a Christian insight into the Old Testament text since it speaks of the law as being given through Moses, but grace and truth as coming through Jesus Christ (see Jn 1:17–18). The reference to "veiled faces" (from 2 Cor 3:18) contrasts the old with the new covenants and is reminiscent of the veiled face of Moses mentioned in Wednesday's reading. Israel saw God's revelation through a veil, as it were. Christians see God's revelation clearly in and through Jesus Christ.

The text from Tertullian on prayer also contrasts the worshipers in the old and new covenants. Prayer is not just intended to get favors from God but gives strength to understand what "suffering for the name of God" means. All creatures pray, says Tertullian, but in their own way. Our prayer through Christ is unique and especially efficacious because, through him, our worship is "in spirit and truth" (as stated in the responsory from John 4:23–24).

At morning prayer today, Psalm 87 emphasizes Jerusalem as the center of the faith of Israel and Psalm 99 the holiness of the Lord our God. The psalm prayer after the first psalm offers a contrast between the old Jerusalem and new Jerusalem:

"Lord God, your only Son wept over ancient Jerusalem, soon to be destroyed for its lack of faith. He established the new Jerusalem firmly upon rock and made it the mother of the faithful. . . ."

The antiphon for Zechariah's canticle is based on the verse of today's gospel about the coming of God's reign: "If it is by the power of God that I cast out devils, says the Lord, then the kingdom of God has come to you already."

At evening prayer the psalmody is Psalm 132, presented in two sections, about God's promises to the house of David and the salvation that will come from this lineage.

Interestingly, the antiphon for the canticle of Mary is not taken from the gospel reading of the day (as has been the custom throughout Lent thus far). Like today's gospel the text is from chapter 11 of Luke, but from verses 27 and 28, and affirms the importance of God's word and our adherence to it: "A woman in the crowd called out: How happy your mother must be, she bore you and fed you at her breast. But Jesus answered: Happier still those who hear the word of God and live by it."

Celebration of the Hours

Since Psalm 95 is used as the responsorial psalm at the eucharist today, it would be preferable to use another, Psalm 100 for example, as the invitatory. This particular psalm reflects the joy of those who "are his people, the sheep of his flock."

The psalmody at the office of readings is from Psalm 89 (vss. 39–53, continuing from yesterday) and Psalm 90. The latter speaks of the Lord as the center of all life, especially the life of those who believe in his covenant and his faithful love.

For morning prayer a general Lenten hymn would be a helpful introduction. The intercessions could mention the elect as they are coming into the light of Christ and will be baptized at Easter. In addition, a prayer for those who seek reconciliation with God and the church would also be helpful today.

At evening prayer a general Lenten hymn would suitably introduce the hour. The Lord's Prayer could well be introduced by a special invitation to prayer, and it could be enhanced by singing. The prayer over the people (no. 11) suggested as a conclusion to the eucharist today could also be used to conclude this hour.

Reflection—"Affiliation or True Allegiance"

The American way of life enshrines some cherished organizations and clubs to which we can belong. All of these organizations require time and effort on the part of members. Fines are often levied should one miss a meeting and one's membership may lapse if the absences are too frequent. One cannot just be affiliated with an organization. One has to offer allegiance and to live by that commitment.

If such is the case with civil organizations, how much more crucial is our self-examination this Lent about our attitude toward our belonging to the people of God. Are we merely affiliated or are we members whose allegiance is secure? Do we honor God with our lips and enjoy a firm but neutral stance where the implications of Christianity are concerned? Does religion truly mean that we offer wholehearted allegiance to Christ?

The time for self-scrutiny is now. After all, it is the person who meditates on the law of the Lord and who lives that law day and night who is the faithful servant of God. It is that person who is truly committed and not just affiliated.

FRIDAY OF THE THIRD WEEK OF LENT

Liturgical Context

Today the eucharist continues the emphasis on the word of God that has been central to the liturgy since Wednesday.

Today's responsorial psalm capsulizes the important relationship between God and his revealed word: "I am the Lord, your God: hear my voice" (Ps 81:9,11). If we truly listen to God's voice, we will respond by loving God and our neighbor not only in words, but by deeds.

Liturgy of the Eucharist

Today's entrance antiphon (not found in the former Roman Missal) praises God for his supreme power: "Lord . . . no god [can] compare with you: you are great and do wonderful things, you are the only God" (Ps 86:8,10).

The opening prayer asks for the grace "to rise above our human weakness." The Latin version asks God to fill our hearts with his grace so that our "human excesses" may be rooted out, and we may follow his commands that lead us to heaven.

The first reading from the prophet Hosea (14:2–10) and the gospel from Mark (12:28–34) are new to today's liturgy. The prophet offers a summary of common prophetic themes when he exhorts Israel to return "to the Lord, your God" (vs. 2). The way to God is made easier when believers realize that the Lord "will heal their defection," "will love them freely," and will turn his wrath away from them (vs. 5). Verse 10 is more sapiential in style than the preceding verses of this reading, but is nevertheless appropriate because it emphasizes conformity to the word and the will of the Lord:

"Let him who is wise understand these things;
    let him who is prudent know them.
Straight are the paths of the Lord,
    in them the just walk,
    but sinners stumble in them" (Hos 2:10).

The responsorial psalm reiterates many of the themes that have already appeared in the reading from Exodus at today's office of readings. There is to be no strange god among this people because there is but one revealed Lord: "I, the Lord, am your God who led you forth from the land of Egypt" (Ps 81:10).

The gospel reading for today (Mk 12:28–34) is also one of the options that the Lectionary provides for the Rite of Penance and for the Rite for Infant Baptism.

In reply to the scribe's inquiry as to "which is the first of all the commandments," Jesus refers to traditional Jewish teaching. Love of God was a basic command of the old law. The law required Jews to love their coreligionists as well as peoples of other cultures who dwelled among them. But it remained for Jesus to place these two laws together and to give them a new scope. The scribe recognizes this fact and says that loving God and loving our neighbor as ourselves is more important than any burnt offering or (temple) sacrifice.

Jesus' teaching is at the core of today's liturgy of the word and is reflected in the communion antiphon (which summarizes the sense of the gospel without quoting it explicitly): "To love God with all your heart, and your neighbor as yourself, is a greater thing than all the temple sacrifices."

The prayer over the gifts speaks of them as "a lasting source of salvation." When offered with proper disposition and when blessed by God, the bread and wine become Christ's body and blood, which is indeed the source of our salvation.

The Latin text of the prayer after communion asks that we may be graced in body and soul by the eucharist and through the liturgy come to share in the fullness of redemption.

The two prayers just mentioned point out that through our common prayer we share in the reality of the paschal mystery, the source of our eternal salvation, until we come to see God face-to-face in his kingdom forever. It is in that kingdom that we will "know fully the redemption we have received."

Celebration of the Eucharist

At the introduction today the presider could use Christ's obedience to his Father's will as the model for our obedient response to the Word.

The verse before the gospel could be number 10 from those offered (Lectionary 224) since it states: "Happy are they who have kept the word with a generous heart, and yield a harvest through perseverance" (see Lk 8:15).

For the intercessions today, petitions about our need for forgiveness and reconciliation, about the elimination of racial prejudice, about an end to social stratification based on economic status, and about the allurements of our consumer culture would be in order.

Of the prefaces for Lent, the first (Lent I) would be an appropriate choice since it indirectly reflects the teaching of Jesus on love of neighbor: "You give us a spirit of loving reverence for you, our Father, and of willing service to our neighbor."

Eucharistic prayer 3 would also be a fitting choice today because of its reference to Christ," whose death has reconciled us to yourself [the Father]" (appropriate for a Friday in Lent with its obvious emphasis on the passion), and because the prayer that, "We may be filled with his Holy Spirit, and become one body, one spirit in Christ," is a reiteration of the gospel's command to love our neighbor.

The Lord's Prayer and the sign of peace could be emphasized today by a special introduction to each. The addition of invocations of Christ who reconciles and who is the word incarnate would be appropriate additions to the Lamb of God.

Liturgy of the Hours

Today's reading from Exodus (35:30–36:1; 37:1–9) concerns the building of the ark of the covenant and the sanctuary. We know that God has been with his people through his loving covenant with them. Now he tells them to build a special dwelling place for him.

The notion of God's dwelling with his people is reflected in the responsory today from Psalm 82 (vss. 2,3) and Psalm 46 (vss. 5,6):

"How dear to me your dwelling place, Lord God of hosts.
My soul is yearning for the courts of the Lord. . . ."

"How holy is the sanctuary of the Most High!
God fills it with his presence and his eternal strength."

The text from Gregory the Great's "Moral Reflections on Job" emphasizes the place of Lenten Fridays as times to reflect on the passion of Christ. The author applies the notion of Christ's suffering and the blood of the lamb of God (using many old covenant images and examples) to the Christian church's celebration of the eucharist and challenges his readers: "If the sacrament of the Lord's passion is to work its effect in us, we must imitate what we receive and proclaim to mankind what we revere."

The responsory to this reading likens the blood of Abel that cried out to God from the earth to the blood of Jesus that "blessed the Earth" that drank it in. The blood of Christ is "more eloquent than the blood of Abel" because it has superseded the bloody sacrifices of the old covenant and has won salvation for the whole world.

Psalm 69 (2–22,30–37), used as the psalmody in the office of readings, speaks of reliance on God and our crying to him for help, especially as we suffer for his sake. The first and second antiphons mark this Friday (and indeed all Fridays) as a time when Christian prayer and meditation reflect on Jesus' passion and death.

The short reading from Isaiah (53:11b–12) is usual on Lenten Fridays and speaks of the suffering servant who, in the light of the gospels, is a figure of Christ.

The antiphon to the Canticle of Zechariah continues the custom of echoing the gospel of the day as it repeats the inquiry: "What is the greatest commandment?"

At evening prayer, a note of praise and thanksgiving is struck by the use of Psalm 135 (in two sections), recalling the history of God's deeds for Israel, and leading to the hymn of adoration from Revelation (15:3–4).

The short reading from James (5:16,19–20) invites us to own up to our sins that we "may find healing."

The antiphon to the Canticle of Mary is a summary statement of the gospel message today: "It is far more important to love your neighbor as yourself than to offer sacrifice."

Celebration of the Liturgy of the Hours

The invitatory to the liturgy of the hours with Psalm 95 would be a traditional and very appropriate introduction today. Should another psalm be substituted for 95, it should not be Psalm 100 since it will be used as the third psalm at morning prayer.

For morning and evening prayer, a hymn reflecting the passion of Christ and our share in his sufferings would be appropriate considering the special emphasis given to the passion on Lenten Fridays.

The scripture reading from Isaiah 53 at morning prayer could easily be expanded, thus continuing its passion orientation but also varying a text that has been used since the Friday after Ash Wednesday.

Since the antiphon to the Canticle of Mary reiterates the love-of-neighbor theme from the gospel, special emphasis should be given to the Lord's Prayer.

Reflection—"Who Is My Neighbor?"

A fundamental openness to others, of all races and kinds, is demanded by the gospel. But even more difficult to do is to live up to the demands that love for neighbor places on us.

Love means bearing burdens and being aware of our responsibilities toward others. It means that there may well be "neighbors" who live as far away as the third world countries and who need our contributions of money to provide them with food. It means that there may be neighbors who need our support in lobbying big business for justice to employees, female as well as male, of whatever race or color. Being neighbor means more than polite conversation in an apartment hallway or over a back fence. Being neighbor means accepting others as we want to be accepted, loving others as we love ourselves.

SATURDAY OF THE THIRD WEEK OF LENT

Liturgical Context

Today's liturgy deals with the true meaning of worship. The attitude of believing communities before God is that of humility, not pride. It is interesting to note that today's liturgy echoes the theme of worship in spirit and truth, as proclaimed in last Sunday's gospel about the Samaritan woman.

Liturgy of the Eucharist

The entrance antiphon encourages us to strive to live better lives by asserting that God is rich in kindness and pardons all our faults (Ps 103:2–3).

The opening prayer relates this Lenten eucharist to the "joy of

Easter" that will be experienced especially at the liturgies of the Easter vigil.

The first reading from Hosea (6:1–6) contains a penetrating insight into God's justice and mercy. The Lord who calls us to return to him (vs. 1) will discipline his people but will heal them as well; he will strike them because of their misdeeds, yet he will also bind up their wounds. The prophet tells the people that they must deepen their commitment to the Lord through purified worship and through lives that reflect their conversion to the Lord: "It is love that I desire, not sacrifice, and knowledge of God rather than holocausts" (vs. 6).

The responsorial psalm is taken from the familiar Psalm 51, which deals with sacrifices that are pleasing to God (vs. 18) and with contrite, humbled hearts before him (vs. 19). The response itself is taken from the last line of the first reading, thus making this a fitting reflection on the words of Hosea.

The gospel from Luke (18:9–14) about the Pharisee and the tax collector is also found among the readings in the Lectionary for the Rite of Penance. The parable is addressed to those "who believed in their own self-righteousness while holding everyone else in contempt" (vs. 9). The Pharisee, who was a religious person, observed the required forms of Jewish religion and even added some extras to show his piety. The tax collector, a figure of a class despised by the Jews, had nothing to offer God except his sincere prayer, "O God, be merciful to me, a sinner" (reminiscent of Psalm 51). In God's sight, the tax collector was more virtuous because of his interior attitude of humility and reliance on God.

The prayer over the gifts asks that we come "to these mysteries with renewed lives." The importance of the proclamation of the word should be recalled here since it is through hearing, pondering, and praying over God's word that we are prepared to celebrate the sacred mysteries, that is, the sacraments. Each time the deacon, priest, or bishop proclaims the gospel he says in a low voice at its conclusion: "May the words of the gospel wipe away our sins." Both word and eucharist together form a celebration that cleanses us from sin and leads us to fuller union with God.

That Christians are to follow the example of the tax collector is indicated by the fact that his prayer forms today's communion antiphon (Lk 18:13).

The prayer after communion recalls the sense of the entrance antiphon in that it addresses the God of mercy. It then asks that we may worship him in truth.

Celebration of the Eucharist

The tone of today's liturgy should be simple and serious since tomorrow there will be the second scrutiny for the elect and a more solemn celebration of the liturgy. The introduction to today's liturgy, then, could simply address the need for purity of worship.

The second form (B) of the penitential rite could be used, for it acknowledges simply that "we have sinned against you" and we ask God to show us his "mercy and love."

Of the verses before the gospel, number 6 (Lectionary 224), about returning "with all your heart . . . [to the Lord because] he is tender and compassionate" would continue the sense of the entrance antiphon and would also lead up to the message of the gospel.

Among the general intercessions today, petitions about religious observances as expressions of internal conversion, about God's mercy offered to all sinners, and about the scrutiny to occur tomorrow would be appropriate.

The Lenten preface IV, about our observance of Lent and the prayer that it might help us "grow in holiness" and lead us to the "reward of everlasting life," would be a good choice.

The Roman Canon might afford a welcome change from the other eucharistic prayers generally used. Its reference to purity of worship makes it particularly appropriate: "Bless and approve our offering; make it acceptable to you, an offering in spirit and truth."

The use of the first introduction (A) to the Lord's Prayer, about calling God our Father, expresses the confidence we have in God who calls us to true and authentic religious worship.

Liturgy of the Hours

The verse before the readings at the office of readings today continues the text used on Lenten Saturdays: "The man of God welcomes the light.—So that all may see that his deeds are true." The fact that this text reflects the gospel at today's eucharist should not be ignored.

The text from the book of Exodus at the office of readings is the last reading from this book to be used in Lent. The building of the "dwelling" is described with Moses doing exactly as the Lord had commanded him (vs. 16). The ark of the covenant deserves reverence because it contains the law that enshrines and symbolizes the covenant relationship (vs. 20). The liturgical allusions should not be passed over (vss. 25,26,35) since we still use lamps, incense, and an altar in our worship. The glory of the Lord filled the dwelling and the Lord was with his people (vs. 34). The book of Exodus ends on a note of pilgrimage with God leading his people by a cloud during the day and by a fire in the cloud at night (vs. 38).

The text from Gregory Nazianzen interprets the prophet's saying: ". . . it is love I desire not sacrifice," to apply not only to the cultic worship of God, but to the worship we offer him when we "show him mercy in the persons of the poor." Love and mercy toward the neighbor, says Gregory, are worth more in God's sight than "myriads of fattened lambs," the sacrifices of the old laws.

The responsory from New Testament sources gives new covenant examples of the love that Christians should bear to others: "I was hungry and you gave me food" (Mt 25:35); "When you did these things for the most neglected of my brothers, you did it for me" (Mt 25:40), all summed up in Jesus' command: "Love one another as I have loved you" (Jn 15:12).

At morning prayer today the scripture reading is taken from Isaiah 1:16–18, which itself echoes the message of the readings at the eucharist: if we sacrifice our pride and our goods to help the widows—that is, the downtrodden—our sins will be forgiven, though they "be like scarlet."

The antiphon to the Canticle of Zechariah repeats the gospel text about the tax collector's humility.

Celebration of the Hours

The invitatory with Psalm 95 would be a fitting introduction to the hours today because this is the last day on which texts from the book of Exodus are read during Lent, and because this psalm refers so often to events of the Exodus.

The psalmody at this hour is from Psalm 107 about the deliverance of Israel by God. The fact that there are three sections of the single psalm make the option of reciting it through with pauses after each section and a psalm prayer at its conclusion appropriate today.

At morning prayer a general Lenten hymn would be a good introduction to the hour. The assigned psalmody (portions of Ps 119 and all of 117) speak of God's love expressed in his commandments.

In between these psalms is the canticle in praise of wisdom, asking that we will be endowed with her so that she "will guide [us] discreetly . . . and safeguard [us] by her glory."

The intercessions today might well include a prayer for the deepening and continuation of Lenten asceticism for those who will celebrate the second scrutiny tomorrow, and for an honest acknowledgment of sin before God and a plea for the gift of his forgiveness.

Reflection—"Liturgy and Life"

During the 1960s there came to be a new emphasis on the social dimensions of the Christian gospel and its relationship to the celebration of the liturgy. Social issues such as race prejudice had come to the fore and communities were challenged to see in the breaking of the bread and praying together a new opportunity to share Jesus' love and mercy with all peoples. The liturgy came to be seen as not only a personal source of communication with God but as cosmic event that all men and women were called to experience.

In the light of these facts we must ask ourselves whether we truly believe in the liberating power of God's message and in the celebration of liturgical rites in his name. Communities must determine where they stand on the question of worship. Is worship to be separated from life in the world or integrated with life in the world? What is our approach to relating liturgy and life?

Chapter Five

Fourth Week of Lent

FOURTH SUNDAY OF LENT

Liturgical Context

At one period of liturgical development the Fourth Sunday of Lent marked the beginning of a three-week fast before Easter and inaugurated the reading of sections from the gospel of John at the eucharist each day. (This custom is attested to in the present Lectionary, which assigns portions of John's gospel from tomorrow until Tuesday of Holy Week). At a later stage in the evolution of Lent, however, the six-week Lenten season was preceded by a three-week period devoted to preparing the Christian community for the penitential prayers and practices that were to come. This period was marked by the Sundays of Septuagesima, Sexagesima, and Quinquagesima. Hence, after three weeks preparing for Lent and three weeks of Lent, this fourth Sunday came to mark a joyful respite in the midst of a very long time of preparation for Easter. This Sunday was called *Laetare* Sunday ("rejoice"), from the first word of the Latin entrance antiphon (still used in our Sacramentary). The option of using rose-colored vestments this day as a change from the violet that had been used throughout Lent was a visual reminder that this Sunday was somewhat the same and yet somehow different from the other Sundays of Lent: it offered a moment of refreshment in the midst of the arduous work of penance. Looking back, we can understand how this evolution of Lent took place. With the demise of the catechumenate and the loss of the obvious connection between initiation and the season of Lent, it was only natural that other themes and spiritual values would substitute for this relationship. Once the medieval emphasis on penance and a rigorous plan of observance evolved, it was natural that believers would look to this Sunday as a break in the regimen.

The present reform of the Lenten liturgy has brought about a return of the catechumenate and its linkage with Lent (hence, the election and scrutinies on Sunday).

The fact that "Rejoice" is still the first word of the entrance antiphon and that rose vestments may still be worn are examples of how the liturgy (even the reformed liturgy) retains its traditional and evolutionary character.

Cycle "A"

Today's verse before the gospel, while not a part of the gospel reading itself (John 9), helps bring out its main point that Jesus, who is "the light of the world," gives sight, that is, light, to the man born blind, as well as to all who follow Jesus.

The repeated references to "light" indicate how this text is related to the scrutiny for baptism and how the season of Lent came to be called the period of "purification and enlightenment." Physical healing leads the man to recognize Jesus as Lord, the source of real light. That sin (either personal or collective) is the cause of this man's blindness is denied by Jesus, who maintains that this condition is present "to let God's works show forth in him" (vs. 3). Almost immediately John emphasizes that through Jesus, so closely identified with the Father that they are one, we come to know the power of God in our midst.

Jesus' use of saliva, a material thing, in healing the blindness symbolizes the importance of material elements as signs of God's power at work. The man washes in the pool of Siloam, which means "one who has been sent" (vs. 7), referring to Jesus, the source of light and enlightenment.

It is at this point that the drama really begins, the protagonists being the man and the Pharisees. Through the dialogue with the Pharisees, the man himself grows in understanding as he commits himself to Jesus in faith. At first the blind (now seeing) man says that Jesus is "a man" (vs. 11), next he affirms that Jesus is a "prophet" (vs. 17), and finally he affirms that Jesus is "Lord" (vs. 38). The Pharisees, however, cannot admit that Jesus is the Messiah as this would involve a faith confession (vs. 22), and so they rest content to affirm who they are, disciples of Moses (vs. 29). Their unbelief makes the man's profession of faith all the more significant. In the face of resolute opposition to Jesus as Messiah, the man cured of his blindness goes beyond his physical cure to its source and affirms that Jesus is not only a wonder-worker, he is Messiah and Lord.

In interpreting this text, the following motifs seem most applicable to the situation of today's liturgy at which a scrutiny takes place. This ceremony is an act of intercession on behalf of the elect by those already committed to the faith. But this act itself requires that those who believe must believe firmly and completely. It is a means whereby the already initiated reflect on what initiation means and what surrender to Jesus as Lord and Messiah really means in their lives.

To move from the darkness of sin to the light of Christ usually requires a progressive movement of allegiance to Jesus. Today's gospel and scrutiny ask the baptized to continue in their progression to faith in the messiahship of Jesus. Similarly, the structure of the Lenten scrutinies attests to the progressive assimilation of the elect into the ranks of the faithful.

It is important to recall the design of the Lenten Lectionary to understand and interpret the first reading today from 1 Samuel (16:1,6–7,10–13). These Old Testament readings have been selected because they mark significant moments in the history of salvation. Today's text, about the selection of David as king of Israel, the least likely candidate, reiterates a common (though continually confounding) theme in salvation history—the choice of the least likely for the most important positions. This youngest son of Jesse (vs. 11) is anointed by Samuel (vs. 13). From now on "the Spirit of the Lord ruled upon David."

While not wanting to impose on this text an unwarranted interpretation, we can say that just as David was chosen by God, so we are chosen by God. We respond to his initiative as we continue from initiation to death. The anointing of David, when the Spirit of the Lord "rushed upon him," is the anointing of the elect that will take place at Easter when the Spirit will come upon them and God will be the source of life and love.

The responsorial psalm, Psalm 23, "The Lord is my shepherd, there is nothing I shall want," is used here and will be used on Monday of the fifth week in Lent to remind us that it is the Lord who chooses, elects, and sustains us in his light, even when we find ourselves in the "dark valley" (vs. 5).

Christ is frequently referred to in the liturgy, especially when John's gospel is proclaimed, as a reminder of his initial and sustaining call to us his chosen ones. In him we can confidently pray, "I fear no evil; for you are at my side" (vs. 5), and through him we have the sure hope that we "shall dwell in the house of the Lord for years to come" (vs. 6).

The second reading from Ephesians 5 (vss. 8–14) reiterates the light/darkness motif of the gospel today. It reminds the initiated that there was a time when we were in darkness, but now we live in light (vs. 8); hence we are to live as children of the light. The goodness, justice, and truth that we receive from Christ (vs. 9) are to be evident in our lives, especially as they are obviously gifts that empower us to stand against the deeds of darkness (vs. 11).

Cycle "B"

The verse before the gospel today, taken from the text that will be proclaimed (Jn 3:14–21), expresses the heart of its message: "God loved the world so much, he gave his only Son, that all who believe in him might have eternal life" (vs. 16).

Just as many were saved, as Exodus tells us, while Moses "lifted up" the bronze serpent (vs. 14), so many will come to be saved when the Son of Man is "lifted up" on the cross. Those who looked upon the serpent and lived (old covenant, Moses) prefigure those who believe in Jesus' redeeming death (new covenant, Jesus) and are saved. But the old covenant pales in comparison with the new because in the new it is God's own Son who gives his life for us (vs. 16). Through the cross and resurrection Jesus is revealed as the one who brings us eternal life. When we commit ourselves to God's ways and to the life of God in Christ, we also commit ourselves to deeds and actions that reflect this affirmation.

The reading from 2 Chronicles (36:14–17,19–23) continues the proclamation of readings dealing with significant events in the history of salvation. It recalls the sin of the people of Judah (vs. 14) and equally clearly it recalls that "early and often did the Lord, the God of their fathers, send his messengers to them, for he had compassion on his people" (vs. 15). These messengers were mocked even by the king of the Chaldeans, who slew them and destroyed the house of God. The king then sold into servitude those who had escaped the sword. The reading ends on a note of optimism by telling how Cyrus, the Persian king, restored the temple and allowed the people to return to Jerusalem. God was caring for his people through the good will shown by King Cyrus. The responsibility to choose the ways of the Lord and to receive his love remains open to us as it did in every age. How we choose will reflect our faith and our allegiance, to the Lord or to other "gods."

The responsorial psalm, Psalm 137, with the responsory, "Let my tongue be silenced, if I ever forget you!" echoes the laments of the people carried into captivity by the wicked king mentioned in the reading from Chronicles. The "foreign land" is contrasted with "Jerusalem," the center of cult worship and religious significance for Israel.

The text from Ephesians 2:4–10 reminds us that we have been brought to life with Christ (vs. 5). We who "were dead in sin" are saved by God's favor. With and in Christ Jesus we are raised up and given a place in the heavens (vs. 6). "This is not your own doing, it is God's gift . . ." (vs. 8). Christ is our life and our redemption. We are offered these gifts so that we may believe in the Father and live our lives in conformity with his will.

Cycle "C"

The gospel readings of the "C" cycle of the Lectionary are, by design, chosen to exemplify the need for reconciliation in the life of the community especially during Lent. Today's gospel is a prime example of this choice, as has already been noted in the commentary for Saturday of the second week in Lent, when this same text was proclaimed (see that commentary for a review of the salient features of this passage).

Proclaimed today as a text about reconciliation in Christ and the process of conversion during Lent, this text stands as a significant reminder of the forgiveness offered to us through the church's liturgy. The introduction to the Rite of Penance, which uses this text and the rest of Luke 15 as its source, speaks of absolution as follows:

"Through the sign of absolution God grants pardon to sinners who in sacramental confession manifest their change of heart to the Church's minister; this completes the sacrament of penance. For in God's design the humanity and loving kindness of our Savior have visibly appeared to us and so God uses visible signs to give salvation and to renew the broken covenant.

"In the sacrament of penance the Father receives the repentant children who come back to him, Christ places the lost sheep on his shoulders and brings them back to the sheepfold, and the Holy Spirit resanctifies those who are the temple of God or dwells more fully in them. The expression of all this is the sharing in the Lord's table, begun again or made more ardent; such a return of children from afar brings great rejoicing at the banquet of God's church" (no. 6d).

The image of the Father welcoming back his repentant children is important in the revised Rite of Penance and in the church's understanding of this sacrament, as is evident in the sample penitential service in Appendix II, no. 31, "The Son returns to the Father," and in the prayers that refer to the names for God used by those engaged in this act of worship. The prayer at the beginning of the service states:

"Almighty God,
you are the Father of us all.
You created the human family
to dwell forever with you
and to praise your glory.
Open our ears to hear your voice
so that we may return to you
with sincere repentance for our sins.
Teach us to see in you our loving Father,
full of compassion for all who call to you for help.
We know that you punish us only to set us free from evil
and that you are ready to forgive our sins.
Restore your gift of salvation
which alone brings true happiness,
so that we may all return to our Father's house
and share your table
now and for ever.
℞. Amen."

The first reading at today's eucharist, from Joshua 5:9,10–12, reaffirms God's sustaining presence to Israel. The Passover rite is referred to in verse 11 as is the feeding with manna in the desert in verse 12. This feeding has now ceased because Israel's desert wanderings have ended. They are now in the land of Canaan where they can eat the yield of the land. It is the same God who, through his Son, leads his people to the promised land of heaven.

The responsorial psalm (Ps 34, also used on Tuesday of the first week in Lent) is seen liturgically as referring to the eucharist and our being fed by the Lord. "Taste and see the goodness of the Lord." Even in our weakness and sin ("when the afflicted man called out, the Lord heard, and from all his distress he saved him"), the Lord continues to call us to himself. It is for this reason that we bless, praise, and glory in the Lord.

The second reading is from 2 Corinthians 5:17–21, the last section of which was already read on Ash Wednesday (vss. 20–21). Paul is insisting on our being a "new creation in Christ" (vs. 17). The old order has passed away (vs. 17) and the new order has begun. "All this has been done by God," through Christ (vs. 18), who has reconciled us to the Father. Just as we have experienced this reconciliation through Christ, so are we to share it with others because we have been given the "ministry of reconciliation" (vs. 18). The point here is that reconciliation is not just a gift for ourselves; it is the gift of God that we offer to each other in love.

Lent as a time for reconciliation in the community becomes the cutting edge of today's readings and reflection. Lent is not a private retreat or a personal journey alone. Lent is our communal renewal and Christian response to God reconciling us through Christ in our world. The challenge of penance and reconciliation is what makes today's recounting of the story of the wayward son a reminder of God's generosity to us and of our love offered to each other.

Sacramentary Texts

The entrance antiphon for today (as has already been noted) is the same as that which was used on this Sunday in the prerevision Lenten liturgy, referring to the comfort and consolation that will come to Jerusalem. Jerusalem is the center from which salvation will come for all peoples (Is 66:18ff.), that is, it is the place where Jesus will suffer, die, and rise again, winning redemption for the world.

A definite shift away from the previous liturgical prayers of
Laetare Sunday is seen in today's Mass formula since it is derived
from more ancient sources than those upon which the previous
Roman Missal depended. The opening prayer is from the earliest
collection of Sacramentary texts and a sermon of St. Leo the Great.
The Latin text speaks about the Word accomplishing the work of
reconciling the human race with God and asks that Christians
"may hasten, with eager devotion and lively faith, toward the
celebrations that are to take place" at Easter.

The prayer over the gifts, also from an early collection of prayers, asks that the gifts offered will be for the salvation of the whole
world, an essential aspect of eucharistic theology that goes beyond
any individual community's celebration of liturgy.

The preface (P 15) assigned for use when the "A" cycle readings
are used speaks about Christ who leads "mankind from darkness
into the light of faith," and then continues:

"Through Adam's fall we were born as slaves of sin,
but now through baptism in Christ
we are reborn as your adopted children."

This Sunday's liturgy helps prepare the elect for the rites of "baptism in Christ" by the celebration of the second scrutiny.

The communion antiphon, like last week's, offers three options,
each corresponding to the Lectionary cycle. The first is derived
from the text of John 9:11 but is not a quotation. Instead the text
applies the event in the gospel to our situation by stating: "I went
away washed; then I could see, and I believed in God." The
second text is from Psalm 121 and emphasizes the place of Jerusalem in the events of redemption. The last text is a quotation from
the parable of the prodigal son in Luke 15:32 and reminds us to
welcome home the erring brother or sister who "was lost and is
found."

The prayer after communion is an example of the Johannine
"theology of light." It expresses faith in the Father who enlightens
"by the light of [the] gospel" all who come into the world.

The celebration of the scrutinies on these Sundays demonstrates
how Lent leads to the sacraments of enlightenment at Easter—
baptism, confirmation, and eucharist.

Second Scrutiny

The format of the scrutiny today follows that established last week. Once more the prayer texts themselves reflect the Johannine gospel read this Sunday and apply it to the situation of the elect. Once again, the "prayer for the elect" may be reworded, but the basic themes must be stressed: the truth of Christ, the apparent foolishness of the cross, the role of the Spirit, doing what is holy and just, suffering for the sake of Christ, belief in the gospel, and witness in the world.

The exorcism prayer itself (RCIA no. 171) eloquently expresses the import of the gospel for the community:

"Father of mercy,
you helped the man born blind to believe in your Son
and through that faith to reach the light of your Kingdom.
Free your chosen ones from the falsehoods that surround and blind
    them.
Let truth be the foundation of their lives.
May they live in your light for ever.
We ask this through Christ our Lord.
℟. Amen.

Lord Jesus,
you are the light that enlightens all men.
By the Spirit of truth,
free all who struggle under the yoke of the father of lies.
Arouse the good will of these men (and women)
whom you have chosen for your sacraments.
Grant them to enjoy your light
like the man whose sight you once restored,
and inspire them to become fearless witnesses to the faith,
for you are Lord for ever and ever.
℟. Amen."

In addition to these prayers for the scrutiny itself, the RCIA offers texts for the Mass when the first, second, and third scrutinies are celebrated (see RCIA, nos. 377, 381, and 385). Understandably, these texts are rather general in theme as they are for use at any season of the liturgical year. For this reason the texts for the Fourth

Sunday of Lent should not be forsaken too quickly in favor of other texts.

Celebration of the Eucharist

Cycle "A"

The introductory rites to the liturgy could allude briefly to the importance of the prayer for the elect at the scrutiny and exorcism. It should also refer to the gospel theme of enlightenment as this will help focus attention on the scripture readings. If the third form of the penitential rite is used, the fifth sample set of invocations about the dead being raised to life, pardon and peace being given to sinners, and the gift of light being bestowed on those in darkness, would lead to the gospel text to come.

The text of today's opening prayer is particularly appropriate since it speaks of Easter and faith in the Lord Jesus. As was suggested last week, since the gospel text is rather long and there is precedent for using more than one reader of the passion account, the use of several readers could help enhance the richness of the gospel text today.

For the celebration of the scrutiny, it is important that ministers and the elect are aware of what is to happen, when and by whom, and so planning, and possibly rehearsal, is necessary.

Because some of the texts of the Sacramentary coincide with the readings from this cycle of the Lectionary, the use of the preface of the Fourth Sunday of Lent and the first communion antiphon is required.

Should the Lamb of God need to be extended today to cover the action of the breaking of the bread and preparing the cups for the distribution of the eucharist, some of Jesus' titles from the gospel of John could be used to begin these strophes; light of the world, Word made flesh, and bread from heaven are all Johannine in character and hence would be useful this Sunday.

Solemn blessing number 5 for the Passion of the Lord could again be used today, to establish continuity with the preceding Sundays of Lent.

Cycle "B"

The introduction to the liturgy could prepare the people for today's gospel by noting the contrast in our lives between darkness and light, sin and virtue, discord and harmony. The use of the third form of the penitential rite with the fifth or sixth set of invocations, reflecting much Johannine imagery, would be appropriate here. A combination of these two sets, utilizing the light/darkness, life/death, forgiveness/sin motifs, would be very helpful.

The alternative opening prayer would coincide well with the readings today since it mentions the Word and states that "by the suffering and death he endured" he "brought mankind the gift of reconciliation."

In the intercessions today, petitions about Lent as a season for coming into the light of Christ, about this season as one of reconciliation, about our participation in the dying and rising of Jesus through liturgy, and about the sick and suffering who seek comfort and consolation from the risen Christ, would all be appropriate today.

The use of the first Lenten preface would be suitable today since it refers to the paschal mystery as the source of salvation and notes that our sharing in the liturgy helps us be conformed more fully to Christ.

The use of the second eucharistic prayer with its phraseology, "Before he was given up to death, a death he freely accepted," would be appropriate. The second memorial acclamation, "Dying you destroyed our death . . . ," reiterates our identification with the paschal mystery of Christ.

If the solemn blessing of the Passion of the Lord has been used already on the Sundays of Lent, it would provide a fitting conclusion to the liturgy. If not, the use of the prayer over the people (no. 17) provided in the day's Mass formula would be fitting since it refers to the love Christ showed for us as he "suffered the agony of the cross."

Cycle "C"

The introductory rites today could replicate those of last week by commenting on the liturgy to be celebrated, using the "I confess," and a sung "Lord, have mercy," thus stressing the reconciliation theme of these Sundays.

The alternative form of the opening prayer is more expressive in its mention of reconciliation, and hence it would be a good choice today: "May our faith, hope and charity turn hatred to love, conflict to peace, death to eternal life." For the general intercessions today, one could refer to the first set of sample prayers (Lent I) in the Sacramentary appendix and to those used last week, and combine them to reflect the readings about reconciliation today.

The use of the second eucharistic prayer for Masses of Reconciliation would be most appropriate today, especially because the theology reflected in the preface indicates that all our efforts at reconciliation are inspired by the Holy Spirit.

The third sample introduction to the Lord's Prayer, asking for forgiveness from God and the grace to forgive others, would be appropriate.

The rites before communion, including the sign of peace and the Lamb of God, could be enhanced today by a special invitation to exchange the sign of peace. Emphasis on titles of Christ as "reconciler" and as the Lord who forgives our sins could figure among the invocations for the Lamb of God prayer.

The solemn blessing of the Passion of our Lord (no. 5), with its reference to "service of God and neighbor," could fittingly conclude the liturgy, which is so concerned with reconciliation with God and each other.

Liturgy of the Hours

Evening Prayer I is a particularly good example of the way this hour of prayer inaugurates the Sunday celebration. The antiphons speak of awaking from sleep and death to rise in the light of Christ (second) and of the life that is ours in Christ Jesus (third).

In the first psalm, 122, its antiphon and psalm prayer point to the Lord who died and rose, forming the church, the new Jerusalem.

The antiphon to the Canticle of Mary is taken from the gospel read in the "B" cycle on Sunday (Jn 3:16), "God loved the world so much . . . ," which same text is the verse before the gospel at the eucharist. Taken as a whole, this hour of prayer reflects the nature of Sunday as a day of rejoicing in the resurrection as well as a day to realize that from this central mystery comes "life" and "light."

The verse before the readings in the office of readings is from John 6:69, "Lord, your words are spirit and life.—You have the words of everlasting life." Significantly this Johannine text is used to begin the liturgical day on which two of the three gospels assigned are from John.

The scripture reading at the office of readings shifts today to the book of Leviticus (8:1–17; 9:22–24). Sections from this book and Numbers will be read this week; next Sunday a continuous reading from the letter to the Hebrews will begin and continue until Wednesday of Holy Week.

Today's text concerns the ritual for anointing priests by Moses. The candidates are Aaron and his sons. Moses washes them with water, robes Aaron with the vestments, and anoints him with oil. He then robes Aaron's sons "as the Lord had commanded him to do." A bullock is then slaughtered as a sin offering.

As has been seen before, the responsory today contrasts the old and the new covenants by using Hebrews 7:23,24 with its contrast between "many priests" in the old dispensation and "an eternal priesthood" in Christ.

The text from Augustine mentions the gospel story of the man born blind and uses much Johannine imagery in elaborating on our relationship with and through Christ who is the way, the truth, and the life.

The responsory includes part of the same text as that of today's invitatory to the hours. Along with Psalm 119:104–105, "Your word is a lantern which guides my step/a light for the pathway before me," this text asserts the priority of the word of God in our conversion and faith renewal in Lent.

At morning prayer the themes of rising with Christ and praising him for the glory of his resurrection mark the antiphons and selection of today's psalms. The antiphon to Zechariah's canticle is based on the message of the gospel reading at the eucharist in the "A" cycle: "It was unheard of for anyone to open the eyes of a man born blind until the coming of Christ, the Son of God." Clearly, there is a balance here between traditional themes that characterize morning prayer (the resurrection) and the theme of light proclaimed in the gospel from John 9.

At Evening Prayer II, greater stress is placed on Christ's sufferings, as seen in the antiphons to the psalms, especially the third antiphon before the canticle from 1 Peter 2:21–24: "Those things, which God foretold through his prophets concerning the sufferings that Christ would endure, have been fulfilled."

The antiphon to the Canticle of Mary is taken from the Lukan gospel proclaimed in the "C" cycle. This is a departure from last week's pattern where this antiphon was taken from the Johannine text from the "A" cycle. This particular antiphon emphasizes the father's dealings with the elder son who refused to rejoice at his brother's return.

Celebration of the Hours

Evening prayer on Saturday and Sunday could be introduced by singing a Lenten hymn emphasizing the passion and triumph of Christ and our participation in this mystery.

The scripture readings at evening prayer these days could be taken from scripture passages from the Lectionary for Mass provided for the two cycles not used today. This would avoid repetition of the texts provided in the hours since the First Sunday of Lent.

At Evening Prayer I it would be helpful to incorporate petitions concerning the scrutiny to occur tomorrow and the reconciliation that ought to be ongoing through Lent. Also petitions about our communal response in word and deed to the Lord would be useful as a reminder of general Lenten themes.

The verse before the readings today is important from the perspective of the Johannine themes it enunciates simply and briefly. Either Psalm 95 or 100 would serve well as the invitatory psalm with this text today since the former deals with listening to the Lord through salvation history and the latter is a praise psalm, especially useful on the Lord's day. If, however, Psalm 24 is chosen, then another invitatory psalm should take its place as the first psalm at the office of readings.

At morning prayer the use of a hymn about the resurrection, new life, and light from Christ would be a good beginning to this hour of prayer that reflects the resurrection so carefully. Intercessions could mention the scrutiny and reconciliation. In addition a prayer about authentic worship on this Lord's day would also be appropriate.

At Evening Prayer II (in addition to the suggestions already made) the intercessions could contain references to our participation in the death and resurrection of Christ, especially the humiliations we have to endure in admitting our weakness and sin. This hour of prayer has traditionally been associated with the forgiveness of sins, thus making such a petition most fitting today. Also at Evening Prayer II, emphasis placed on the Lord's Prayer (by singing or by a special invitation to prayer) and the addition of a sign of peace exchanged by all present could help underscore the reconciliation emphasis of the "C" cycle readings.

Reflection—"Eyes Open but Shut Tight"

The healing of the man born blind offers many levels of interpretation and much food for our reflection. But we who have never been unable to see might well be in a good position to appreciate one aspect of the phenomenon of blindness—that not *wanting* to see is as crippling, if not more crippling, than not being *able* to see. Despite physical ability to see, we may well be shutting our eyes to real issues and concerns that need attention in our lives and in the world in which we live.

Today's gospel points us toward this kind of reflection because the man who was cured received more than physical sight, he achieved spiritual insight that Jesus was "Lord" and one to whom he owed loyalty.

Do we, who are able to see physically, want to see the implications of the spiritual insight we gain in being created by God? Do we want to face the moral dilemmas of nuclear armaments as squarely as we face the lack of harmony in our individual lives? Do we want to face the fact that there is gross inequity in the distribution of the world's supply of food? How much of this inequity are we, as Americans, responsible for? Do we want to see that political and social structures, sometimes by default, continue to oppress "minorities" because of color, race, religion, or sex? Do we want to face the fact that an ever growing percentage of our society is dependent on drugs (and alcohol) to the extent that abuse of our physical health and psychic balance are taken for granted as "normal" ways of living?

Do we want to see that we are required by the teachings of Jesus and of the church to be aware of these moral evils and to do what we can about them, whether by influencing legislators, living according to the principles of justice and peace even when that is difficult, and accepting the challenge of raising such issues with our family and friends?

Illuminating, seeing, living, reconciling, and forgiving are on the evangelists' agenda today. Are they on our agenda for living today? The man born blind received more than his sight; he received a new way of looking at life. We who can see are challenged in today's liturgy to open our eyes to the wider dimensions of what we celebrate.

MONDAY OF THE FOURTH WEEK OF LENT

Liturgical Context

The liturgy of these three weeks prior to Easter is reminiscent of the time when Lent lasted just three weeks and a continuous reading of the gospel of John prepared the elect for initiation. Now the gospel of John is read from today until Tuesday of Holy Week (exclusive of chapters that are more appropriate to the Easter season, e.g., John 6 on the bread of life and John 10 about the good shepherd). As the Lectionary Introduction states: "Beginning with Monday of the fourth week of Lent, there is a semicontinuous reading of the Gospel of John, made up of texts that correspond more closely to the themes proper to Lent . . ." (no. 98).

Liturgy of the Eucharist

Today's liturgy emphasizes the union of the believer with God, that is, a sharing in the life of God through trusting in his word. The entrance antiphon from Psalm 31 (vss. 7–8) affirms our trust in the Lord: "I shall be glad and rejoice in your mercy, because you have seen my affliction."

The opening prayer speaks of the "new life" we receive through the sacraments. These are the church's normal means of leading us to eternal life. The "life" mentioned in the prayer can also refer to the life often spoken of in John's gospel, available through faith in Christ.

The first reading from Isaiah (65:17–21) anticipates the gospel reading today from John (4:43–54). The Isaian text emphasizes the creative work of God that includes his providential care in sustaining in life and vitality what he has made. This providence extends to those who are in sorrow or who are ill, and thus is germane to the gospel account of the cure of the royal official's son. For the believer who trusts in God's providence, the active presence of God is apparent in all aspects of life, and his healing hand is at work to sustain us in sharing his own life and love.

The responsorial psalm (Ps 30) with the responsory, "I will praise you Lord, for you have rescued me," reiterates this notion of God's providence by emphasizing his intervention as he preserves us from destruction (vs. 4) and changes mourning into dancing (vs. 12).

The gospel reading from John 4 follows the account of Jesus' meeting with the Samaritan woman (4:5–42), read on the Third Sunday of Lent "A" cycle. Today's text refers to Jesus's turning the water into wine at Cana, which is the "first sign" of Jesus' power. The healing of the royal official's son, narrated here, is the "second sign," which John locates also at Cana (vs. 46). John then tells of the royal official's request that Jesus "come down and restore health to his son who was near death" (vs. 47). Jesus seizes the opportunity to point out that oftentimes people look for "signs and wonders" before they are willing to believe in him. The attitude of this man, however, is different in that he "put his trust in the word Jesus spoke to him" (vs. 50) rather than insisting first on a miracle. At the end of the story, when it is evident that the Lord cured the boy as he said he would, the official "and his whole household thereupon became believers" (vs. 53). The fact that the official approached Jesus in his need and believed in the Lord's powerful word offers a model for the elect who are preparing for initiation and for the already baptized. All of us are to grow ever more firmly convinced of the power of God's word and through this holy word to grow in holiness.

The fact that catechumens are welcomed to the Sunday liturgy of the word and dismissed before the eucharist begins is a liturgical practice that demonstrates the formative place of the word in becoming a Christian.

The prayer over the gifts uses the Johannine term "life" in two places; it asks that we receive the grace to cast off our old ways of life in order to be redirected to "the life of heaven."

The communion antiphon, taken from Ezekiel (36:27) rather than from either of the day's scripture readings or the book of psalms, refers to the Lord's spirit living in us and our response to his presence by obeying the Lord's laws and decrees.

The prayer after communion again refers to the Johannine theme of "life" by speaking of "life and holiness" and being led "to the happiness of eternal life" through the sacraments we celebrate.

Celebration of the Eucharist

By way of introduction to the liturgy today, the presider could well speak of how we come to union with God through the Word who is Jesus, the source of life and vitality. Of the sample invocations to accompany the third form of the penitential rite, the fifth or sixth is most appropriate in that both use the Johannine vocabulary of life.

Of the verses before the gospel, number 12, (taken from John 3:16) (Lectionary 224), speaks of God's love for us through Christ: "God so loved the world . . . that all who believe in him might have eternal life."

Among the petitions in the general intercessions today, some might include our communal and individual response to the word of the Lord, our need for healing from God for our weakness and failures, and the deeper conversion of the elect who were prayed for at the eucharist yesterday and whose final stages of preparation for baptism have begun.

Of the Lenten prefaces, part of the second (Lent II) could be understood to reflect the message of John's gospel when it states: "You teach us how to live in this passing world/with our heart set on the world that will never end."

Should the Lamb of God be extended beyond three invocations, additional titles of Christ can be taken from those used at the penitential rite today or from the titles of Christ in John's gospel.

To conclude the liturgy the presider might want to use number 16 of the prayers over the people, which refers to being consoled "in this life" and being brought "to the life to come."

Liturgy of the Hours

The verse before the readings at the office of readings today is the same as that used already on Mondays of Lent: "Turn away from sin and be faithful to the Gospel.—The kingdom of God is at hand." These sentences recall the great significance given to the gospel in the revised liturgy of Lent; they also emphasize the very important notion of actively turning from sin toward God. It is not a matter of less sin and more grace—it is turning away from sin entirely and toward God more completely.

The psalmody at the office of readings (Ps 73) addresses the temptation to envy others who seem to be more favored by God than we are. One way to overcome such temptations is to place greater trust and confidence in God who will not abandon us.

The readings at this hour begin with a selection from Leviticus (16:2–28), about the Day of Atonement. (Recall here that the Lenten readings from the book of Exodus were completed last Saturday and that the readings for this week come from Leviticus and Numbers.) The reading begins with the Lord telling Moses how Aaron, his brother, is to prepare himself to offer sacrifice to the Lord. Aaron is to wear sacred vestments, first bathing himself in water. Then he is to take various animals, some of which are to be slain and their blood sprinkled on certain parts of the sanctuary. All the bloody sacrifices, described in detail in this reading, are meant to atone for the sins of Aaron and his family and for the whole Israelite community.

Today's reading also describes the ritual of Aaron's laying both his hands on a goat's head and confessing "over it all the sinful faults and transgressions of the Israelites and so put them on the goat's head." It is doubtful that this rite was a prefigurement of Christ's taking upon himself the sins of all the world's people.

It is clear, however, that when Christ suffered, died, and rose again, the bloody sacrifices of the old law had become obsolete as atonement for sin and worship of the Father. It is in this light that we must understand the responsory to this reading from Hebrews 9:11,12,24: "Christ came as the high priest of the good things which are to be. Not with the blood of goats or calves, but with his own blood . . ." he entered the holy place once for all, and won our eternal salvation.

Next week continuous readings from the letter to the Hebrews will be proclaimed at the office of readings to show the relationship between the Jewish Passover ritual and the new Passover of the people of Christ.

The text from Origen's treatise *On Leviticus* refers to Christ as our high priest who gave his blood in atonement for the sins of all people. Origen points out that just as the Jewish high priest sprinkled the sacrificial blood toward the east, so it is from the east that we receive redemption, from him whose name is Dayspring, the mediator between God and men.

At morning prayer the psalmody asks God to fill us with his love each morning (Ps 90), while Psalm 135:1–12 praises God for all his wondrous works on behalf of his people.

The text from Isaiah 42:19–16, used as a canticle between these psalms, addresses God as victor, who leads the blind on their journey and who turns their darkness into light.

The short scripture reading from Exodus 19:4–6a, about the chosenness of Israel, is a text that has been used on Mondays since the beginning of Lent.

The antiphon to Zechariah's canticle is from the gospel of the day about the royal official's plea for his son's cure.

At evening prayer the psalmody is from Psalm 136 recounting God's ever faithful love for Israel and the refrain that this same love "endures forever."

The canticle from Ephesians (1:3–10) praises Christ as the fullness of God's redemptive love for us. The scripture passage from Romans 12:1–2 is a brief but poignant reminder that true worship is offering ourselves as living sacrifices to God.

The antiphon to the Canticle of Mary is from today's gospel (Jn 4:53) and speaks of the cure of the official's son and the turning of his whole household to Jesus in faith.

Celebration of the Hours

The verse before the readings and Psalm 95 would be a good introduction to the hours today, especially in the contrast provided between the verse, which speaks of the command to turn to the Lord, and the psalm, which reminds us of the times when Israel did and did not turn to God.

Since just one psalm is used in the office of readings, it could be recited straight through, or with pauses between the sections, or with doxologies and antiphons. Because of the significant theological content of the responsory to the first reading, it should be emphasized in celebration (perhaps by singing, by a meditative recitation, and/or by silence before and after it is sung/said).

A general Lenten hymn would appropriately begin morning prayer. The use of a longer reading or another text would be an appropriate option since the assigned text has been used since the beginning of Lent.

Among the intercessions today, the petitions about true repentance and about continuing Christ's mission of justice and peace are especially useful. In addition, mention might be made of those preparing for initiation at Easter.

A general Lenten hymn would be an appropriate introduction to the hour of evening prayer. Instead of using the reading from Romans 12, which has been assigned to Monday evening prayer since Lent began, a longer reading (from Romans 12) or another suitable text could be proclaimed.

Reflection—"Signs Are Things That Mean Something Else"

Many times in our lives we do something for the sake of something else. Athletes, for example, run and flex muscles not for the sake of the exercise but in order to develop the proper endurance and flexibility needed to play strenuous games; athletes do one thing for the sake of another.

People in love offer each other rings at their wedding not for what pieces of metal mean in themselves, but for what these round pieces of jewelry signify—their love for one another.

The coming together to share a meal signifies unity, care, love, and interest in one another. People dine together, but the event means far more than just eating.

All the actions just mentioned have several levels of meaning. The same thing is true of the gospel narratives. In John's story of the healing of the official's son, the cure is almost overshadowed by other, ultimately more important elements. What is of interest to the author is the man's faith, the power of Jesus' word to effect what he said, and the response of others who became believers.

The same is true of Lent. We make sacrifices not just for their own sake, but as ways of showing our love for God and our neighbor. In Lent the church leads the catechumens on their journey to initiation by means of the scrutinies. But we, the baptized, must remind ourselves of how much more we need to be conformed to the image of Christ. We gather at liturgy to pray for and with each other, but we do so in such a way that we all grow in unity with one another as living witnesses and as living signs of God's presence with his people on earth.

We are involved in sign-making all the time. Are we willing to accept the responsibility to make appropriate and meaningful signs in Lent—signs that really mean interior and spiritual conversion to God? Unless we are, we may well be abusing the signs we perform at liturgy.

TUESDAY OF THE FOURTH WEEK OF LENT

Liturgical Context

The reading from John's gospel continues today with the account of the cure of the man in the pool of Bethesda (Jn 5:1–3,5–16). The liturgical context established on the Sundays of the "A" cycle with its scrutinies and the nature of the Lenten liturgy as leading to initiation and reconciliation should be recalled in order to appreciate the full meaning of the cure described in John's gospel. Images of water purification and believing in Jesus as a response to his word provide suitable ways of applying and appropriating the meaning of today's liturgy.

Liturgy of the Eucharist

The symbolism of water, with which the liturgy is filled today, is introduced by the entrance antiphon, from Isaiah 55:1, with the invitation to "come to the waters, all who thirst . . . come and drink with joy." Especially during Lent, the church invites the elect to come closer to Christ through prayer, penance, and the last phase of the catechumenate. It is also a time for all the faithful to drink more deeply from the font that is God himself.

The opening prayer, derived from traditional sources, speaks of embracing the paschal mystery and proclaiming the salvation that God has granted through Christ.

Today's first reading from Ezekiel 47:1–9,12 also is among those offered in the Lectionary (no. 188) for the rite of baptism for children. The church sees in this reading a figure of the saving waters of baptism. Not only does the prophet see a flowing river, he says that "wherever the river flows, every sort of living creature that can multiply shall live . . . for wherever this water comes the sea shall be made fresh" (vs. 9).

The responsorial psalm reflects the message of the Isaian text by acclaiming God as the author of life: "The mighty Lord is with us;

the God of Jacob is our refuge" (Ps 46:8). Verse 5 of the psalm refers to "a stream whose runlets gladden the city of God." We acclaim the Lord for the "astounding things he has wrought on the earth" (vs. 9).

The gospel from John recounts the cure of the man by the Bethesda pool, but characteristically it deals with a number of related issues as well, among them the growing animosity of the Jewish establishment toward Jesus. The waters of the pool were credited with the power to cure sick people. But Jesus cures the sick man without his having to go into the pool, which he has so long desired to do. Jesus here shows his power; he can cure the sick by his word alone. This angers his enemies. "It was because Jesus did such things on the sabbath that they began to persecute him" (vs. 16).

John further points out that the cured man had no idea who Jesus was (vs. 13). But we Christians do know who Jesus Christ is. Nonetheless, we must be ever on the alert to "give up [our] sins so that something worse may not overtake [us]," a lesson we may take to heart, especially during Lent.

The prayer over the gifts today is taken from a very early collection of prayers and points out that the gifts we give to God are gifts that he has already bestowed on us so that he can transform them into a new creation, into food for everlasting life.

The Lord who leads us on our way to union with God by faith is referred to in the communion antiphon: "The Lord is my shepherd . . . he leads me beside the waters of peace" (Ps 23:1–2). This brief quotation from the psalms again draws our attention to the symbol of water. We reaffirm our trust in the Lord who as shepherd leads us through Lent to share the joy of Easter. The liturgical aspects of today's liturgy of the word are reflected in the prayer after communion where we ask: "May your holy sacraments cleanse and renew us. . . ."

Celebration of the Eucharist

The introduction to the liturgy could speak of the power of God inherent in the liturgy, which brings us into a closer spiritual union with him. The eighth set of sample invocations acclaims the Lord who healed the sick, who forgave sinners, and who brings us strength.

The verse before the gospel number 15 (Lectionary 224), taken from the raising of Lazarus in Jn 11:25,26, speaks of Christ as the resurrection and the life for those who believe in him, an appropriate introduction to the Johannine text today.

Among the petitions in the general intercessions, prayers for believers seeking deeper meaning in their lives, for those preparing for baptism at Easter, for all Christians who want to make the Lord the center of their lives, and for the sick and terminally ill would be appropriate.

The first Lenten preface (Lent I), with its reference to this season "when we prepare to celebrate the paschal mystery" (when initiation will occur and the renewal of baptismal promises will be made) would be a suitable choice.

Should the liturgy conclude with a prayer over the people, number 18, about being reborn to lead a new life, would be an appropriate way of emphasizing that we are to "Go in peace to love and serve the Lord."

Liturgy of the Hours

The scripture reading at the office of readings, from Leviticus 19:1–18,31–37 is, as it were, a commentary on the commandments, especially regarding one's conduct toward the neighbor. The holiness to which the community of Israel is called is the holiness that is from God and is God (vs. 2). The people are to bear no hatred toward their brothers (vs. 17) and they are explicitly commanded to "love your neighbor as yourself" (vs. 18), a text to which Christianity assigns great prominence, for it is the complement to the love of God (Mt 22:39; Mk 12:31). Respect is to be shown to the elderly (vs. 32). The responsory to the text, derived from Galatians 5:14,13 and John 13:34, emphasizes love of neighbor: "All God's commands are summed up in one: love your neighbors as yourself.—Love one another as I have loved you."

The patristic reading is from Leo the Great on charity. Since God is love, charity should have no limit, for God is illimitable. These days of Lent, Leo says, should "provide a special encouragement" to do charitable works, which themselves are a sacrificial offering.

Whereas today's text from Leviticus stresses the law, Leo stresses love as the motive for dealing with our neighbor. The psalmody at the office of readings is Psalm 102 about searching for God, yet being confident in him who "will endure for ever."

At morning prayer the first psalm (101) deals with dedication to the Lord. It is followed by a psalm prayer that links the holiness of God with doing what is right before him. The Canticle of Azariah from Daniel 3 speaks about coming before God with a contrite and humbled spirit. The last psalm (144) speaks of trust in God's mercy and confidence in his triumph. This is a particularly appropriate sentiment in Lent when we celebrate our communal preparation for the paschal mysteries of the triduum that commemorates Christ's triumphant death and resurrection. Some of this understanding is reflected in the psalm prayer that follows.

The short scripture reading from Joel 2:12–13 recalls the first words heard in Lent, at the eucharist of Ash Wednesday, about returning to the Lord with our whole hearts.

The antiphon to Zechariah's canticle is taken from the gospel today: "The man who cured me told me to pick up my sleeping mat and go in peace" (Jn 5:11).

The psalms at evening prayer, from Psalms 137 (vss. 1–6) and 138, deal with the song of an exile (137) and a song of thanksgiving (138). The use of the familiar canticle from Revelation (4–5) praises the Lord, who with his blood, "purchased for God men of every race and tongue, of every people and nation" (5:9). The uniqueness of Israel over against other nations is transcended here since all peoples are welcomed into God's love through Christ. All nations are able to call on God and acclaim:

"Worthy is the Lamb that was slain
to receive power and riches,
wisdom and strength,
honor and glory and praise" (5:12).

The short scripture reading from James 2:14,17,18b, used on other Tuesday evenings in Lent, exhorts us to good works as an expression of faith in Christ.

The antiphon to the Canticle of Mary is taken from the gospel of the day and reiterates the importance of our response to God's intervention in our lives: "Now that you are well again, do not sin any more, or something worse may happen to you" (5:14). This is especially fitting since one of the traditional themes of evening prayer is petition for the forgiveness of sins.

Celebration of the Liturgy of the Hours

Psalm 100, with the seasonal invitatory antiphon, strikes a confident note in the liturgy today. The psalm fittingly emphasizes the mercy and love of God and his enduring fidelity. The use of Psalm 102 in three sections once again offers options about how to recite the psalmody with or without doxologies and antiphons. Whatever the choice, silence should be maintained after the psalm. Because of the scriptural and liturgical significance of the responsory to the Leviticus reading, this part of the liturgy deserves special emphasis in celebration.

At morning prayer a general Lenten hymn to introduce the hour would be appropriate. A longer version of today's scripture reading today would offer a good alternative to the repeated use of these same verses.

The first intercession refers to the relationship between Lent and Easter and the fourth asks that the church might become "an ever greater witness to you."

At evening prayer a general Lenten hymn would be appropriate to begin the hour. The psalm prayer following the first psalm could be reworded to be more direct and precise and thus more fitting for celebration today.

The first intercession speaks in Johannine terminology of Jesus as the way, the truth, and the life and the second of Jesus as living water. The addition of prayers about sin forgiveness and the necessity of good works would be helpful additions to these intercessions.

Reflection—"Cleansing Means Changing"

The notion of "cleansing" has had a long and traditional association with baptism. Commentators from the fathers of the church to present-day catechists describe baptism as a cleansing, especially cleansing from original sin. By the water bath of initiation we are freed from original sin and made members of the body of Christ, the church.

But there is a real difference involved in the cleansing performed in the sacrament and other kinds of cleaning. To clean means to make something spotless only on the outside. Such, however, is not what the cleansing of baptism means. Baptism makes us a wholly new creation and gives us a share in the very life of God. But for this to occur we have to at least want to have a change take place in our lives. The sick man at the pool wanted to be changed from a life of sickness to a life of health. Jesus, by his power, accomplishes this. The man is healed physically. But John's gospel is concerned with another kind of change in the man's life—an internal change. Jesus requires that the man give up his sins.

The same requirements apply to us. For us to be forgiven our sins and to remain freed from them means that we have to change our ways. Like the sick man in the gospel who admitted his infirmity, the first step for us is to admit our infirmity. The second step is to change our ways so that habits of sin and our shoddy ways of acting are surrendered to the Lord who cleanses us from sin.

The issue in today's gospel is not merely about physical healing. It is about the new life we share with God through Christ's healing and cleansing power. But cleansing means changing.

WEDNESDAY OF THE FOURTH WEEK OF LENT

Liturgical Context

The reading from the gospel of John continues today, showing that Jesus is one with the Father. Those who hear Jesus' words and profess faith in the Father gain eternal life. This text is particularly appropriate for this Lenten Wednesday since Wednesdays have held a significant place in the catechumenate and scrutiny process prior to baptism at Easter. Hence hearing the voice of the Lord at the liturgy is an ongoing preparation for initiation and the renewal of baptismal promises at Easter.

Liturgy of the Eucharist

The entrance antiphon today reflects a longing for God and an appeal for his mercy.

The opening prayer contains a strong repentance theme. We pray that God will grant us forgiveness of our sins as we acknowledge them humbly and with sorrow.

Today's first reading reflects the longing for God established in the entrance antiphon and it paves the way for the judgment theme of the gospel by emphasizing the Lord's mercy and love toward all peoples. This section of Isaiah (49:8–15) speaks of the restoration and liberation of Zion. Read in our liturgical gathering in Lent, it assures us of the mercy and salvation of the Lord, even in times of trial (vs. 8), and the constant mercy and love of God for all peoples (vss. 10,13). The reference to those who hunger or thirst (vs. 10) may well be an echo of the book of Exodus (already proclaimed in the office of readings) in which it is told how Israel was fed by manna and sustained by water from the rock. The Lord promises that "his people shall not hunger or thirst . . ." (vs. 10) and that even should a mother forget her child (incredible as that would be) the Lord will never forget his people (vs. 15).

The responsorial psalm (Ps 145) reflects the kindness and mercy of God and asserts that he is "slow to anger" and has "great kindness" (vs. 8). Unlike people who might take advantage of the oppressed and downtrodden, the Lord lifts the falling and raises those who are bowed down (vs. 13). Just as Isaiah assures the Lord's presence to all nations, so the psalm reiterates that he is "near to all who call upon him" (vs. 18).

This positive and encouraging note provides a fitting context for the strong statements in John's gospel that require our faith and commitment to the Lord (Jn 5:17–30). The miracle of the cure of the sick man recounted in yesterday's gospel reading is a scandal to the Jews for two reasons: first it was done on the Sabbath, and second, Jesus made himself God's equal. In today's reading Jesus says: "Just as the Father possesses life in himself, so has he granted it to the Son to have life in himself" (vs. 26). The criteria for those who want to share the very life of God is to hear the Word of the Lord and to profess faith in him (vs. 24). Clearly, while this text is perennially valid, it has special relevance in this Lenten season when baptismal preparation and renewal is paramount in the church's prayer. Baptism requires the active commitment to life lived on God's terms. When our choices are made in conformity with God's Word then we enter upon the path that leads ultimately to union with him. But to make a decision to follow Jesus is never made only once at baptism. It is made again and again, especially in Lent, so that Easter can be an authentic and true celebration of what we really believe.

The prayer over the gifts asks that the celebration of the eucharist might "wash away our sins" and "renew our lives and bring us to salvation."

The communion antiphon refers to another Johannine passage (Jn 3:13) and reminds us that the Son was sent into the world, not to condemn it, "but so that the world might be saved through him." We share in Christ's work of salvation by offering ourselves totally to him.

In the prayer after communion, we acknowledge the eucharist as "a source of life and salvation." The Latin original of the prayer fittingly calls eucharistic bread and wine "heavenly gifts," for these lead us to eternal happiness with God in heaven.

Celebration of the Eucharist

The introduction to the liturgy today could speak of the importance (stressed in the gospel) of hearing the "voice of God's Son," the eternal Word.

The use of the sixth set of sample invocations at the penitential rite, about "new life," being forgiven our sins, and being fed with the body and blood of the Lord, would be appropriate. For the verse before the gospel, the use of number 12 (Lectionary 224), referring to John's notion of eternal life, would be fitting.

The prayer of the faithful might well include intentions for those preparing for baptism, for our communal submission to the word of the Lord in Lent, and for the faithful departed that they may be mercifully judged by God.

The use of the fourth Lenten preface with its reference to the purgative nature of Lent would be a good choice: "You correct our faults and raise our minds to you. . . .".

Should the presider want to conclude the liturgy with one of the prayers over the people, number 1, referring to "the everlasting life you prepare for us," would be appropriate.

Liturgy of the Hours

At the office of readings, the scripture text from Numbers (11:4–6,10–30) recalls the time when Israel complained about having no food save for the manna provided by God. Moses acts as mediator and intercedes with God, who then promises meat for a month (vs. 20). In addition to this food controversy, the text recounts the giving of the spirit to Joshua and the seventy elders, along with Eldad and Medad (vss. 24–29), indicating that God's presence was not to be restricted to a small in-crowd or a clique of leaders. It was intended for all who heard and believed.

The responsory emphasizes this spirit-endowing aspect of the text as it is drawn from the vision of Joel (2:28–29) and the gift of the Spirit on the early church (Acts 1:8).

The patristic text, from Maximus the Confessor, deals with the mercy of God to the penitent. The mercy of God is emphasized: "God's desire for our salvation is the primary and preeminent sign of his infinite goodness." Maximus uses the examples of the lost coin, the good Samaritan, the lost sheep, and the profligate son as ways of imaging and exploring this divine mercy. The implications for the believer include forgiveness, conversion, and reconciliation, all of which are emphasized clearly on the Sundays of Lent in the "C" cycle.

The psalmody at the office of readings is the complete text of Psalm 103, which contains an important summary of our relationship to God in the scriptures. We "bless" and "give thanks" to the Lord (vss. 1–2) and acknowledge "all his blessings" (vss. 1–2) because he forgives and redeems his people (vs. 3). God made his ways known to Moses and "his deeds to Israel's sons" (vs. 7), for which we acclaim him whose love is everlasting (vs. 17). By recounting examples of his love in liturgy (vss. 10–11), we experience the active presence of this gracious God; before him our humble prayer begins and ends with thanks and praise (vss. 20–22). This pattern of Jewish prayer has influenced Christian prayer as seen in both liturgical and personal prayer. The psalm prayer ties together the Lord's forgiveness with this Lenten season.

The psalmody at morning prayer recalls God's love and pleads for his help (Ps 108). Psalm 146 describes the new and eternal Jerusalem (in the imagery of the intimacy of marriage between God and his people) and praises God for his steadfast love.

The short scripture reading from Deuteronomy 7 (vss. 6,8–9) once again asserts the particularity of the election of Israel.

The gospel text is used in the antiphon to Zechariah's canticle to reassert the criteria necessary for life in union with God: "Whoever hears my words, says the Lord, and believes in him who sent me, has eternal life" (Jn 5:24).

At evening prayer Psalm 139 is used as the first two sections of psalmody, which speak of God's knowledge of us and his invitation to faithfulness:

"O Lord, you search me and you know me,
you know my resting and my rising,
you discern my purpose from afar.

O search me, God, and know my heart.
O test me and know my thoughts.
See that I follow not the wrong path
and lead me in the path of life eternal" (vss. 1,23–24).

The canticle from Colossians 1:12–20, about Christ's preeminence, concludes this section of the prayer.

The short scripture text from Philippians (2:12b–15a) repeats Paul's exhortation to prove ourselves "children of God without reproach."

Celebration of the Hours

Since the verse before the readings begins with the words "Turn back to the Lord," the use of Psalm 95 with this antiphon would be a good way to begin the hours; the repetition of this psalm points up the call of the chosen people and their response to the Lord.

At the office of readings the psalm prayer following the three sections of Psalm 103 may be used as is or it may be expanded to apply the meaning of this text more directly to the community during Lent.

At morning and evening prayer a general Lenten hymn would appropriately begin these hours of prayer. The scripture readings could each be expanded (since they have been used since Ash Wednesday) or changed to provide variety. The third and fourth petitions presented for the intercessions at morning prayer are suitable for this season as they speak about sharing with the needy and the real life received from the wounds of Christ. Additional petitions might mention fidelity to the word and the witness of those elected as members of the household of Christ.

Reflection—"Personnel: Inventory and Evaluation"

A major concern of business and education today is how to get the most efficient work out of employees. Efficiency experts, work supervisors, and annual performance evaluations are standard operating procedures for businesses, however large or small. But among the most difficult questions to face when evaluating another's performance or one's own performance on a job is what criteria should be used.

Self-evaluation is part of what the scriptures call us to do in Lent. The gospel of John especially is concerned with reflection on how we will be judged by God on our fidelity to him and to his gospel. The criteria are two: hearing (and thus keeping) the word of Jesus and having faith in him. These lead to eternal life.

These criteria are precisely those mentioned throughout the catechumenate and they are the criteria to be used when evaluating sponsors as well as the elect, the community as well as those seeking admission to the church. The gospel states simply: those who have done right shall live, shall rise to the fullness of life in Jesus; those who have done evil will rise to be damned (Jn 5:29).

The church is not big business, nor is it a collection of employees whose contracts are up for renewal. The church is the community of those who have heard the voice of the Lord and have followed him in faith. Lent is our annual review, our annual self-scrutiny and self-evaluation to determine to what extent we have professed our faith and still do so today. It is also the season when the faithful (faith-filled, literally) welcome those seeking faith, the catechumens. It is time for their self-scrutiny as they approach the bath of baptism. Today's liturgy reminds us of the criteria by which we will be judged. Between now and Easter, and from then until the end of our lives, we have to evaluate ourselves in the light of these criteria: How have we "heard" the word and followed the Lord in faith?

THURSDAY OF THE FOURTH WEEK OF LENT

Liturgical Context

The continuation of John 5 sets the context for today's eucharist. The gospel contains a rather lengthy exposition of Jesus' claim to identification with the Father and to being the one "about whom

Moses wrote." These claims are met with unbelief by the Jews. The lesson for us Christians is to deepen our conversion to Jesus, the Lord.

Liturgy of the Eucharist

Today's entrance antiphon was used in the previous Roman Missal: "search for the Lord," "seek the Lord," and "always seek the face of the Lord" (Ps 105:3–4).

The opening prayer is a general Lenten prayer that, in its Latin version, asks for God's mercy that the good works done in penance may lead us to the paschal celebrations.

The first reading, from Exodus (32:7–14), has already been used in the office of readings in Lent (Tuesday, week 3, vss. 1–20). This account of the golden calf was chosen for proclamation today as a prelude to today's gospel reading in which the Jews of Jesus' time are likened to their ancestors who refused to put their complete trust in God. In the Exodus story, God was forsaken for a molten calf; in Jesus' time he was unrecognized as the Messiah. The infidelity of Israel was not matched by God's wrath; rather, in response to Moses' intercession and pleading, God "relented in the punishment he had threatened to inflict on his people" (vs. 14). This "remembrance" of the covenant forged with Israel caused God to extend love and mercy to his people, as is seen in the responsorial psalm (Ps 106) with the refrain, "Lord, remember us, for the love you bear your people." The worship of the golden calf at Horeb is recalled in the psalm (vs. 19) and the attitude of Israel is summarized: "They forgot the God who had saved them, who had done great things in Egypt" (vs. 21).

The gospel, in a sense, parallels the Exodus reading (chosenness abused, the Lord relenting and not punishing the people). The stage is set from the beginning for a dramatic exchange because Jesus discourses "to the Jews" (vs. 31). The testimony of John is transcended in Jesus, who did the works his Father sent him to accomplish (vs. 36). If the ancestors of Israel had believed Moses, the people of Jesus' day would then believe him (vss. 45–46), but because of their continued stubbornness of heart they have not yet come to trust him. The idolatry described in Exodus and the attitude of the Jews at the time of Jesus are offered for our communal reflection this Lent. To share in the election of God's people implies that we are to trust his ways and word fully and forthrightly.

The prayer over the gifts indicates the strength and guidance that the eucharist offers us in our lives; we pray that this sacrifice may strengthen our weakness and purge us of those things that hinder us from following the Lord. The word challenges us to greater fidelity; the bread and wine of the eucharist strengthen us to live that word in faithfulness.

That our relationship with God is based on the covenant is emphasized in the communion antiphon from Jeremiah (31:33), recalling that the law of God is to be written in our hearts, and by extension to be lived wholeheartedly in our lives.

The prayer after communion refers to "your family" (Latin) as a way of linking the community of Israel with that of the first followers of Jesus and with the present liturgical assembly. We pray that we will be freed from all faults and rejoice in the fullness of eternal blessedness.

Celebration of the Eucharist

The introduction to the liturgy could speak about God's faithfulness to us and our fidelity to him as we respond to his promises to Israel and to the reality of salvation given to us in his Son. The "I confess" form of the penitential rite could be used today as it is an acknowledgment that we, like Israel, have not always been faithful and fully committed to the Lord.

Appropriate petitions in the prayer of the faithful could include those that ask for a more complete response to him in our lives, as well as a prayer that our communal observance of Lent go beyond externals and be deeply rooted in our lives.

The use of the second Lenten preface (Lent II) that speaks of this season as a gift "to your family," and of the strength that the Lord gives us to purify our hearts, to control our desires, and so to serve [Him] in freedom" would be appropriate. An alternative would be to use the first prayer for Masses for Reconciliation since its preface speaks of the disobedience of Israel to the covenant and of the forgiveness of God to us, especially in this season, to turn to him in faith: "Now is the time for your people to turn back to you and to be renewed in Christ your Son. . . ."

The communal aspect of liturgy, of this season, and of our lives could be underscored by a special introduction to the Lord's Prayer noting the "our" in the Our Father. A special introduction to the sign of peace could also express our relatedness to each other as we continue our journey to the kingdom.

Liturgy of the Hours

The verse before the readings today repeats the one used on Thursdays since the day after Ash Wednesday: "Whoever meditates on the law of the Lord . . . will bring forth much fruit at harvest." It is a fitting introduction to the liturgy of the hours because this scriptural prayer asks that we come to know God and his ways, and by extension, that we come to know of his will for us. Hence, meditation on his ways ("on the law of the Lord," Ps 1) will yield a rich harvest.

The scriptural text in the office of readings, from Numbers 12:16–13:3,17–33, recounts the journey of a select group to Canaan to find a homeland for his people. Those to scout the land are twelve, the leaders of the twelve tribes; this itself is significant for they represent all the tribes and eventually all who will share the Lord's goodness and favor. The assessment took "forty days" (vs. 25), again a significant number, after which time they returned to announce a land flowing with milk and honey (vs. 27). The description of the inhabitants, however, was not so positive; they were "fierce" (vs. 28), hence those who scouted "spread discouraging reports among the Israelites about the land they scouted" (vs. 32). This last section leads to tomorrow's reading, which mentions the murmuring of Israel and their complaints against God.

Today's text, however, emphasizes the land of promise and the near completion of the Exodus. That the people are not yet home free is significant for those who celebrate Lent. We are nearing Easter; the end of the journey is in sight. But we, too, have challenges to accept and difficulties yet to face. The Lord who has begun in us this good work of Lent, we pray, will bring it to fulfillment both at Easter and in our eternal homeland of heaven.

The patristic text from Leo the Great on the Lord's passion describes the way in which liturgy brings us into real and immediate contact with the saving mysteries of Christ's death and resurrection. The saint states: "True reverence for the Lord's passion means fixing the eyes of our heart on Jesus crucified and recognizing in him our own humanity."

In true patristic fashion Leo collates some significant biblical passages when he says: "The sacred blood of Christ has quenched the flaming sword that barred access to the tree of life. The age-old night of sin has given place to the tree of life." The sin of Genesis has been undone by the death of Jesus on the wood of the cross, the new and definitive "tree of life." A final and most significant parallel between Christ's death and our own is stated clearly: "The body that lay lifeless in the tomb is ours. The body that rose again on the third day is ours." The complete likeness of our bodies with Christ's will only be accomplished when we rise through his power. Lent, and the whole of a Christian's life, is meant to be a time to prepare for that day. The resurrection is here depicted as our union with God through Christ.

At morning prayer the first psalm (143:1–11) is a prayer uttered in distress yet in confidence: "In the morning let me know your love for I put my trust in you" (vs. 8). The canticle from Isaiah 66 (vss. 10–14) describes the joys of eternal life with God. The fact that it is placed after the first psalm makes it an effective balance to the distress reflected there. The antiphon to Zechariah's canticle refers to John's testimony on behalf of Jesus (Jn 5:34). This is particularly appropriate since it precedes the canticle of John's father who announces the significance of his son's birth: "You my child, shall be called the prophet of the Most High . . ." (Lk 1:76–77).

At evening prayer the psalmody includes two sections of Psalm 144, a prayer for victory and peace. The Revelation canticle (Rev 11–12) then follows, giving a glimpse of the significance of the death and resurrection of Christ—the reign of God has come in Jesus and the powers of evil have been definitively overcome by the blood of the Lamb.

Celebration of the Hours

Psalm 24 could be used as the invitatory psalm today, thus offering variety at the beginning of the hours. It speaks of coming to the Lord with clean hands and a pure heart, and that we come to God by climbing the mountain of the Lord. These sentiments are most appropriate for the introduction to the liturgy of the day through which we come near to God and are purged of impurity of heart.

At the office of readings, Psalm 44 is followed by a particularly well constructed psalm prayer, thus making it a fitting way to conclude the psalmody section of this hour. The way of singing or reciting the psalmody at the hours should be reviewed periodically to avoid a routine celebration. The options include alternating sides, responsorial psalms, or a solo recitation with the whole congregation involved at the beginning and end with antiphon and concluding doxology.

At morning prayer the intercessions reflect general Lenten themes: that the church live its vocation as the "sacrament of salvation" and that baptism and penance might be occasions of true renewal and new life. At evening prayer the petitions are less pertinent to Lent since they reflect a eucharistic theme (especially the first and second). The pattern of the general intercessions at Mass is followed at evening prayer. It would be appropriate, however, to address the needs of the particular community as it journeys through Lent, along with petitions for the whole church as it moves to initiation and reconciliation at Easter.

Reflection—"Doing the Deeds of Jesus"

John would expect us to be shocked at the behavior of the Jews in today's gospel who refused to see in Jesus their Messiah and Lord, for such is part of the evangelist's editorial design. But are we so willing to be shocked at how we sometimes ignore Christ? The Jewish establishment is indicted in this gospel because these leaders, skilled in religious observance, closed their spiritual eyes to Christ. They distanced themselves from him because this vision would make demands on them. Do we distance ourselves from the Christ present among us because of the demands he will place on us?

Are we really very different from the unperceiving Jews of John's gospel in Lent? Do we work on fine-tuning externals while allowing the core of our being and convictions to remain untouched by Jesus? To hear the word means to put it into practice; to put faith in Jesus means to do what is his will for us.

There is a story about the famous biblical translator, St. Jerome. Once he had been asked to write a commentary on a section of the scriptures and after having missed a deadline he explained that he was unable to complete his writing because he took the words of the scripture seriously. He could not write because so many needy people kept coming to his door. Jerome heard and saw Jesus present in those in need.

On this Lenten weekday we are asked whether we can see Jesus among us or whether we are blind to the ways he manifests himself in today's life. He comes often in the poor, the lonely, the uncared for. Some Jews of Jesus' time turned from acknowledging his presence and preferred to perform religious observances and enjoy their special status as the chosen of God. Are we so very different when it comes to living out the implications which the gospel reveals to us?

FRIDAY OF THE FOURTH WEEK OF LENT

Liturgical Context

In the continuous reading from John's gospel, today's text tells how Jesus, who was teaching in the temple, tells the people that he has been sent by God. Jesus is the "just one" heralded in today's first reading from Wisdom. It is he whom the wicked want to condemn to death. Today the liturgy moves closer to that day, Good Friday, when we Christians commemorate the death of the "just one."

Liturgy of the Eucharist

The entrance antiphon is the prayer of one in need: "Save me, O God . . . hear my prayer, listen to my plea" (Ps 54:3–4).

The opening prayer, acknowledging that God knows our human weakness and gives us aid to cope with it, asks that we may experience the effects of his help with joy and may have frequent recourse to it.

The first reading from Wisdom 2:1,12–22 coincides with today's gospel. Conflict and dissension are revealed here as the wicked say, "Let us beset the just one because he is obnoxious to us" (vs. 12) because his life "is not like other men's, and different are his ways" (vs. 15). Among the reasons why this just man is hated is because he claims that God is his Father (vs. 16b). The mockery of the crowd culminates in the derisive remark: "Let us condemn him to a

back there (vss. 1–4), the very place from which they sought escape. Moses and Aaron try to reassure them by saying that they need not fear the people in Canaan and that the "Lord is with us" (vs. 9). The community of Israel, however, still wanted to stone these leaders for leading them to a new series of trials. As if this were not enough, God himself appears and declares his wrath against his chosen people (vss. 11–12) for their ingratitude after all he has done for them. Moses intercedes and asks that the Lord "pardon . . . the wickedness of this people in keeping with your great kindness" (vs. 19).

While on the one hand we might ourselves be impatient with Israel for what we see clearly to be its infidelity and ingratitude, on the other hand, this text may well mirror our own fickleness and ingratitude before God. We believers are challenged to examine the ways in which Israel's reactions are our own; we are thus challenged to greater fidelity in following a God who treats us as tenderly as a father treats his children (Ps 103:13). The responsory draws on Psalm 103 (the same psalm used on Wednesday of this week at the office of readings) to proclaim that "the Lord is merciful and loving, slow to anger and full of compassion" (vs. 8).

The patristic text from Athanasius' Easter letter speaks about the annual new beginning which Christians experience through the commemoration of the paschal mystery of Christ. This is our blessed Passover. Fittingly this commemoration takes place as spring buds forth in new life and as Israel commemorates its liberation in the Exodus.

Sacramentally we feed on the "food of life" and we refresh our souls on "precious blood, as from a fountain." But still we "are always thirsting, burning to be satisfied." Easter this year and every year looks beyond itself to the eternal Easter where there will be no more hunger or thirst, when we will meet the risen Lord and be united with him forever.

The psalmody for the office of readings is from Psalm 78 (1–39), a review of salvation history with special reference to the Exodus. The story, familiar in the Lenten scripture readings, is repeated here—the infidelity of Israel and the faithfulness of God.

At morning prayer the pattern established early in Lent is completed in this fourth week of psalm distribution since the first psalm is Psalm 51. This important text invites us to acknowledge our sins and to accept the Lord's mercy for us. Thanksgiving for deliverance marks the canticle from Tobit 13:8–11,13–15, and the final psalm (147:12–20) speaks of the restoration of Jerusalem. Israel is again described as uniquely privileged: "He has not dealt thus with other nations; he has not taught them his decrees" (vs. 20).

Once more the scripture text is from Isaiah 53:11b–12, about the suffering servant; by extension we reflect on our redemption won through the death and resurrection of Jesus.

The antiphon to the canticle of Zechariah is taken from the gospel of the day (Jn 7:28), about Jesus' origin in God, a rebuff to those who had heard the prophets' words and warnings and thus should have been prepared to accept Jesus as from God. Perhaps we Christians at times still refuse to submit totally to God despite our having heard the word again and again.

At evening prayer Psalm 145 is divided into two sections praising the majesty of God.

The canticle from Revelation 15:3–4 is devoted to adoration of the Almighty, our Redeemer and Lord.

The scripture text from James 5:16,19–20 speaks about the reality of sin and points out the reward for bringing back a sinner from his way.

The antiphon to Mary's canticle repeats the text of the gospel that Jesus' "hour" had not yet come (Jn 7:30).

Celebration of the Hours

Today's verse before the readings ("Turn back to the Lord . . .") and Psalm 95 form a fitting introduction to the celebration of the hours since they combine the evangelical exhortation with the psalm recounting God's dealings with his chosen people. By implication we can apply this revelation and the attitudes of Israel to ourselves who pray for the grace to turn to the Lord in this season.

Because of the traditional emphasis on Friday as a day commemorating the passion and death of Jesus, at both morning and evening prayer an introductory hymn about the Lord's passion and our participation in it would be most appropriate. At both morning and evening prayer an expanded scripture reading would be in order since the texts provided have been used since Lent began.

The intercessions provided at both these hours are appropriate especially because they join the objective fact of the passion and death of Christ with our present experience of redemption. Such a parallel should be continued in any additional petitions that might speak even more concretely of our share in the paschal mystery.

Reflection—"The Persecution of the Just"

"Why?" "Why me?" "Why did this have to happen to me?" "After all, I am a good Catholic, and a good, decent-living person. I don't cheat or steal. I go to church. I say my prayers. Why did this have to happen to me?"

How often have we heard these or similar statements? How many times have we said them to ourselves? When we try our best to live decently we do wonder whether God has abandoned us in our time of need—when tragedy strikes or misfortune sets in.

Today's readings at the eucharist reflect just such a situation before God—the "just one" of Wisdom and Jesus the Messiah. Why should Jesus have to suffer? Why did the God-Man have to die for us? To reply, human logic must give way and one must submit to the mysterious ways of God. Through the eyes of faith we learn that suffering leads to real life, life in union with God. Through the eyes of faith we learn that health and fortune in this life are nothing compared to eternal life with God.

The readings tell us that suffering happened to the "just" Jesus. Suffering will occur in our lives too. And "why, why me" will likely remain a repeated refrain when suffering sets in. Curiously, we humans often need to experience setbacks in this life so we can come to rely more fully on God.

This Lenten Friday reminds us that our own sufferings and setbacks will lead to union with Christ in heaven.

SATURDAY OF THE FOURTH WEEK OF LENT

Liturgical Context

The setting for today's liturgy closely parallels that for yesterday. The continuous reading from the gospel of John, with its emphasis on plots against Jesus and his enemies' concern over his growing popularity, dominates today's eucharist. There is also growing emphasis these days on the events leading to the passion and death of Jesus.

Liturgy of the Eucharist

The entrance antiphon sets the liturgical tone by quoting Psalm 17:5–7, which speaks of "the snares of death," thus calling our attention to the passion and death of Jesus. The opening prayer asks the Father to direct our hearts by his mercy, for without such guidance and his abiding grace we cannot please him. Once again, the prayer reminds us that all we do, especially during our Lenten observances, is done at God's initiative and through his sustaining presence.

The first reading, from Jeremiah 11:18–20, is a prelude to today's gospel since it deals with the plot against Jeremiah. In the eyes of the church the text contains unmistakable references to the passion and death of our Lord. The prophet states that he was "like a trusting lamb led to slaughter" (vs. 19); in Christian prayer we refer to Jesus as the Lamb slain for our salvation. The prophet's enemies conspire and say: "Let us destroy the tree in its vigor; let us cut him off . . . so that his name will be spoken no more . . ." (vs. 19). While admitting a certain exegetical license, it would not be inappropriate to point out that liturgical tradition assigns great emphasis to the entrance of sin into the world through the tree in the garden of Eden and the overturning of its effects through the tree of the cross of Christ. Like the prophet, we who pray at worship trust in the Lord for it is to him that we have entrusted our cause (vs. 20).

This giving over of our lives in trust is a theme continued in the responsorial psalm (Ps 7:2) as we say that we take refuge in the Lord, who is "a shield before me . . . [and] who saves the upright of heart" (vs. 11).

The gospel today forms the conclusion of chapter 7 of John (vss. 40–53). (Since yesterday's text ended with vs. 30, it would be helpful to read vss. 30–40 to determine the exact setting for these verses.) Once more the author considers the origins of Jesus (vss. 40–44) because the crowd spoke of his origins. The Pharisees are shown to be particularly angry again at Jesus (vss. 45–48). They prefer to cling to the law (which they manipulate) for security. One of their number, Nicodemus, reappears here (the one whose conversation with Jesus led to the significant teaching on being born "from above" in Jn 3) and tries to defend Jesus by asking how the

Law could condemn him since it is stated that no one is condemned without first "hearing him and knowing the facts" (vs. 51).

As is frequently the case in John's account, the "Jews" reflect those who should know better and who choose not to put faith in the Messiah. Their negative example should lead us to a more positive commitment to Jesus as our Lord.

The prayer over the gifts admits that our wills resist Jesus, but we pray that he will make us obedient to him and faithful in his service.

The references to the passion continue with the use of 1 Peter 1:19 as the communion antiphon, which states that we are "ransomed with the precious blood of Christ; as with the blood of a lamb without blemish or spot." The reference in Jeremiah to the "lamb" is reiterated here to remind us of the liturgical importance of biblical categories in describing Christ's death. These notions should be kept in mind when acclaiming Christ as the Lamb of God.

The prayer after communion asks that the eucharist may purify us and work within us so that we become more and more pleasing to God.

Celebration of the Eucharist

In light of the third scrutiny, to take place tomorrow, and the usually more solemn celebration of the Sunday liturgy, today's eucharist should be simple in comparison. At the introduction the presider could speak about our salvation accomplished through Christ's humiliation and our acceptance of the humiliations that are inevitable for those who witness to Christ.

The second penitential rite ("Lord, we have sinned against you. . . .") would be an appropriate option especially because it is simpler and more direct than the others.

For the verse before the gospel number 12 (Lectionary 224), from John 3:16, would be appropriate.

Today's intercessions might include petitions relating to our lives in witness to the Lord, our willingness not to control the power of the gospel but to be transformed by it, and the important final scrutiny of the elect to take place tomorrow.

The purpose of this season is stated in the second Lenten preface

(Lent II): "to control our desires and to serve you in freedom," thus making it a fitting option today.

The second eucharistic prayer would add to the simplicity of the celebration because of its comparative brevity.

The use of the second memorial acclamation, "Dying you destroyed our death . . . ," would be a subtle reminder of our union with Christ's paschal victory through the liturgy.

Special mention of knowing the Father's will and having the grace to do it would be a way of introducing the Our Father.

Liturgy of the Hours

The verse before the readings today recalls the important light symbolism used throughout Lent, especially for those preparing for baptism and their sponsors: "The man of God welcomes the light.—So that all may see that his deeds are true." This again points toward the scrutinies as important rites before initiation at Easter.

The first reading at the office of readings is again from Numbers (20:1–13,21:4–9) and recounts the incidents of Israelites contending against God at Meribah and of the placing of the bronze serpent upon a pole so that those who had been bitten by real serpents could look upon it and be cured. The incident about the water from the rock has already been used in the Lenten office of readings (Wednesday, second week of Lent, Ex 17:1–16). Today it serves as a fitting completion to the reading of the Old Testament at the office of readings because it summarizes the fidelity of God toward his people and their response—faithful at times, and far from faith at others.

Moses and Aaron plead with the Lord for help (vss. 7–13) and receive the desired water. However, since Moses struck the rock twice, not once as the Lord commanded, he would not be allowed to lead the community into the promised land (vs. 12).

The incident at Meribah is recalled whenever Psalm 95 is used as the invitatory (vss. 8–9), a continual warning that this "contention against God" is not to be repeated in later generations.

The reading, however, ends on a positive note because the attack by saraph serpents is overcome by the raised bronze serpent (vs. 9), a sign that functions as an enduring example of God's love and intervention for his people.

The responsory takes up the image of the bronze serpent and quotes from the gospel of John to the effect that as Moses lifted up the bronze serpent, "so the Son of Man must be lifted up—so that all who believe in him, may have eternal life" (Jn 3:14,15,17). (It should also be noted that the section from which this responsory comes is used as the gospel for the Fourth Sunday of Lent in the "B" cycle, Jn 3:14–21.)

The second reading at the office of readings is taken from the Pastoral Constitution on the Church in the Modern World about human progress and the temptations to pride and inordinate self-love. Properly understood, human progress is a manifestation of Christ at work in our world for the good of all.

The psalmody at this hour is a continuation of Psalm 78 begun yesterday (vss. 40–72), a kind of summary of salvation history; it is again presented in three sections.

At morning prayer the first psalm praises God as creator and Lord (Ps 92). The second is taken from the vision of Ezekiel (36:24–28), offering strength and hope, for it envisions clean water, a new heart, and a new spirit all coming from God. In the midst of trial and adversity, such as that spoken of by the prophet, this text reminds the people of God's faithfulness.

The third psalm (8) is traditional for Saturday and praises God the creator of nature and of humanity. We acclaim him as maker of all and Lord of everything he has made.

The scripture passage from Isaiah 1 (vss. 16–18) exhorts us to put off misdeeds, to do good, and to allow the justice of God to flourish.

The antiphon to Zechariah's canticle is taken from today's gospel (vs. 46) and refers to the uniqueness of Jesus as seen through the eyes of the temple guards: "Never before has anyone spoken like this man."

Celebration of the Hours

The appropriate choice for invitatory psalm today would be Psalm 95 because it summarizes material from the readings from Exodus, Leviticus, and Numbers, which has been used at the office of readings thus far in Lent. It also refers specifically to the incident recounted in the passage from Numbers read today.

Psalm 78 could be recited in three sections as already noted, but with significant silences between sections. Opting for fewer words and attentive silences here can help emphasize our appropriation of what is prayed in common. After the first reading, the responsory from John 3 might well be emphasized in celebration because its theme is that of the Son of Man being lifted up as our source of salvation.

At morning prayer a general Lenten hymn would provide a good introduction to the hour. The first of the prescribed psalm prayers is better in theme and structure than the second. Should the latter be used it might well be expanded by mentioning the Lord of creation and mediator of new life and the new creation, Christ, the Messiah and Lord.

The scripture reading might well be expanded so that any monotony at hearing the same text each week can be avoided.

At the intercessions, general Lenten petitions about the discipline of the season and the celebration of initiation at Easter could be added. Also special mention might be made of the third scrutiny to occur tomorrow.

Reflection—"Religion's Real Demands"

There is an ever present danger that religion can become domesticated, that is, tamed and fashioned according to the image and likeness of its manipulator. In today's gospel we again meet the Pharisees who had manipulated religion to serve their needs and whose notion of fidelity meant performing what they determined should be done. We can react with shock at their situation and with perfect hindsight say that they attempted to play God.

But are we very different? Do we ourselves domesticate the demands of Jesus by taking what we like and leaving the rest? The American bishops have taken some strong positions on moral and lifestyle issues and are often criticized by practicing Catholics who think that they have "gone too far." Sometimes such people need to have their religious horizons expanded as well as challenged by the gospel. The bishops think that their pastoral instructions are an important means to do just that.

For example, the bishops have spoken out strongly and consistently on the scandal of racial prejudice. Everyone, they maintain, can claim relationship to us as brother and sister. But what is our response? Do we want to do what the Pharisees did and cling to our prejudices? Or are we willing to open our eyes at the sign of peace and see others who are part of the community we call "brothers and sisters in Christ"?

As this Lenten season leads us to reflect on his atoning death for the forgiveness of our sins, we may well want to reflect on the fact that his blood was shed "for all" so that sins might be forgiven. May we ask forgiveness for the times in our lives when we did not look to "all" and discriminated against others because of color, sex, and economic or social level.

Chapter Six

Fifth Week of Lent

FIFTH SUNDAY OF LENT

Liturgical Context

Prior to the reform of the liturgy the Fourth Sunday of Lent was called Laetare Sunday; this Sunday was called Passion Sunday and ushered in a two-week period called "Passiontide." These two weeks before Easter were marked by a liturgy whose tone was somber and severe. All statues and crucifixes were veiled with purple cloth that was removed at the Easter vigil (save for the crucifix, which was uncovered as part of the Good Friday liturgy). These external observances were viewed as signs of penitential preparation for Easter.

The present reform, however, is a return to an older tradition in which initiation and reconciliation were the ways that communities observed Lent as they prepared for Easter. The communal observances of Lent stressed sacramental celebrations rather than external and ceremonial details.

Today's Sunday is called the Fifth Sunday of Lent and the term Passion Sunday is given to next Sunday, formerly called Palm Sunday. This shift reflects the fact that one of the synoptic accounts of the passion of our Lord is proclaimed next Sunday.

In the reformed Lenten liturgy, today's eucharist celebrates and concludes the scrutiny liturgies and begins to turn our attention toward the death and resurrection of Jesus at the liturgy of the hours.

Cycle "A"

Today's verse before the gospel, "I am the resurrection and the life, says the Lord; he who believes in me will not die forever" (Jn 11:25,26), is well suited as an introduction to this celebration.

The narration of the raising of Lazarus (Jn 11:1–45) completes the trilogy of Johannine texts that together form the basis for the celebration of the scrutinies prior to initiation.

Today's narrative deals with the symbol of life, the new life into which a candidate is initiated at baptism and the new life to which the already initiated recommit themselves at Easter. The association between this incident and eternal life after death is signaled by the use of part of this text (11:17–27) as an option for the Mass of Christian Burial.

As is to be expected in a Johannine narrative, the event of the raising of Lazarus provides the setting for the evangelist's exposition of his theology for the benefit of Christian believers.

At the beginning of the text we are surprised at Jesus' apparent disinterest in his friend's illness when he states: "This sickness is not going to end in death; rather it is for God's glory, that through it the Son of Man may be glorified" (vs. 4). Yet, as we have often seen in Johannine theology, such words are pregnant with meaning. God's glory will be revealed through Jesus who will raise his friend from physical death. It is another of the signs in John's gospel through which Jesus does the works of God and by which he reveals the power of God.

Jesus says that Lazarus is dead, and then adds: "For your sakes I am glad I was not there, that you may come to believe" (vs. 15). This is an interesting statement because these disciples first came to believe at Jesus' first sign at Cana (Jn 2:11); now he states that they are to grow in this faith. Faith is not a static gift but a quality that grows and progresses. It is fitting, therefore, that the scrutiny is held today, another step in the catechumen's coming to faith profession at Easter.

The dialogue with Martha reveals a further insight of Johannine theology. Martha affirms her faith in "the resurrection on the last day" and says that her brother will eventually rise again. But Jesus interjects that he is the resurrection and the life. All that is promised to those who believe in eternal life is now present in him: "Whoever believes in me, though he should die, will come to life" (vss. 25–26). Eternal life is present already in Jesus and through him is shared by those who follow him in faith. Martha replies that she has "come to believe" (vs. 27) that he is the Messiah. Once again the same expression is used to denote a growing, deepening notion of faith, as was used in verse 15.

The rest of the text relates the raising of Lazarus using some significant Johannine phrases. Jesus "looked upward" (vs. 41), thus using a prayerful posture that was common in Jewish piety and referred to in the Roman Canon: "The day before he suffered he took bread in his sacred hands and looking up to heaven, to you, his almighty Father. . . ."

John then tells us of Jesus' prayer: "Father, I thank you for having heard me . . ." (vs. 42), once again reaffirming the intimate connection between him and the Father. It is the will of the Father that is to be done and is always to be accomplished by Jesus (see Jn 4:34). Jesus asks that Lazarus be raised "for the sake of the crowd, that they may believe that you sent me" (vs. 42). Lazarus comes forth from the tomb, but the result of Jesus' work is more than a physical restoration to life. This act is a manifestation of the power of God at work in Jesus, a power shared with his followers who, like Lazarus, share his life. Jesus is the source of real *life* for those who have faith despite the obstacles, disappointments, and setbacks in professing faith.

The first reading from Ezekiel (37:12–14) is from a section of the book dealing with the prophet's vision of dry bones being en-fleshed and enlivened. It is the Lord who will open graves and have the dead rise (vs. 12) and it is the Lord who will pour forth his spirit that they will live (vs. 14). These verses are especially significant for initiation because of the obvious references to "spirit" and "life." While these passages refer to salvation for Israel, they also affirm that the Lord is the origin of true life.

The responsorial psalm, 130, with its refrain: "With the Lord there is mercy and fullness of redemption," aptly reflects the experience of believers whose only trust, at times, is in the Lord alone. As Israel waited for the Lord so do we, knowing that he who redeemed Israel "from all their iniquities" (vs. 8) will redeem us from our sins.

The reading from the letter to the Romans (8:8–11) provides a connection between today's other two scripture texts. The comments about flesh/spirit deal not with a duality of body/soul but rather with choosing that which is to be the dominant principle of our lives: our selfishness or God. For those who believe, Paul affirms that the "Spirit of God" dwells in them and that anyone who does not have this Spirit of Christ cannot belong to Christ.

This enlivening spirit is the gift of Christ. "If Christ is in you the body is dead because of sin, while the spirit lives because of justice" (vs. 10). Initiation into the death and resurrection of Christ at baptism is what the elect prepare for during Lent, and this is the reason why the scrutinies take place these Sundays. Conversion to God in Christ means that we give priority to the Spirit over flesh throughout our lives.

Cycle "B"

Today's verse before the gospel aptly introduces the text from John 12:20–33 that will be proclaimed today: "If you serve me, follow me, says the Lord; and where I am, my servant will also be" (Jn 12:26). This gospel is the third in this Lectionary cycle to deal with our identification with Christ's paschal victory. In typical Johannine fashion it instructs us that glory comes from dying to self. The Son of Man is about to be glorified, and the glory that has already been seen in Jesus' signs and wonders in John's gospel will culminate in his life-giving death and resurrection. The "hour" (vs. 23) long awaited and frequently mentioned in the gospel is about to occur. The culminating moment, the final and ultimate sign of God's love for us is about to unfold. But the price for our sharing in this mystery is nothing less than imitating Jesus, who himself imitated the cycle of nature: unless the grain of wheat "falls to the earth and dies" it remains a single grain. But if it succumbs to death in the earth it brings forth much fruit. Jesus' death and burial are required for life and eternal goodness to shine forth.

The narrative next turns to Jesus' own conflict as he experiences distress before the approaching "hour." "My soul is troubled now" (vs. 27) reflects the same distress he felt at the death of Lazarus his friend, and it is the same dread that he experienced in the garden as portrayed in the synoptics. Yet he freely accepted his death. The Johannine account returns to Jesus' resolute acceptance of his Father's will. "What shall I say—Father, save me from this hour? [No] it was for this that I came to this hour" (vs. 27). Jesus puts aside his hesitancy and accepts the coming humiliation, for from it his glory will be fully and finally revealed. John does not depict any agony in the garden, and this statement, which comes closest, is quickly overturned by his actively accepting his Father's will. Once Jesus is "lifted up from the earth" (a reference to the Nicodemus dialogue) he states, "[I] will draw all men to myself" (vs. 32). John concludes that "this statement of his indicated the sort of death he was going to die" (vs. 33).

The picture of Jesus shrinking in the face of his approaching death and his acceptance of the consequences of the approaching "hour" has a parallel in the lives of the faithful. To identify with Christ in the struggle and to commit oneself to the Father despite distress and pain is one way for the believer to identify with the Lord.

The first reading from Jeremiah (31:31–34) contains the oft-cited reference to the new covenant with Israel. It is a fitting conclusion to the series of Old Testament texts used in the "B" Lectionary cycle as they have all dealt with an aspect of the covenant relationship with God: Noah and his family (first Sunday), Abraham's sacrifice of Isaac (second), the giving of the law (third), the exile of the chosen people (fourth), and now Jeremiah's reference to a new covenant (fifth). The reading opens with a reference to the Exodus and states that this new covenant will be very different from the old one (vs. 32). The law will no longer be written on tablets of stone but in the hearts of the chosen people. The familiar formula solidifying the relationship between Yahweh and Israel is again stated here: "I will be their God, and they shall be my people." This same God will "forgive their evildoing and remember their sin no more" (vs. 34). That the Lord will actively cherish and continue to sustain his chosen people applies to the contemporary community that hears these words this Sunday.

The responsorial psalm is Psalm 51, with the refrain: "Create a clean heart in me, O God." In acknowledging our need for God we are also to acknowledge, especially in Lent, specific areas of our lives that need his forgiveness and strength. In the words of the psalmist: "Thoroughly wash me from my guilt and of my sin cleanse me" (vs. 4), and "A clean heart create for me O God, and a steadfast spirit renew within me" (vs. 12).

A significant link between these readings is provided by the second reading from Hebrews (5:7–9). The reality of anguish before God (whether Jesus as seen in the gospel, or our own as experienced in our lives) is portrayed clearly: "Christ . . . offered prayers and supplications with loud cries and tears to God" (vs. 7). These, however, were not without hope because "God was able to save him from death." The author asserts that Jesus "learned obedience from what he suffered" (vs. 8) and through his suffering became the "source of eternal salvation for all who obey him" (vs. 9). Jesus continues this mediating role for us in and through the liturgy, our communal participation in the paschal mystery.

Cycle "C"

Today's gospel reading recounts the story of the woman caught in adultery and of her being forgiven by Jesus. This particular text was used traditionally for penance rites and it is found as an optional reading in the present Rite of Penance. In true Johannine fashion the evangelist begins by setting the scene in the "temple area" (vs. 2) where the "scribes and Pharisees" would gather. Here Jewish religious institutions and practitioners of religion (teachers of the law) came into contact with Jesus. In this incident law and gospel will clash once more.

The Old Testament penalty for the act of adultery is death to both parties (Lv 20:10) with stoning a probable method (Ez 16:38–40). The crowd wants to trip up Jesus and so they call him "teacher" (vs. 4), meaning arbiter of the law. Significantly they do not use the names that the man born blind used of Jesus: man, prophet, and Lord. Jesus as teacher is reminded of what the law says and is asked what to do with the woman. Instead of giving an immediate answer, Jesus traces on the ground with his finger (vs. 6). Whatever commentators make of this tracing, it is at least significant that Jesus is apparently disinterested in their questioning. When he stands up Jesus states clearly, and somewhat hyperbolically: "Let the man among you who has no sin be the first to cast a stone at her" (vs. 7). At this the audience drifts away "one by one" (vs. 9). Then Jesus, realizing that no one condemned her, says that he will not either: "You may go. But from now on, avoid this sin" (vs. 11). The drama here points to the forgiveness of God bestowed on the woman when the law would have required her death. Yet the conclusion to the text should not be forgotten; in fact it points to a significant aspect of Jesus' dealing with the woman. She is forgiven but told to stop sinning.

Forgiveness should not be abused, nor should one presume God's forgiveness when no effort is made to avoid sin. We turn to the Lord in penance to be forgiven and filled with his grace. Thus we are empowered to avoid sin because the love of God is active in us. We are forgiven so that we can continue to do the will of God and to live according to the gospel.

The first reading from Isaiah (43:16–21) is from a section on the promises of redemption and restoration for Israel. God's saving work at the Exodus is recalled. Then the prophet, speaking in the name of the Lord, says: "See, I am doing something new" (vs. 19), and "I put water in the desert for my chosen people to drink" (vs. 20). What the prophet speaks of here is the sustained relationship of the Lord with Israel, not the historical past events. Now, in their exile in Babylon, the people are promised new liberation and new freedom.

This parallels our use of scripture at the liturgy. Texts are read for our instruction and are to be applied to our present experience. The celebration of initiation and penance depend on these texts as ways of reminding contemporary congregations that the Lord who acted in history in Israel and through Jesus acts now in the sacraments.

The responsorial psalm echoes the above sentiments (at least indirectly): "The Lord has done great things for me, we are filled with joy" (Ps 126). What occurred in the past now occurs for us. To accept this fact requires deep faith and commitment to the Lord.

The moving text from Philippians (3:8–14) states so much so simply: Paul has forefeited all for Christ (vs. 8). All that is important is to know Christ and "the power flowing from his resurrection" (vs. 10). It is only with deep faith that we can affirm with Paul that this identification requires suffering and humiliation. That all of this takes a lifetime is expressed clearly by Paul: "It is not that I have reached it [the goal] yet" (vs. 12), but "my entire attention is on the finish line as I run toward the prize to which God calls me—life on high in Christ Jesus" (vs. 14).

On this Fifth Sunday of Lent we are not at the finish line of the season (much less the finish line of life) but we are hopeful that, with Paul, we may share in the vision and reality of Christ's risen life in Lent and most fully at Easter.

Sacramentary Texts

The entrance antiphon today follows the usage of the former Roman Missal, Psalm 43:1–2, affirming our confidence and trust in

God whose justice will save and protect us "against the wicked" and "from deceitful and unjust men."

The opening prayer asks that we may be like Christ, and that we may be guided by his example.

The prayer over the gifts, from an early collection of Lenten prayers for the catechumenate, asks that those who have been steeped in the teachings of Christian faith may be cleansed by the operation of this sacrifice.

The preface of the Fifth Sunday of Lent is to be used when the Lazarus gospel of the "A" cycle is proclaimed. This preface sums up the message of the gospel:

"As a man like Lazarus, Jesus wept for his friend.
As eternal God, he raised Lazarus from the dead. . . ."

Three communion antiphons are provided for use, depending on the Lectionary cycle.

The prayer after communion refers to the sacramental life of the church. In it we ask that we who share in this eucharist may truly be numbered among those who are the body of Christ on earth.

Third Scrutiny

The third of three scrutinies (See RCIA, no. 177) takes place today for the elect preparing for baptism at the Easter vigil. Like the first two scrutinies, the structure involves a "prayer for the elect" with the community responding as they do to intercessions at the prayer of the faithful, and an exorcism. The exorcism prayer mentions the raising of Lazarus and asks that "all who seek life from your sacraments" may be rescued from death:

"Father of eternal life,
you are a God, not of the dead, but of the living:
you sent your Son to proclaim the good news of life,
to rescue men from the kingdom of death
and to lead them to resurrection.
Free these chosen people
from the power of the evil spirit who brings death.
May they receive new life from Christ

and bear witness to his resurrection.
We ask this through Christ our Lord.
R̝. Amen."

Lord Jesus,
you raised Lazarus from death
as a sign that you had come to give men life in fullest measure.
Rescue from death all who seek life from your sacraments
and free them from the spirit of evil.
By your Holy Spirit fill them with life;
give them faith, hope and love
that they may live with you always
and come to share the glory of your resurrection,
for you are Lord for ever and ever.
R̝. Amen."

This final scrutiny concludes with the dismissal by the celebrant:
"Go in peace, and may the Lord be with you always." The next
special communal liturgy for the elect will be sacramental initiation
at Easter.

Celebration of the Eucharist

Cycle "A"

The introductory rites today could refer to the gospel proclamation and the scrutiny to follow by mentioning the life we receive in
Christ at baptism and at Sunday eucharist.

The use of the third penitential rite with the sixth set of sample
invocations would be appropriate here since they refer to the Lord
raising us to new life, forgiving our sins, and feeding us with his
body and blood. This is also an indirect way of referring to the
notion of sacraments continuing the work of Christ in our lives,
just as his power was operative to raise Lazarus from the dead.

The alternative opening prayer expresses in some detail the
mystery of suffering of the cross of Christ and the coming "life and
joy" we share in at Easter. This last reference also points to the
term of the catechumenate process, initiation at Easter.

It might be well to use more than one reader for today's rather
lengthy Johannine text in order to hold the attention of the hearers.

In addition, careful planning of the scrutiny, seeing that silences are observed and the laying on of hands is done carefully, can go a long way toward emphasizing the importance of this ritual action.

The prayer for the elect can be used as printed in the ritual or it may be adapted for local circumstances. Should adaptations be desired, the phrasing and structure of the original form should be noted and used as a model.

The preface for the Fifth Sunday of Lent, designed for use with the Lazarus gospel, should be proclaimed today.

The text of the Lamb of God may be elongated if necessary to accompany the ritual action of breaking bread and pouring wine for communion. Strophes about Jesus and the rising of Lazarus would be appropriate.

The first of the communion antiphons, from today's gospel, is assigned for use today: "He who lives and believes in me will not die for ever, says the Lord" (Jn 11:26).

If the solemn blessing of the Passion of the Lord has been used on the other Sundays of Lent it could well be used today to mark the unity of these weeks and to provide a fitting dismissal today.

Cycle "B"

The introductory rite today could help orient the community to the mystery of death leading to life, humiliation leading to glorification in Christ, who was humbled for our sakes. The invocations that accompany the third penitential rite could be taken from (or adapted from) the fifth sample set about Christ raising the dead to life in the Spirit, granting pardon and peace to the sinner, and bringing light to those in darkness.

The opening prayer refers succinctly to our lives as being patterned after Christ's, thus making it a good choice for the liturgy today.

The general intercessions could include petitions about appropriate renunciation in a land of prosperity, about self-sacrifice in a culture of self-fulfillment, about suffering leading to glory for those who believe, about those who first shared the covenant relationship with God, the Jews, and about those preparing for initiation at Easter.

The Lent II preface would seem to reflect most appropriately the paradox of the gospel today: "You teach us how to live in this passing world with our heart set on the world that will never end."

The Roman Canon would be a good choice for the eucharistic prayer since it states very simply that Jesus celebrated the Last Supper "the day before he suffered. . . ." (Verse 8 of today's reading from Hebrews reminds us that we share life with God made possible through the suffering of his Son.)

The last sample introduction to the Lord's Prayer, about the "coming of the Kingdom," would signify that we look beyond this life to complete union with God in heaven.

The second communion antiphon is assigned for use today since it is drawn from the gospel of this cycle.

The use of the solemn blessing of the Passion of the Lord is a fitting conclusion to this liturgy, especially because of the text of the third section reflecting today's gospel:

"He humbled himself for our sakes.
May you follow his example
and share in his resurrection."

Cycle "C"

The introduction to the liturgy today could speak about God's forgiving and reconciling love as has been seen these past two weeks and as exemplified in his forgiveness of the adulterous woman. The fourth set of sample invocations that speak about Christ reconciling us with one another and the Father, and his healing the wounds of sin and division, would make this a logical choice when the third penitential rite is used.

The alternative opening prayer is a more expressive treatment of the "suffering of the cross" that is a central theme these days, especially as the liturgy begins to give greater attention to the paschal mystery of Jesus.

The verse before the gospel today could be number 5, which states: "I do not wish the sinner to die, says the Lord, but to turn to me and live" (Ez 33:11).

Petitions in the general intercessions might well include our need for reconciliation in Christ and Christ's forgiving love extended to those who are marginal Catholics. Ideas for the petitions can be found in the "penitential intercessions" in the Rite of Penance (no. 204) and ideas for the composition of a concluding collect could be taken from the prayers contained in this rite, especially number 89:

"Lord Jesus,
you opened the eyes of the blind,
healed the sick,
forgave the sinful woman,
and after Peter's denial confirmed him in your love.
Listen to my prayer:
forgive all my sins,
renew your love in my heart,
help me to live in perfect unity with my fellow Christians
that I may proclaim your saving power to all the world."

The eucharistic prayer today could be chosen from the two provided for Masses for Reconciliation.

In introducing the Lord's Prayer the presider might want to emphasize the connection between God forgiving us and our forgiving others in him.

The sign of peace could receive a special introduction today stressing the forgiveness theme of the gospel.

The third communion antiphon is assigned for use today with its very appropriate reference to the grain of wheat dying and producing good fruit (Jn 12:24–25).

The solemn blessing of the Passion of the Lord would provide an ample and fitting conclusion to the liturgy today.

Liturgy of the Hours

As was noted above (in the "Liturgical Context" section), today's liturgy of the hours reflects some of the passion overtones that were traditionally associated with this Sunday and with the next two weeks in the liturgy. This is seen especially in the scripture reading used at Evening Prayer I. Taken from 1 Peter 1:18–21 it speaks about Christ's blood, "the blood of a spotless and unblemished lamb. . . ."

The antiphon to the Canticle of the Blessed Virgin, from the gospel of John (12:24), is used at the eucharist in the "B" cycle: "Unless the grain of wheat falls to the ground. . . ."

The antiphons to the psalmody at this hour are all taken from texts assigned as second readings at the Sunday eucharist: Jeremiah 31 (first), Philippians 3 (second), and Hebrews 5 (third). While obviously reflecting the close association between the hours and the eucharist, it is significant that the passion motifs prevail in this hour of prayer and none of these themes coordinate with the scrutiny gospel about the raising of Lazarus.

The verse before the readings at the office of readings today applies the death motif in John's gospel to the community: "If anyone obeys my teaching—He will never die." The careful weaving together of the Johannine theme of death giving way to life and the Hebrews theme of the obedience of Jesus to the Father as an example for us is a most significant introduction to the office today.

Today the office of readings begins a continuous reading from Hebrews (1:1–2:4) that will last until Wednesday of Holy Week. This letter, with its emphasis on Christ as the fulfillment of the Old Testament covenant, leads to the liturgy of the paschal triduum.

The responsory states: "Our faith rests on Jesus, who endured the cross for the sake of the joy that lay before him." It is this joy that we share through him as we are united in his paschal suffering and triumph.

The text from Athanasius' Easter letter offers a useful parallel between Old Testament background and Jesus. Christ is now the Passover, the way, the lamb who takes away the sins of the world. By selecting this text the editors have deviated from the pattern established the past two weeks when this reading reflected the "A" gospel about initiation. Here the main element is the passion of Christ and our sharing new life through this saving act.

At morning prayer the third antiphon from John (12:23), "The hour has come for the Son of Man to be glorified," shows the growing emphasis on the passion of Jesus.

The scripture reading provided is a change from that used on the first four Sundays of Lent (Nehemiah). Now the text from Leviticus (23:4–7) refers to the commemoration of God's intervention on behalf of Israel, especially in the feasts of Passover and Unleavened Bread. These feasts together are combined in the Christian celebration of new life in the paschal triduum to come.

The antiphon to the Canticle of Zechariah is taken from the Lazarus gospel: "Our friend Lazarus has fallen asleep; let us go and wake him." Again the liturgy offers us a number of references to ponder in prayer, specifically the coming commemoration of the passion of Jesus and our being raised as was the dead Lazarus.

Their juxtaposition in today's morning prayer reflects the desire to offer complementary, not necessarily uniform, themes in the liturgy.

At Evening Prayer II the first and third antiphons refer to the passion of the Lord: "The Son of Man must be lifted up" (referring to John 3) and the union between the faithful and Jesus' sacrifice: "By his wounds we are healed."

The scripture reading from Acts (13:26–30) refers to the passion and death of Jesus, especially verses 29–30: "They took him down from the tree and laid him in a tomb. Yet God raised him from the dead." Once again the scripture text assigned for the first four weeks of Lent is changed and that which is used today is also assigned for next week, Passion (Palm) Sunday. The antiphon to the Canticle of Mary, "When I am lifted up from the earth, I will draw all people to myself," applies the salvation won in Christ to all believers.

Celebration of the Hours

At both Evening Prayer I and II, an introductory hymn about the passion of Christ and our being redeemed by his sacrifice would be a good way to emphasize the passion context of the liturgy these days.

Appropriate psalm prayers that refer to the passion and death of Christ in the light of the psalms prayed would also provide another way of reiterating this emphasis.

Among the intercessions at evening prayer some might include the scrutiny to be celebrated (or that has been celebrated), the urgency of these last two weeks of preparation before Easter, our identification in the suffering, dying, and rising of Jesus, and the renunciation required of those who profess the Christian faith.

The use of a prayer over the people as a dismissal to this hour could also help emphasize the passion of our Lord. One particularly appropriate choice would be number 17.

At the invitatory to the hours today, the use of Psalm 24 with the invitatory verse would be most appropriate since it refers to the Lord as the king of glory. When used in a Christian context the images applied to God in Psalm 24 can appropriately be understood to refer to Jesus.

A hymn at the office of readings and (or) at morning prayer to emphasize the death and resurrection of Jesus and our identification in this mystery would be most fitting today.

At morning prayer today, intercessions could mention the scrutiny to come as well as the new life in Christ that the community is preparing for at Easter.

The use of a prayer over the people or the solemn blessing of the Passion of the Lord would be a fitting way to conclude this hour of prayer today.

Reflection—"Life: How Human?"

We Christians believe that we share the very life of God in Christ and that in our day and age we are to be witnesses on behalf of life, both human and divine. The task is on us to witness to these values as Jesus did. On the everyday human level it means taking each other seriously, not taking each other for granted, and loving each other because we are loved by God. It also means that illness and old age offer special opportunities for us to witness to the value of health and life in Christ. Yet, is it not here that we often fail to live out the implications of our having received the life of God in Christ?

The elderly are increasing in numbers in our society and their need for care, both physical and emotional, are growing. Browning said:

"Grow old along with me,
the best is yet to be,
the last of life for which the first was made,"

but it seems all too apparent that this last of life (often called the "third age" today) brings with it more isolation than happiness, more fear than freedom from fear, more psychological burdens than unburdened spirits. How do we who profess and live the life and love of God address such an issue? Do we wish it to go away or do we witness to the value of life by being with, visiting, helping, and praying with the elderly. We may not be their peers, but are we not spiritual sons and daughters? Does our notion of Christianity include action and prayer for and with the aged?

Another problem in our culture that may well need our witness and reflection is the approach to life that states, explicitly or implicitly, "You are what you do." Increasingly a dehumanization occurs when the only real issues are the "bottom line" and "productivity." The phenomena of "midlife" crises and their ensuing paralysis of spirit derives from a culture that exploits those who can produce and ignores those who cannot. How do we deal with each other? Do we plot and plan to get things done through others? Or do we respect the fundamental equality of all persons whatever their God-given talents and gifts?

The life for which we yearn is the life of God in Christ. And the place where this is given us here and now is in the liturgy. We are all equals at the Lord's table and we are all in need as we come to share the life of God at worship.

May we who come near to this altar come nearer to each other in Christ so that we will know what really matters in life and cherish each other as God cherishes us.

MONDAY OF THE FIFTH WEEK OF LENT

Liturgical Context

As noted previously, the former "passiontide" has been eliminated. However, some elements of the former passiontide have been retained; for example, the preface prescribed for this week is that of the "Passion of the Lord I," which speaks of the suffering and death of Jesus and the power of the cross revealing his judgment on the world. The gospels are still taken from the semicontinuous reading from John (chapter 8 and sections of 10 and 11), leading up to the betrayal and the events of the passion. In addition, the scripture reading at the office of readings is from the letter to the Hebrews, an epistle that offers parallelism between the old covenant (commemorated especially in the Passover) and the new covenant in Jesus and his role as high priest and mediator.

As the drama of the events leading to our redemption unfold, the liturgy invites us to deeper prayer and to a fuller realization and experience of the paschal mystery. At liturgy we do not dramatize what was once accomplished for our salvation; rather we enter into these saving events and experience anew the mystery of Christ died and risen, and ourselves dead to sin and alive in Christ Jesus.

Liturgy of the Eucharist

The entrance antiphon today is taken from that formerly used in the Roman Missal: "God, take pity on me. My enemies are crushing me . . ." (Ps 55:2). As applied to Christ this refers to his betrayal. As applied to the community gathered for prayer it can refer to the price which they often must pay for witnessing to Christ in their lives.

The opening prayer, from Leo the Great, is a text that describes God as the "source of all blessings," through whom we "pass from our old life of sin to the new life of grace." But we also look toward the eternal Easter and lasting joy after our mortal lives have ended, for we pray that God will prepare us for the glory of his kingdom.

Today's first reading, Daniel 13, recounts the story of Susanna as an antitype of the woman who had been caught in adultery in today's gospel (John 8:1–11). (If this gospel was used yesterday in the "C" cycle, then Jn 8:12–20 is used.) Susanna is condemned by two men who wanted her to lie with them (vs. 20). In order to determine her guilt, Daniel asks to interrogate these men separately regarding where this event took place. The two have conflicting stories; hence they are found guilty of perjury and condemned instead of Susanna (vs. 61).

The confidence and security that a believer should experience in the Lord despite trials and false accusations is reflected in the responsory: "Though I walk in the valley of darkness, I fear no evil, for you are with me" (Ps 23:4).

The gospel of the woman caught in adultery has already been treated (in the commentary for the Fifth Sunday of Lent "C" cycle), but the juxtaposition of this text with the incident of Susanna from the book of Daniel leads to some further reflection. In the gospel it is the one who is without sin who is invited to cast the first stone; in the first reading those who sinned by lying were themselves condemned for their sin. In the gospel the accusers leave the woman unpunished; in the first reading the men who wanted to escape punishment are themselves punished and killed for their misdeeds. The judgment of God, showing his mercy to the oppressed, is seen in both readings. Susanna is freed because she did not sin; the adulterous woman is freed because of God's mercy and forgiveness.

The alternate gospel from John (8:12–20) begins with the statement, "I am the light of the world" (vs. 12). The revelation of the "light" is significant in Johannine theology; in this text it is applied to God's judgment through Jesus, judgment that is true because it comes from God (vss. 15–16). The evidence of two witnesses is usually determinative in the law (hence the importance of two men in the Daniel reading); Jesus asserts that his judgment is valid because the two witnesses are himself and his Father (vs. 17). The assertion that Jesus and the Father are one confounds the Jews (vs. 18), and later on it will be the cause of his being condemned. John asserts that Jesus' "hour had not yet come" (vs. 20). We are left with another in a succession of scenes leading to the coming of his "hour," when Jesus will suffer and die to manifest his final judgment on the world and the fullness of his life and light for all who believe in him.

Lent is a privileged time for coming closer to the Lord who is life and light. An important means is self-accusation, not abiding by others' accusations and assessments. The reading from Daniel reminds us of how fleeting and unreliable are the judgments of others when they do not reflect the judgments of God or fidelity to his word, which themselves are significant Johannine themes.

The prayer over the gifts (especially in the Latin form) asks that we might offer the fruit of bodily penance and show to him a joyful purity of heart. The liturgy can be a way of purifying self and coming into more complete union with God.

The communion antiphon today recalls important verses from the gospel: "neither do I condemn you . . ." (Jn 8:11); "I am the light of the world" (Jn 8:12).

The prayer after communion speaks of the power and the grace of the sacraments, which strengthen us to follow Christ more faithfully and come to give us the joy of the kingdom.

Celebration of the Eucharist

The introduction to the liturgy could address our tendency to accuse others when what is really important is accusation of self and how we live in the light of Christ.

The use of the fifth set of invocations for the third penitential rite, about Jesus bringing "pardon and peace to the sinner" (first gospel) and "light to those in darkness" (second gospel), would be appropriate.

To introduce the gospel, number 14 of the verses before the

gospel (Lectionary 224), "I am the light of the world" from John 8:12, would be effective.

For the petitions and the structure of the general intercessions today, the second form of sample intercessions for Lent in the Appendix to the Sacramentary would be useful as reference.

The prescribed preface of the Passion of the Lord I is especially significant when the gospel of John is read since it refers to the *kingship* of the crucified Christ, not a suffering servant; it also refers to his *judgment* on the world coming from his cross.

Because of the passion emphasis in the readings this week the use of the fourth memorial acclamation, "Lord, by your cross and resurrection . . . ," would be useful, as would the second "dying you destroyed our death." (However, it should be remembered that this latter text is found prominently in the Easter liturgy, soon to occur, thus making the first option preferable.)

The introduction to the Lord's Prayer could direct attention to our forgiving one another as Christ forgives us, unlike the wicked men in the readings who chose to condemn rather than to forgive.

Liturgy of the Hours

The verse before the readings today has been used each Monday in Lent, but will be replaced by another next week. To "turn away from sin and be faithful to the gospel" as this text asserts is what the Christian life is about and what the liturgy of Lent is meant to lead to—a life lived in greater fidelity to God's word and will.

The scripture reading from Hebrews (2:5–18) in the office of readings speaks of Jesus being crowned with glory because "he suffered death 'for the sake of all men'" (vs. 9); he is our "leader in the work of salvation" because of his suffering for our sake (vs. 10). Jesus was fully human and was like us in every way (vs. 15–17). Therefore we have "a merciful and faithful high priest before God . . . to expiate the sins of the people" (vs. 17). Because "he was tested through what he suffered, he is able to help those who are tempted" (vs. 18). Jesus, the mediator of the new covenant, frees us from sin and death by submitting himself to the human condition and death for us.

The teaching of Hebrews is reflected in the second reading at this hour from St. John Fisher. He takes the notion of "high priest" from Hebrews and uses it as a basis for developing an understanding of redemption. "Our sacrifice is his precious body which he immolated on the altar of the cross." This sacrifice is available to us in the eucharist. It is this sacrament of his body and blood (the blood "of the most innocent lamb") that we share in at the liturgy.

With yesterday's liturgy of the hours we returned to the first week of the psalter; hence today's psalms at the office of readings are Psalms 6 and 9. The first speaks of our condition before God, our need for him in our distress, and the confidence that comes from knowing that his care is continually offered to us (vss. 7,9,10). In the second we offer praise and thanks for his victory and triumph; for us he is a "stronghold in times of distress" (vs. 10). We trust in him who will never forsake those who seek him (vs. 11).

At morning prayer the scripture texts begin a new two-week cycle with today's reading from Jeremiah 11:19–20. These verses formed part of the first reading at eucharist last Saturday. Like a "trusting lamb led to slaughter," Jesus, through whom we pray in liturgy is the mediator of the new covenant.

The antiphon to the Canticle of Zechariah is taken from the alternate gospel text today, John (8:12): "Whoever follows me . . . will have the light of life."

The intercessions at morning prayer begin with the important phrase: "By his death he has opened for us the way of salvation." The emphasis in the liturgy these days is the sacrifice of Jesus through whom we gain access to the Father; through him we are strengthened to live his life and live in his light.

Traditional Lenten themes mark the petitions today: baptism, generosity to the needy, and the forgiveness of sins.

At evening prayer the use of Psalm 11, about the Lord our refuge, and Psalm 15, about those admitted to God's presence, reminds us of the graciousness of God to us: "He who walks without fault [and] he who acts with justice" will be admitted to the Lord's presence (Ps 15:2).

The familiar canticle from Ephesians (1:3–10) has a richer meaning these days since it speaks of our redemption which, through the blood of Jesus, forgives sins (vs. 7).

The scripture reading from Romans (5:8–9) is a section of the second reading for the Fourth Sunday "A" cycle and emphasizes that we were justified through the blood of Christ when we were still sinners. Through him we are saved from God's wrath.

The antiphon to the Canticle of Mary is taken from the alternate gospel today (as was seen at morning prayer), emphasizing the notions of the Father's testimony given on behalf of Jesus (Jn 8:18).

The petitions at the intercessions here speak of the church born of water and the word, of baptism, of our compassion toward each other, and of intercession for the dead.

Celebration of the Hours

The invitatory verse today could be joined with Psalm 24 as a fitting way to begin the hours. It speaks of coming before the Lord without sin—a fitting act of dedication as a new day begins in prayer and praise.

If the psalm prayers are used at the office of readings, the second might be made more specific to reflect our needs as we come before the Lord by interpolating the "our wounds" of the text.

Whether or not the responsory to the second reading is necessary would seem to depend on the use that the community will make of these same verses as found in the short scripture reading at evening prayer.

At morning and evening prayer the use of a hymn referring to Christ's passion and death would be appropriate introductions to these hours.

Both scripture readings might be either expanded or changed because of their being used again in the Lenten liturgy. Since, however, one of the functions that these repeated texts serve is to underscore particularly significant scripture texts through a season, the decision to change a text should be done only after careful consideration.

Reflection—"Self-Accusation"

How we appear to others can sometimes be a good indication of how we are doing and what we are about. Friends, loved ones, husbands, or wives can often tell when something is wrong, or at least when things are not just right. But this is not always the case. There are times when we cover what we really believe, think, and are and put on a good show for our audience. We play a part, we do not act naturally; we carry off a sleight of hand and no one is the wiser.

Today's scriptures tell us to judge ourselves, not others. This is especially true at this point in Lent when we have perhaps "done well" and have been "good." Have we really been so virtuous?

We may be fasting, a good thing. But are we fasting so that we can experience a real share in the poverty that afflicts so many millions on our earth? Or are we fasting to lose weight and to have others notice how much better we look? We can fool others by the gesture; we cannot fool ourselves by the motivation.

We may be helping in parish programs of outreach or education. But are we doing it so that the gospel can reach many more people? Are we really convinced that the gospel is worth all the effort? Or are we doing it because it looks good on a résumé or because we find a certain prestige in it? The action is the same. Others can be duped by it. But only we can tell that it is authentic and for the sake of God.

We can fool others and we can fool ourselves. Lent is a time when we should stop the playacting and do what the Lord wants and for his sake alone. The only real judge of this is ourselves and God.

TUESDAY OF THE FIFTH WEEK OF LENT

Liturgical Context

The continuous reading from the gospel of John together with certain passion emphases in the liturgy continue strongly in today's eucharist.

Liturgy of the Eucharist

Today's entrance antiphon is traditional. The text of Psalm 27:14, "Put your hope in the Lord. Take courage and be strong," invites the praying community to put its confidence in the same loving God whom Jesus trusted as he went to death for our salvation.

The Latin text of the opening prayer contains a reference to the importance of perseverance in doing the will of God, a notion especially important at this point in Lent.

The first reading from Numbers (21:4–9) also forms the second part of the scripture reading on Saturday at the office of readings and the first reading proclaimed on the feast of the Triumph of the Cross. The reference to the Son of Man being "lifted up" in the gospel accounts for the choice of this text for today's liturgy. The summary of Israel's complaints against the Lord is followed by punishment by saraph serpents. Yet the Lord does relent in this punishment and allows Moses to place a bronze serpent on a pole so that "whenever anyone who had been bitten by a serpent looked at the bronze serpent, he recovered" (vs. 9). The bronze saraph cures only because the people admitted their sin and acknowledged their guilt before God. This particular image provides the background for one way of understanding the reference in John's gospel to the power derived from the dying and rising of the Son of Man.

The responsorial psalm (102), "O Lord, hear my prayer, and let my cry come to you" (vs. 2), is frequently used in the liturgy to begin prayers or to introduce blessings. The liturgical community identifies with the experience of Israel in the first reading as we pray:

"The Lord looked down from his holy height;
from heaven he beheld the earth,
To hear the groaning of the prisoners,
to release those doomed to die" (vss. 20–21).

The gospel today (John 8:21–30) continues the Johannine drama played out between the unbelieving Jews and Jesus. The Johannine notion of being born from above and from below (from John 3, the Nicodemus dialogue) is again used here to contrast the world and believers; the world is "below" and the realm of Jesus is "above." Jesus states: "You belong to this world—a world which cannot hold me" (vs. 23). The way one comes to the realm of God ("above") is to believe that Jesus is the fullness and revelation of God (hence the use of the significant formula "I AM"—the reality of God). Jesus clearly identifies himself with the Father and acknowledges that he can do nothing on his own. His life and mission is permeated with doing the Father's will, even to accepting death on the cross: "When you lift up the Son of Man, you will come to realize that I AM and that I do nothing by myself" (vs. 28). Unlike the experience of Israel in the first reading, Jesus affirms that the Lord remains with him to sustain him: "He has not deserted me since I always do what pleases him" (vs. 29). The evangelist John concludes by speaking of the effect of Jesus' words on many of the people despite their leaders' enmity to Jesus: "Because he spoke this way, many came to believe in him" (vs. 30).

For us in this week before our solemn commemoration of the passion of Christ, we are spurred on to deeper faith in the Lord. That we experience the fullness and lasting effects of this redemption is seen in the prayer over the gifts, which speaks of the forgiveness of our sins and asks that God would guide our wayward hearts to him. The present translation ("the gift of reconciliation") stretches the meaning of the Latin prayer, which asks that we might be absolved from our sins by the sacrifice we offer—the eucharist.

That the key insight in the liturgy of the word today is the lifting up of the Lord is confirmed in the communion antiphon, which speaks about the coming "hour" when the Lord will be "lifted up from the earth." Then he assures us that he will draw all peoples to himself.

This eucharist strengthens us in the process of coming to believe more and more firmly in the Lord. It is also the lasting pledge of what we hope to share in the "gift of heaven" (prayer after communion).

Celebration of the Eucharist

The introduction to the liturgy could compare the Old and New Testament readings today by speaking about the important place that signs and symbols have in our religious observance and tradition. The liturgy we celebrate is our participation in the central sign of salvation, the sign of the cross of Christ.

The seventh set of sample invocations for the third penitential rite uses significant Johannine phrases and images (but they do not repeat the verses of today's gospel). Jesus is acclaimed as the "way to the Father," the "consolation of the truth," and the "Good Shepherd leading us into everlasting life."

For the verse before the gospel, another Johannine text would be a good option, number 12 (Lectionary 224), from John 3:16, which speaks of God who gave his only Son "that all who believe in him might have eternal life."

The general intercessions today could draw on those in the Sacramentary Appendix for "Lent II," with the possible addition (or incorporation) of petitions about the Jews who will soon be commemorating the Passover, and about our doing the will of God especially in Lent.

The prescribed preface today is the Passion of Our Lord I.

To introduce the Lord's Prayer, a special comment about the will of the Father and the strength we gain from this prayer would be helpful.

Liturgy of the Hours

The first reading at the office of readings continues from the letter to the Hebrews (3:1–19). It contrasts Moses and Jesus and shows how Jesus is superior to Moses. The writer tells us that we are "partners of Christ" only if we continue to maintain our confidence in him. What we are to do is to "fix [our] eyes on Jesus, the apostle and high priest whom we acknowledge in faith" (13:1).

The text today from St. Leo the Great deals with many of the scriptural images used this week to describe the cross of Christ. Leo asserts that "the glory of the cross" shines on in heaven and earth, a glory that we share when we appropriate to ourselves the redemption won by Christ when his "hour" had come and when he accepted death on the cross for our salvation. The animal sacrifices and blood rituals are now ended and transcended because the one offering of the body and blood of the Lamb of God is "the fulfillment of all the different sacrificial offerings" of the old law. More importantly, Christ "did away with the everlasting character of death so as to make death a thing of time, not of eternity."

Significantly, the responsory to this reading combines a reference to Colossians (2:14–15) with the verse from today's gospel: "when you have lifted up the Son of Man . . ." (Jn 8:25).

The psalmody at this hour is taken from Psalm 10 (in two sections) and Psalm 12. The former is a prayer of thanksgiving where the poor who trust in God are saved from the wicked; the latter is a plea for God's help especially because "good men have vanished and truth has gone from the sons of men" (vs. 1).

At morning prayer the first psalm, 24, is offered as the invitatory psalm of the liturgy of the hours. The antiphon from the text of the psalm (vs. 4) emphasizes its importance in the liturgy of Lent: "The man whose deeds are blameless and whose heart is pure will climb the mountain of the Lord." This season is a time for renewed dependence on the Lord whose grace and mercy will purify us if we submit to him and his rule.

The section from Tobit 13:1–8; used as a second psalm, reminds us that "God afflicts only to heal"; thus there is always hope and encouragement for us even when we feel afflicted and abandoned by God.

The third psalm, 33, is a prayer of praise and trust in the word of the Lord. It reminds us of the powerful and enduring power of the word of God: "By his word the heavens were made, by the breath of his mouth all the stars" (vs. 6).

The scripture reading from Zechariah (12:10–11a) is from a section of the prophet's words about "Messianic Jerusalem." It has been used in Christian literature to refer to Christ himself, for the prophet states: "They shall look on him whom they have thrust through," and "they shall mourn for him as one mourns for an only son . . ." (vs. 10). The antiphon to Zechariah's canticle recalls the important text from today's gospel: "When you have lifted up the Son of Man you will know that I am he" (Jn 8:28). It is through and with him that we offer our morning praise to the Father.

The psalmody at evening prayer includes invoking the Lord's blessing in time of need: "May the Lord answer in time of trial; may the name of Jacob's God protect you" (Ps 20:1), and a psalm of thanksgiving for the king's victory (Ps 21). The redemption hymn from Revelation (4:11; 5:9–10,12) takes on greater import this week as the events leading to Jesus' passion and death are recounted; it gives a summary of what we have received in the paschal victory of Christ:

"Worthy is the Lamb that was slain
to receive power and riches,
wisdom and strength,
honor and glory and praise" (vs. 12).

The fact that we have received "life in Christ Jesus" (vs. 30) is the central message of the scripture reading assigned for evening prayer from 1 Corinthians (1:27b–30).

The antiphon to the Canticle of the Blessed Virgin is also taken from the gospel reading indicating the identity between Jesus and his Father: "The One who sent me is with me; he has not left me alone, because I always do what pleases him" (Jn 12:29). By extension we can apply this text to those who are united with the Father through Christ in faith, a faith affirmed at baptism and renewed every Lent for those already initiated.

Celebration of the Hours

The invitatory verse and Psalm 95 would form a fitting introduction to the day's liturgy of the hours. At the office of readings, adapting the psalm prayer to include a reference to the cross and resurrection would be in keeping with the paschal orientation of the liturgy in these days.

At both morning and evening prayer a passion hymn would be suitable.

The reading assigned for morning prayer from Zechariah could easily be expanded since verses 1–10 form a section of the chapter about Jerusalem as God's chosen instrument. Since the introduction to the intercessions speaks of Christ as "the bread from heaven" and this reference usually refers to the eucharist, it might be more appropriate to reword the introduction and to rewrite the first petition, (which mentions the eucharist) to stress such Lenten themes as the suffering of those who are drawn into the mystery of the passion and redemptive death of Christ.

At evening prayer the psalm prayers speak of sections of the psalm that refer to our share in the paschal mystery and eternal life with God.

The introduction to the general intercessions urges us to observe the Lord's command to watch and pray to avoid temptation, as he warned his disciples in the garden of Gethsemane.

Reflection—"The Reality of Signs"

It is a fact that we communicate many messages by gestures rather than by words. A wink, a shrug of the shoulders, a smile can communicate what dozens of words cannot: acknowledgment, indifference, acceptance. The language of nonverbal communication through gesture helps reveal what we really mean when we "speak" to another.

In addition there are key code words and phrases that mean

volumes to the initiated but which can mean very little to an outsider. Such is the meaning attached to the simple phrase "lifted up" in the gospel today. Those who hear the scriptures proclaimed time and again become familiar with the story of how the people who had been bitten by the serpent were healed by looking upon the bronze serpent, and how all this was a figure of the fullness of life eternal coming from the cross of Christ. What is involved here is the sacred authors' use of signs, which reveal God's love for us. We know that eternal life has been granted us in Christ and that the cross is the sign of what we believe in. Some of the signs we use to show our belief in Christ include going to church more frequently at this point in Lent to show that these last days are no less important than the first and visiting those whose illness confines them to a closed-in life as a sign of our love and caring.

We who believe in Jesus and in the reality of the sign of his cross are called upon to make our whole lives signs of Jesus' cross as we give of ourselves to our brothers and sisters in Christ.

WEDNESDAY OF THE FIFTH WEEK OF LENT

Liturgical Context

John's gospel continues to be a dominant factor in today's liturgy. It should also be recalled that Wednesdays in Lent have been given special emphasis in liturgical tradition as fast days and days for special prayer, instruction, and exorcism for the elect. Hence an appreciation of the liturgy today would emphasize the notion (derived from the gospel) of remaining in the Lord—both for the elect as they continue their struggle with evil and sin prior to baptism and for the initiated as they struggle with these same realities.

Liturgy of the Eucharist

Today's entrance antiphon is traditional; it focuses on the passion of our Lord.

The opening prayer refers to the traditional themes of the church's sacramental practice during Lent as it asks that those who have been sanctified through penance in Lent may be enlightened by the Lord.

The first reading from the book of Daniel (3:14–20,91–92,95) is a foretaste of the gospel, part of which concerns putting trust in the

Lord alone. The text from Daniel deals with the royal official's order that all Jews should worship the golden statue that Nebuchadnezzar had set up (vs. 10). The administrators Shadrach, Meshach, and Abednego refused to serve this idol (vs. 12) and hence were cast into the fiery furnace (v. 15). Instead of being killed by the flames they were spared because they trusted in their Lord. At the conclusion of today's reading the king declares, "Blessed be the God of Shadrach, Meshach, and Abednego who sent his angel to deliver the servants that trusted in him; they disobeyed the royal command and yielded their bodies rather than serve or worship any god except their own God" (vs. 95). Appropriately, this reading is followed by the responsorial psalm taken from this chapter of Daniel with the refrain: "Blessed are you, O Lord, the God of our fathers . . ." (vs. 52). It is significant that the attitude of praise and thanks expressed by "blessed are you . . ." in the canticle is precisely the term used by the king when he came to acknowledge the Lord of Israel.

The acknowledgment of God and the revelation of Christ as the fullness of the very being of God is at issue in the reading from John (8:31–42). The cutting edge in today's passage concerns living according to Jesus' teaching, not just knowing it. It is only then that people will truly "know the truth," the truth that will set them free (vs. 32).

Jesus' enemies find his teaching so repugnant that they want to kill him (vs. 40). It is sometimes hard for us to accept Jesus' teaching, but we, unlike Jesus' enemies, turn to him in love and faith and ask him to help us in our weakness.

The prayer over the gifts reminds us that the gifts we present in honor of the Lord's name come from him; through his grace and blessing they become for us "a source of health and strength."

The responsorial psalm echoes the praise and blessing of the Lord proclaimed in the first reading from Daniel.

The communion antiphon today is atypical since it is not taken from either the psalms or the gospel of the day. Yet these verses from Colossians (1:13–14) aptly describe believers as redeemed and forgiven.

The Latin text of the prayer after communion refers to the eucharist as a "heavenly medicine" that purges us of our vices and is an everlasting protection for us.

Celebration of the Eucharist

The introduction to the liturgy today could address our need to be faithful to the Word of God, personified and revealed through Jesus, and to trust in His presence with us in the face of trials and conflicts that lead us away from the faith that we profess at the eucharist.

The use of the second form of the penitential rite with the simple admission of having sinned against the Lord would be a subtle reiteration of our failures before God and our need for this eucharist to strengthen and heal us.

Number 10 (Lectionary 224) of the verses before the gospel (derived from Lk 8:15), "Happy are they who have kept the word with a generous heart, and yield a harvest through perseverance," would fittingly introduce today's gospel.

In continuing to use the second sample set of general intercessions for Lent as a model for the prayer of the faithful today, petitions reflective of the scripture readings could include prayer for all believers to deepen their commitment to the Lord and to grow in fidelity to his word. Petitions for those who observe religious practices, but who do not have the appropriate spirit to enliven them, and for those who have grown lukewarm in their commitment to Christ would also be appropriate.

The first preface of the Passion of Our Lord, prescribed for proclamation today, refers to the paschal mystery soon to be commemorated in its fullness: "The suffering and death of your Son brought life to the whole world."

An introduction to the Lord's Prayer might mention our commitment to the Lord through prayer and reflection.

Our continual turning to the Lord and being obedient to him is stated in number 15 of the prayers over the people.

Liturgy of the Hours

The verse before the readings today continues the customary phrase used on the Wednesdays of Lent: "Turn back to the Lord and do penance.—Be renewed in heart and spirit." This text can be an effective reminder that Lent is about our renewed commitment to the Lord through works of fasting, prayer, and almsgiving. It is the spirit with which we do them and keeping their end in mind that makes them appropriate ways to God.

The continuation of the letter to the Hebrews (6:9–20) at the office of readings provides an important instruction on the foundation of our faith in Jesus' self-sacrifice, an offering that fulfilled the promises to Abraham and his descendants. We are not "to grow lazy" (vs. 12) in our lives of faith, for by perseverance and ever-deepening commitment to the Lord we can see and experience the fulfillment in Christ of what was promised to Abraham (vs. 13,15). Jesus is the high priest who makes us acceptable to the Father (vs. 20).

This notion of mediatorship is carried through in the text from St. Augustine today. He states that Jesus, the Son of God and the Son of Man, "prays for us as our priest, he prays in us as our head, he is the object of our prayers as our God."

In characteristically insightful fashion Augustine focuses on Jesus as mediator and on us as experiencing union with God through him.

The psalmody at the office of readings is taken from Psalm 18 (vss. 2–30), which acclaims the Lord as our rock, fortress, savior, shield, mighty help, and stronghold (vss. 2–3). He protects the humble and safeguards his people (vss. 29–30). Hence, the office of readings provides many images and likenesses for God whom we worship and through whom we experience salvation.

At morning prayer the first psalm (36) contrasts the malice of sinners and the goodness of God. The psalm prayer speaks of the Lord as the source of "unfailing light"—a light that illuminates those who come together for liturgical prayer.

The hymn from the book of Judith (16:2–3a,13–15) offers praise to God as the Lord of creation.

The last psalm (47) acclaims the Lord as the king of all peoples. He is praised as Lord of creation who offered a covenant to his chosen Israel, but whose mercy and love now extend to all nations and peoples.

The universality of the covenant seen in the letter to the Hebrews and experienced in Christianity is the completion of what is hinted at here. As stated in the psalm prayer, we pray to the "King of all peoples and all ages."

The scripture passage for morning prayer contains the verses from Isaiah 50 (vss. 4b–7), which will be used as the first reading at the eucharist on Passion (Palm) Sunday. As applied to the sacrifice of Jesus we see that the servant of the Lord was resolute and confirmed in his obeying the Father: "I have not rebelled, have not turned back" (vs. 5). Confidently the servant prays, "The Lord God is my help, therefore I am not disgraced" (vs. 7).

The antiphon to the Canticle of Zechariah reiterates the teaching of today's gospel about fidelity to Jesus' teaching; this faithfulness will enable us to "know the truth," which truth alone will make you free" (Jn 8:31).

At evening prayer the first two sections of psalmody are from Psalm 27 and speak of our longing for the Lord and our trust in him. The confident hope and trust in the Lord that was the psalmist's should be our own, especially in these days of Lent:

"I am sure I shall see the Lord's goodness
in the land of the living.
Hope in him, hold firm and take heart.
Hope in the Lord" (vs. 13).

The familiar imagery of darkness/light is used as a way of describing how we experience redemption and the forgiveness of our sins in Christ, as seen in the canticle from the letter to the Colossians (1:12–20). All will be reconciled in him, from whom we have received the forgiveness of our sins. The scripture reading from Ephesians 4:32–5:2 reminds us of our responsibility to show forgiveness to each other in Christ (vs. 32) and to love each other as Jesus loved us (5:5). The antiphon to the canticle of Mary is taken from the gospel and demonstrates that not all of Jesus listeners wanted to hear the truth. In fact his hearers wanted to kill him for the words he spoke (Jn 8:40).

Celebration of the Hours

The use of Psalm 95 with the invitatory today would be an appropriate introduction to the liturgy of the hours.

The use of the responsory after the reading from Hebrews brings out much of the richness of this text and may well be used as a way of confirming its message and implications for contemporary communities.

The use of Psalm 18 in three sections at the office of readings again offers the option of separating them by doxologies and antiphons or by silent pauses.

At both morning and evening prayer a passion hymn would be an appropriate way to begin these hours. The first psalm prayer at morning prayer (following Ps 36) might be expanded to make explicit the initiation implication of the darkness/light theme. The scripture passage from Isaiah 50 might well be expanded to include more verses from this same chapter.

The intercessions at morning prayer speak adequately of our being a new creation in Christ and that our lives are a gift from God.

At evening prayer the psalm prayer following Psalm 27 is particularly well constructed and might well be used as a fitting conclusion to the two sections of the psalm. The scripture reading from Ephesians could be extended through to 5:8, as these additional six verses specify and apply what is contained in printed text of the reading.

The intercessions at evening prayer contain two petitions that are appropriate for Lent (third and fourth) and the structure appropriately reflects the intention of offering prayer for the whole church. As always, the prayer as printed can be altered, provided that its structure is followed.

Reflection—"Freedom Is Not Free"

The way we approach faith and trust in God as well as how we see our lives before God comes from how we view freedom.

We live at a time when freedom and creativity are prized possessions and qualities that should be developed. Yet the wrong kind of freedom and misused creativity can lead Christians down the path to perdition. As we see in the process of becoming a Christian in the catechumenate, for those who seek to follow Christ and want to believe, Christ has to become the center of life and the light in which we view all of reality. Hence coming to know Christ, to love and be loved by Christ, and to follow Christ need to become the central factors of our lives, especially in Lent. Knowing Christ, submitting to Christ, and persevering in this commitment leads to true freedom for the believer. Freedom comes from knowing Christ and doing his will.

For those who do not believe, or whose faith is half-hearted, freedom can often mean the license to do whatever we want to do whenever we want to do it. Such is not real freedom for the thinking person. It is acting on unrestrained impulse and instinct.

For the believer any such behavior is completely incompatible with following the Lord. Whether it is ethics in business, conduct towards family and friends, or sexual morality, what makes us free is not instinct or unbridled desire. What gives harmony to life and authenticity to our lives is following Christ's word, which is the truth that will set us free.

The Word in Christ is the word we hear and receive in liturgy. This same word comes to us in sacraments to assure us of God's presence and guidance as we seek to live according to his truth. One who believes sees beyond instinct or passion to the Lord of all life and love.

THURSDAY OF THE FIFTH WEEK OF LENT

Liturgical Context

That Jesus has transcended the covenant made with Israel through Abraham is clearly described in today's gospel. The drama that has been building all week about origins, allegiance, and coming to believe in Jesus as opposed to trusting only in the prescriptions of the covenant made with Israel comes to a climax today. What the Jews interpret as blasphemy—that Jesus is God—is actually the foundation for the faith we profess as Christians. It is into this faith that the elect will be initiated at Easter. Once again the liturgy invites us to deeper knowledge of and greater commitment to the Lord Jesus.

Liturgy of the Eucharist

The entrance antiphon for the eucharist is taken from the letter to the Hebrews and calls upon Christ, "the mediator of a new covenant" through whom we "receive the eternal inheritance promised" us (Heb 9:15).

The opening prayer asks that we may "remain faithful to a holy way of life" and so finally receive "the inheritance which [the Lord] has promised."

The first reading from Genesis (17:3–9) prepares us for the discussion of "covenant" by recounting the covenant forged with Abraham (vs. 5). The Lord God promises to Abraham and his descendants the land in which he presently lives. Abraham and his descendants must acknowledge God's gift by keeping the Lord's covenant "throughout the ages" (vs. 9).

The Lord's commitment to this pact with Israel is affirmed in the responsorial psalm with the refrain "the Lord remembers his covenant forever." That Abraham himself and his descendants were instrumental in establishing and handing on the covenant is stated repeatedly (vs. 6,8,9) and in poetic language it is clear that the covenant was to endure: "He remembers forever his covenant which he made binding for a thousand generations" (vs. 8).

For the Christian this covenant is personified and summed up in Jesus, who asserts his identity with the Father in the gospel (Jn 8:51–59) using Old Testament language in referring to God; Jesus states boldly that "before Abraham came to be, I AM" (vs. 58). Jesus' enemies responded: "Surely you do not pretend to be greater than our father Abraham . . ." (vs. 53). A major test of Abraham's greatness was that he died faithful to the Lord; Jesus, however, asserts that he offers eternal life to any who are true to his word (vs. 51). Adherence to Christ, the mediator of the new covenant, requires full and total commitment to Him who is the Word made flesh and the only way to the Father.

The prayer over the gifts asks that our conversion might be complete (the sense of the Latin text) and that the celebration of these sacred mysteries might "help us grow in holiness."

The unity of Jesus and the Father is stressed in the communion antiphon from Romans (8:32): "God did not spare his own Son."

The prayer after communion expresses the constancy of divine mercy that sustains us.

Celebration of the Eucharist

The introduction to the eucharist today could deal with the question of our allegiance to Jesus as the origin of our covenant with God and our source of salvation. That the Word came to bring us the Father's grace and love can be expressed by using the second sample set of invocations for the third penitential rite: You "came to gather the nations into the peace of God's kingdom," "You come in word and sacrament to strengthen us in holiness," and "You will come in glory with salvation for your people."

The verse before the gospel, number 12 (Lectionary 224),

"God loved the world so much, he gave us his only son . . ."
(Jn 3:16) would set the tone for the proclamation of the gospel.

The general intercessions today could reflect the word proclaimed and the urgency of Lent with petitions asking that we
might be faithful to the word, that couples might be strengthened
to live faithfully the covenant of married love, that those who have
grown lukewarm in faith might recommit themselves to the gospel,
and that those who have died believing in the promise of eternal
life would live in union with God forever.

The prescribed preface today is that of the Passion of Our
Lord I.

An introduction to the Lord's Prayer that speaks of the community as "brothers and sisters" in Christ by baptism could give
added meaning to this part of the liturgy.

To conclude the liturgy, the use of number 6 of the prayers over
the people, about receiving "a complete change of heart ˙ and
following the Lord "with greater fidelity" would be appropriate.

Liturgy of the Hours

The reading from the letter to the Hebrews continues at the
office of readings with the assertion that Jesus' priesthood resembles that of Melchizedek rather than that of Aaron (Heb 7:1–10).
The Aaronic priesthood in Israel was based on lineage and physical
descent. Melchizedek, on the other hand, is unique in that his
lineage is unknown ("without father, mother or ancestry," vs. 3).
Yet his priesthood "remains forever" (vs. 3). The author of the
letter uses this example as a way of describing Jesus' uniqueness in
the sense that while we know his human parents and can therefore
trace a genealogy, in another sense we do not know his origins and
mission except in faith.

Many fathers of the church used the Old Testament examples of
the sacrifices offered by Abraham and Melchizedek as prefigure-
ments of Jesus' sacrifice of himself.

The responsory to this reading quotes Genesis (14:18) and Psalm
110 (vs. 5) as background for the Christian view of Christ's unique
priesthood.

The second reading is from the Dogmatic Constitution on the
Church (par. 9), which deals with the "old Israel" and with the
"church of God." The new covenant promised and fulfilled in Jesus

is shared among the baptized through the enduring power of God present in and celebrated through the liturgy, specifically baptism and eucharist. Hence, the readings at this hour can be used to reflect and illuminate the situation of the church at this point of Lent looking toward the renewal of the community at Easter.

The psalmody for the office of readings continues yesterday's proclamation of Psalm 18 (today, vss. 31–51). The image of God as "rock" (vs. 32) is continued (noted as "my rock" vs. 47) who sustains and supports those who call upon him. It is this God who is praised for his salvation and for preserving us from our oppressors (vss. 48–50).

The psalmody at morning prayer begins with Psalm 57, which acknowledges our need for forgiveness, a traditional theme of morning prayer. We pray, "Have mercy on me, O God, have mercy/for in you my soul has taken refuge" (vs. 2). Here we assert our trust in the Lord's power to deliver us in our need. The canticle is taken from the section of the book of Jeremiah that speaks about God's deliverance of Israel. These verses (31:10–14) also remind us of our destiny to live with God forever in the kingdom. The last psalm is a prayer of thanksgiving for the safety the Lord gives us throughout our lives (Ps 48).

The scripture reading from Hebrews 2 (vss. 9–10) speaks of the death of Jesus "for the sake of all men" (vs. 9) and the consolation we receive from knowing that God made our "leader in the work of salvation perfect through suffering" (vs. 10). These same verses form part of the longer reading from Hebrews used in the office of readings for Monday this week (2:5–18).

The antiphon to Zechariah's canticle is from John 8 (vs. 47): "Whoever comes from God hears the word of God. You will not listen because you do not come from God." Fidelity to God is reasserted here, a continued reminder of the challenge of Lent to be converted more fully to the Lord.

The petitions of the intercessions speak clearly of Lenten themes, specifically the phrases "that we who sinned in Adam may rise again in Christ," the word of God as a "lamp to guide us," and the command "that your light may shine on the whole human family by means of your church."

At evening prayer the first psalm (Ps 30) speaks of thanksgiving for our deliverance by God with the particularly poignant phrases:

"you have rescued me," "you have healed me," (vss. 1–2), "at night there are tears, but joy comes with dawn" (vs. 6), and "you changed my mourning into dancing, you removed my sackcloth and clothed me with joy" (vs. 12). The Lord as our refuge and the one who forgives sins is addressed in the second psalm (Ps 32).

The New Testament canticle from Revelation (11–12) is a hymn praising the salvation and power of God and the reign of God. We acclaim the Lord as the Lamb whose blood defeated our enemies. It is by the blood of Jesus that we have been cleansed, but this is only because the Lamb was slain and sacrificed.

The scripture reading from Hebrews 13:12–15 assigned for this evening takes up this notion of blood; the death of Jesus is the price paid "to sanctify the people by his own blood" (vs. 12). It is through Jesus that we offer God a sacrifice of praise (vs. 15).

The antiphon to the Canticle of the Blessed Virgin Mary: "Before Abraham even was, I AM says the Lord" (Jn 8:57–58), is an echo of today's gospel. Among the images used in the intercessions this evening are two that are particularly striking: the one asking for "pardon for your executioners," and the other for the catechumens coming to the waters of baptism to the light of Christ as did the man born blind. These texts offer examples of ways in which biblical images can be used to describe the power God exercises on our behalf.

Celebration of the Hours

The invitatory psalm today could be Psalm 100, a joyful song offering examples of God's fidelity to his people from "age to age." It is this fidelity that is emphasized in the two readings at the office of readings and it is this fidelity that we are reminded of throughout Lent. To begin the office with this psalm would both provide a relief from the continued use of Psalm 95 and also strike a correct note for these hours of Lenten prayer.

After the psalmody at the office of readings, the psalm prayer could be elaborated to include reference to the sacrifice of Christ, the mediator of the new covenant as seen in the Hebrews reading.

At morning and evening prayer, the use of a passion-oriented hymn would be suitable. Both scripture texts assigned for these hours could be expanded, especially in communities that do not celebrate the office of readings in common. The texts from the letter to the Hebrews are most important to emphasize at this point in Lent and can provide a depth of background for appreciating the celebration of the Easter triduum next week.

Reflection—"The Blasphemy of Jesus"

Jesus made himself out to be God, and his audience was shocked and horrified. But what about the sins of their forefathers, who turned away from the prophets sent by Yahweh to call the people from their evil ways? What about ourselves? We Christians are called the chosen race, the people of Christ, a holy nation—we have been made so in baptism. Do we not sometimes lapse into evil and sin?

We shake our heads in consternation at those who should know better, the enemies of Jesus, but we forget that our lives should be examples of fidelity. We are shocked and horrified when someone we know does not live up to our notion of Christianity and a Christlike life. But are we so quick or demanding of ourselves? Do we see the apparent contradictions in others while we disregard the real contradictions in ourselves?

These last days of Lent draw us more deeply into the reality of Christ's death and resurrection. They also invite us to trust in him as the fullness of God's revelation to us.

FRIDAY OF THE FIFTH WEEK OF LENT

Liturgical Context

Today's readings at the eucharist tell of the growing hostility toward Jesus, the plotting of detractors against his life. In a sense they point toward the unfolding of the events that comprise the heart of Christian faith—the paschal mystery. In faith what appears to be betrayal and murder is actually triumph and victory.

Liturgy of the Eucharist

The entrance antiphon today (taken from the former Roman Missal) asks that the Lord "have mercy" (Ps 31:10) on those who are "in distress" (vs. 16). The plea for God's help is not uttered in desperation but in the confident hope that he will protect his people in faithfulness to his covenant and to his revealed word.

In the opening prayer we acknowledge our sin and our need for forgiveness before the goodness of God.

In the first reading from Jeremiah (20:10–13), the prophet experiences "an interior crisis" that required him to call for God's help and guidance. As his enemies cry "denounce him," the prophet realizes that these who were originally his friends (vs. 10) are now "on the watch for any misstep of mine." Yet, the prophet's appeal is hopeful and trusting since he declares that "the Lord is with me" (vs. 11). It is to the Lord that he entrusted his life and vocation (vs. 12), the Lord who "has rescued the life of the poor from the power of the wicked" (vs. 13).

This same balance between appealing to the Lord for help in distress and the realization that he will hear us is reflected in the responsorial psalm, Psalm 18. The refrain "In my distress I called upon the Lord, and he heard my voice" (vs. 7) is matched by an attitude of serenity, confidence, and peace of soul in the verses that follow. The Lord is addressed as "rock," "fortress," and "deliverer" (vs. 2).

The gospel reading proclaimed today does not follow immediately after yesterday's gospel since the intervening chapter and a half deal with the cure of the man born blind (Jn 9, used as the gospel on the Fourth Sunday of Lent "A" cycle). The continuity with yesterday's gospel reading is maintained by noting that some of the Jews again "reached for rocks to stone him" (Jn 10:31). The reason why the crowds wanted to stone Jesus was his "blasphemy," that is, that he was claiming to be God (vs. 33). Jesus does not shrink from this assertion; rather he invites the crowd to put their faith in him precisely because he does the will of the Father and that "the Father is in me and I in him" (vs. 38). At this, some tried to arrest him (again), but many others "came to believe in him" (vs. 42).

The prayer over the gifts speaks of the gifts at the altar as the sacrifice of "eternal salvation" for those who share in them.

The communion antiphon recalls the passion context of the liturgy by citing 1 Peter 2:24: "By his wounds we have been healed."

The prayer after communion fittingly concludes the liturgy by speaking of the "protection of this sacrifice." We pray that through it we might be kept safe from all harm.

244   *Friday of the Fifth Week of Lent*

Celebration of the Eucharist

Today's liturgy could begin with an invitation to deeper trust in the Lord especially as this faith requires us to renounce the world's standards of judgment and measures of prestige. The rejection experienced by Jesus should offer us encouragement and hope as we experience similar (though less obvious) rejection for our faith

The common recitation of the "I confess" would stress the special penitential character of a Friday in Lent, as would a reflective tone for a sung "Lord, have mercy."

For the verse before the gospel the use of number 3 from Psalm 130 (vss. 5,7) (Lectionary 224) would underscore the believer's reliance on God amidst misunderstanding and rejection: "I hope in the Lord, I trust in his word; with him there is mercy. . . ."

Suitable petitions in the prayer of the faithful might include the deeper conversion of the elect and the baptized to the word of God, and the plea that we who hear and observe the word might become signs of Christ, even though the world may reject us.

The first preface of the Passion of Our Lord is prescribed for proclamation today. The section dealing with how faith views the death of Jesus is particularly striking on this Lenten Friday: "The suffering and death of your Son brought life to the whole world."

The third eucharistic prayer asks God to "strengthen in faith and love your pilgrim church on earth," thus making it a suitable choice today.

An invitation to the Lord's Prayer that speaks of our being united with each other as brothers and sisters in faith would be suitable today.

Number 9 of the prayers over the people would be a fitting conclusion to the liturgy since it speaks of our prayer "for your people who believe in you." We who celebrate these sacred mysteries join in prayer for the whole church, not just for ourselves or for the local community. Liturgy joins us with the church throughout the world that it might ever be a truer sign and fuller manifestation of Christ's presence in our world.

Liturgy of the Hours

The text of the letter to the Hebrews continues as the first reading at the office of readings (Heb 7:11–28). It emphasizes Christ as high priest and it contrasts the Levitical priesthood and that of Jesus. As was noted above, Jesus stands in the order of Melchizedek, not the hereditary Levitical order, ". . . in virtue of the power of a life that cannot be destroyed" (vs. 16). The Levitical priesthood was established by law, and the law of itself can bring nothing to perfection (vs. 19). While other priests died and did not remain in office to intercede for others (vs. 23), "Jesus, because he remains forever, has a priesthood which does not pass away" (vs. 24).

The author contrasts the Levitical, hereditary priesthood with that of the eternally begotten and true priesthood of Jesus. The daily and continual sacrifices of the old covenant are shadows of the fullness and fulfillment of sacrifices in the one sacrifice of Jesus who offered himself for all (vs. 27).

Significantly on this Friday, a day commemorating the passion, we are reminded that Jesus' death brought life, that we derive life from his sacrificial death and glorious resurrection.

The text from Fulgentius of Ruspe's treatise on faith offers a commentary on the role of Christ as high priest. Jesus not only transcends the sacrifices of the old law; he himself is both priest and sacrifice of the new covenant. The church continues to experience anew this union and communion with God through the liturgy. The sacrifices of the old covenant point to the uniqueness and centrality of what could not be granted to the world before Christ, that is, access to God through God's son as mediator.

The psalmody at the office of readings, from Psalm 35, speaks of the Lord as savior in time of persecution. As applied to Jesus, the psalm speaks of his innocence among his foes, his calling on the Father for assistance, and his experience of mockery and injustice. The believer who tries to live the Christ-life will also experience trials and humiliation in daily life.

The psalmody at morning prayer begins with the familiar Psalm 51, asking for God's mercy as we stand before him admitting our sin and guilt. The second section of psalmody, from Isaiah 45 (vss. 15–25), speaks of the Lord who invites all peoples to his kingdom. The last psalm is Psalm 100, sometimes used as an invitatory psalm to the hours, placed here, as is customary at morning prayer, as a hymn of praise.

The scripture reading assigned for morning prayer, from Isaiah 52:13–15, is part of the longer section from this book that is the first reading on Good Friday (52:13–53:12). The servant of the Lord is described as one who will prosper but only through ignominy and suffering. This text is an appropriate choice for this Friday in Lent and leads us to an awareness that in a week we will solemnly commemorate the passion of the servant Jesus.

The antiphon to Zechariah's canticle is taken from today's gospel text: "The Lord said: I have done you many acts of kindness; for which of these do you want to kill me?" (vs. 32). This deeply ironic statement leads to renewed appreciation of the fact that we too will be rejected should we choose to follow the Lord's commands and live the ways of his gospel.

Fittingly, the introduction to the intercessions refers to the passion of Jesus as that which is lifegiving. The petitions are also well suited to the passion theme and the season of Lent since the first refers to being freed from sin by the passion, the second refers to Lenten self-denial, and the third speaks of penance and works of mercy.

At evening prayer the first psalm (41) is a prayer of the afflicted who trusts in the Lord. The second (46) speaks of God as our refuge and strength. It contains the oft-repeated text: "The Lord of hosts is with us: the God of Jacob is our stronghold," which reiterates the faithfulness of God to his people. The final section of psalmody is taken from Revelation 15 (vss. 3–4) in adoration of the Lord, the Savior.

The scripture reading assigned to evening prayer is the text from 1 Peter (vss. 21–24) that has been used as a canticle at Sunday evening prayer throughout Lent. The union of ourselves with Christ is made explicit here when it states that Christ "left you an example," that "in his own body he brought your sins to the cross," and "by his wounds you were healed" (vs. 24).

The antiphon to the Canticle of the Blessed Virgin is from today's gospel and appeals for faith in Christ: "Even if you have no faith in my words, you should at least believe the evidence of the works I do in God's name" (vs. 38). This deepening faith in the Lord is what draws us together for the liturgy, and it is this faith that enables us to see the shedding of Christ's blood as making us holy (invitation to intercessions) and as a way of accepting the sufferings and difficulties of our lives as mentioned in the petitions at evening prayer.

Celebration of the Hours

The use of Psalm 95 as the invitatory psalm today could remind us of Israel's and our own commitment to the Lord.

The responsory to the first reading combines some scriptural images of Jesus as high priest and hence might well be used at the liturgy as a way of reiterating a main point made in the reading from Hebrews.

Since Psalm 35 is broken into three sections at the office of readings, silence could be maintained between each section to allow for prayerful reflection on the passion.

At both morning and evening prayer a hymn about the passion of Jesus would be most appropriate, especially on this Friday closest to Good Friday.

At morning prayer the first psalm prayer is well constructed and may well be used in celebration; the prayer following the third psalm could be used with an added reference to the death of Christ leading to his triumph.

The scripture reading could easily be expanded to give more emphasis to this important section of Isaiah that will be used on Good Friday.

At evening prayer the fact that Psalm 46 contains the refrain (noted above) could make this a natural occasion to have a cantor or schola do the verses of the psalm and the whole community join in the refrain.

The scripture reading at evening prayer could also be extended beyond the verses assigned; however, the proclamation of this text in a community familiar with the celebration of the hours might itself be a good use of what is already familiar as a canticle at Sunday evening prayer in Lent.

Reflection—"True Miracles"

A lesson of the gospels is that Jesus taught by his example and by his works. Works and miracles, however, were not enough, for some people still withheld faith. They wanted a Messiah according to their imaging and liking, not according to the designs of God.

Miracles are not miraculous unless we believe in their divine origin. Jesus is not Lord of our lives unless we admit the need for direction from God in our lives. Liturgy is not the worship of God unless we admit first our need for God and our love for his ways.

These last days of Lent require deep prayer and reflection on the passion of Jesus and our understanding of that passion as Christ's sacrifice for us and for our salvation. If and when that happens, then Jesus' life and death will indeed be miraculous for us and the source of eternal life.

SATURDAY OF THE FIFTH WEEK OF LENT

Liturgical Context

Today's gospel sets the scene for the betrayal and the execution of Jesus that will be narrated in tomorrow's reading of the passion. With tomorrow's liturgy our Christian passover begins once more.

Liturgy of the Eucharist

The urgency and imminence of Jesus' passion is glimpsed in the entrance antiphon: "Lord, do not stray away; come quickly to help me" (Ps 22:20). This is the same psalm which Jesus quotes as he utters, "My God, my God, why have you forsaken me?" (vs. 1) from the cross.

The opening prayer, from the Leonine Sacramentary, refers to initiation and our personal appropriation of the paschal mystery through baptism. The Latin text speaks of our being "regenerated" and "reborn" through God who "always work[s] to save us," and who gives abundant grace to the chosen (elected) people.

This week, which began with the third scrutiny, now reaches its end as we pray to God for those "about to become your children" and for "those who are already baptized."

In today's first reading, from Ezekiel 37:21–28, the Lord promises to intervene to unite Israel into one nation (vss. 21–22) and to "deliver them from all their sins of apostasy and [to] cleanse them so that they may be my people and I may be their God" (vs. 23). God will dwell with his people and will grant them "an everlasting covenant of peace" (vs. 26). The journey of Lent is a time for us to respond to God's intervention in our individual and communal lives. It is also a time to acknowledge our failures to respond as fully as we ought to this grace of God.

The responsorial psalm is taken from the prophet Jeremiah (chapter 31) and takes up this notion of God's acting on our behalf. The familiar image that is used is that of the "shepherd guarding his flock" (vs. 10, used as the response). We are the ones who need to "hear the word of the Lord" and to realize the fidelity of the Lord who will turn our mourning into joy and console us amid sorrows and disappointments in this life (vs. 13).

The gospel from John 11:45–57 comes after the section about the raising of Lazarus (last Sunday's gospel "A" cycle). The Johannine narrative focuses ironically on Caiaphas, who was "high priest that year" (vs. 49). The one whom we acknowledge as our new "high priest" in Hebrews is himself feared by Judaism's high priest. Jesus is destined to die in order to gather into one all the dispersed children of God (vs. 52). As noted above, the Ezekiel reading foresees the universality noted here.

Jesus' enemies continue their intrigue: "From that day onward there was a plan afoot to kill him" (vs. 53). The chief priests and Pharisees were on the lookout for Jesus in Jerusalem (vss. 55–57). Ironically, Jesus is condemned by "high priests," who seek him out at "Passover" time, in order to put him to death (like the paschal lamb) so that by dying and rising from the dead he could become the new and eternal high priest.

The prayer over the gifts emphasizes baptism by which the Lord restores us to life, that is, to that grace and gifted state from which we all fell by the sin we call original.

The communion antiphon, taken from today's gospel (vs. 52), states that Christ was sacrificed so that he could fulfill his mission and gather the scattered children of God. Significantly this text is used as the antiphon at the action of sharing in the sacrament of unity and communal reconciliation in Christ.

The prayer after communion refers to our share in the eucharist as a real share in the life of God. Our first participation in God's life occurred at baptism; it is continued and sustained in the eucharist.

Celebration of the Eucharist

The celebration of eucharist today should be done simply in the light of the celebration of Passion Sunday tomorrow. An introduction that speaks about the life we share in Christ through faith and commitment to him could lead to the third penitential rite with the sixth set of sample invocations.

The fact that John 11 (vss. 25–26) is the source for number 15 of the verses before the gospel (Lectionary 224) makes this an appropriate choice today: "I am the resurrection and the life . . . he who believes in me will not die forever."

With the general intercessions recommended for Lent II as a model, additional petitions could speak of all who will participate in the liturgies of Holy Week, of those who will be initiated at Easter, and for all believers that their lives might reflect the presence and power of God. The first preface of the Passion of Our Lord is prescribed for use today. The fourth sample introduction to the Lord's Prayer could be used today because of its brevity and reference to the coming of the kingdom.

Liturgy of the Hours

Today is the last time the usual verse before the readings for the Saturdays of Lent will be used this season. In Johannine imagery we who celebrate this liturgy are drawn into the light of Christ, the light which cured the man born blind, which attribute of Jesus causes him to claim that he is the "light of the world."

The reading from the letter to the Hebrews continues at today's office of readings with the significant section dealing with Christ as our high priest (8:1–13). It is fitting that this text about the intercession of Christ with the Father on our behalf and his exalted status at the right side of God should be read on this day that precedes the proclamation of the passion account. The passion is the beginning of the events that will lead to Christ's exaltation in the kingdom of heaven. While other high priests need something to offer and a sanctuary in which to offer it (vss. 3–6), Jesus himself is both offering and offerer. The old covenant's prescriptions and the whole old covenant is done away with in Jesus who "declares the first one obsolete" (vs. 13). At every act of liturgy we pray through, with, and in Christ as our high priest who ever lives to make intercessions for us with the Father.

The text from Gregory Nanzianzen speaks of the commemoration of our Lord's passing through suffering and death to new life. We offer a sacrifice of praise and the sacrifice of our lives in union with Christ. Gregory maintains that here and now we must be ready to be crucified, "imitating [Jesus'] passion by our sufferings and honoring his blood by shedding our own." This is the means of our experiencing salvation and the way our sins are forgiven.

The psalmody at this hour, from Psalm 105, acclaims the fidelity of the Lord, especially his faithfulness to his promises. The covenants with Abraham, Isaac, and Jacob are recalled (vss. 6,8,9), as is the wandering journey of Israel throughout salvation history (vss. 12–22), concretized and typified in the Exodus from Egypt (vss. 23–43).

At morning prayer the first psalm (Ps 119) is more usually found at a minor hour in the tradition of the office. The verses used here (vss. 145–152) speak of the commands and the law and our being close to the Lord when we observe them. Next comes the song of Moses from Exodus praising God for his wondrous works for his people. The theme of the praise of God continues in the concluding psalm, Psalm 117.

The scripture reading from Isaiah 65 (1b–3a) reiterates the notion of God's overarching initiative toward his people despite the refusal of the chosen to respond.

The antiphon for the Canticle of Zechariah is taken from the sentiments expressed in the gospel of the day (Jn 11:52): "Jesus died to gather into one family all the scattered children of God." What was prophesied in Ezekiel about two nations being united into one and in John about the unity of all in Christ is experienced each time we celebrate the liturgy, our privileged experience of the challenge and reality of life lived in union with each other as fellow believers in the one Lord. In the intercessions at morning prayer, the introduction contains references both to initiation and to eucharist and the fourth petition speaks about the forgiveness of sins—three sacramental ways of sharing now in the life of Christ.

Celebration of the Hours

The invitatory today could be recited with Psalm 24, which refers to our being in need of the Lord's forgiveness so that we can grow in virtue.

The three sections of the single Psalm 105 at the office of readings make the option of silence between the sections an attractive way to celebrate this hour simply yet reverently.

The psalm prayer coincides well with the sense of the readings and thus is a helpful way to conclude the psalmody.

At morning prayer a hymn about our sharing in the passion and death of Christ would be an appropriate way to begin this hour of prayer.

The psalm prayer after the verses of Psalm 119 is helpful in that it speaks about the important place which the word of the Lord should have in our lives.

The psalm prayer following Psalm 117 emphasizes the universality theme of the psalm by referring to all the nations that praise the Lord and receive his benefits, not just Israel.

Reflection—"Drama Only or Real Life?"

Often we read ads for works of fiction—books, television shows, plays, or films—that describe plots as reflecting "real life" situations. What appeals to us is how close to real life the romance is, or the vindication of the underdog is. We identify readily when the story strikes close to home. We then more easily become one with the central character. His or her triumph is ours. His or her hurts are ours. His or her loves are ours. The more real the story line, the more we feel we can make the plot our own.

What we commemorate during Holy Week are the actual events of Jesus' passion, death, and resurrection. These (unlike fiction) are facts, recounted in scripture and in the accounts of contemporary historians. But what makes our solemn liturgical commemoration of them so important is that through them we experience in ourselves all that Jesus went through, if we allow the liturgy to be what it is supposed to be and to do what it is supposed to do. Liturgy is not playacting or the yearly unfolding of the familiar passion play. It is our being inserted into Christ's paschal mystery by allowing our lives, loves, joys, hopes, disappointments, and sufferings to be made over by Christ's experience of these same realities. What Jesus accomplished in this act of redemption is done for us in such a way that all that needs redeeming in our lives is transformed by him through his sacrificial death and glorious resurrection. What we commemorate is not just Jesus' dying and rising but our dying and rising in him.

The question we must continually ask ourselves is what things in our lives need redemption, forgiveness, healing, and reconciliation. These are the things we ought to bring to Holy Week this year so that he who was slain for our salvation can forgive us our sins, heal our wounds, and reconcile us again with one another. All these things that are part of our "real lives" should be brought to the unfolding of the events of Jesus' real death and resurrection so that our lives will be touched and deeply affected by this Holy Week.

If we understand Holy Week as a time to "watch" the events of Jesus' passion we lose its real liturgical meaning. The heart of liturgical commemoration is our being assimilated into the saving mysteries of the mystery we call "paschal," especially during this week we call "holy." What is certainly "real" is that Jesus died and rose for our justification. We allow that reality to affect and change us profoundly when we bring our real selves and our real needs to him who is high priest forever.

Chapter Seven

Passion Sunday to Wednesday of Holy Week

PASSION (PALM) SUNDAY

Liturgical Context

Today on Passion (Palm) Sunday we commemorate Christ's triumphal entrance into Jerusalem and his passion and death. The former designation "Palm" Sunday is put alongside "Passion" since both emphases in the eucharist and the liturgy of the hours are clear. The liturgy today recalls the beginning of Jesus' journey to the cross—his riding into the holy city to the acclaim of the crowd and of his followers. But it also emphasizes (in fact more strongly) that the real triumph and glory that Jesus receives comes from the suffering and passion he endured and the ultimate sacrifice—death on a cross.

This Sunday begins our annual solemn commemoration of the events that reconcile us with God and that stand at the heart and center of our faith: "Christ has died, Christ is risen, Christ will come again."

The liturgy focuses on the redemption that Jesus accomplished through suffering, dying, and rising. What we experience in our time is the same saving intervention of God through, with, and in Christ.

Our celebration of Passion (Palm) Sunday helps us see that we not only commemorate Jesus' entrance into Jerusalem; through the liturgy we also commemorate his passion and death (in the reading of the passion account) as well as his resurrection (in the celebration of the eucharist, always the memorial of his suffering, death, and resurrection). On Holy Thursday evening we commemorate the beginning of the sacred triduum by remembering the Last Supper of Jesus with his disciples, the washing of the feet, and the command to live his love, but all within the perspective of his passion and resurrection (as is seen in the prayers of the liturgy). On Good

Friday we commemorate the passion of Jesus, but from the unique perspective of those who know and experience again the power of his resurrection. We do not read the passion on Good Friday and pretend that the resurrection has not happened. Rather, we read the passion from the perspective of the hope and glory that comes from faith in the resurrection. Again the prayers of the liturgy speak about both suffering and glory even on this day that appropriately emphasizes the reality of Jesus' suffering. At the Easter vigil, as we recall the great moments of the history of salvation (the liturgy of the word) and celebrate the sacraments of initiation (baptism, confirmation, and eucharist) we do so in the light of the passion as well as the victorious resurrection of Christ. On Holy Saturday night we do not forget the passion Jesus endured; rather we commemorate the lasting power of his passion and resurrection made available to us in the liturgy. As is succinctly stated in the first Easter preface:

"We praise you with greater joy than ever
on this Easter night (day),
when Christ became our paschal sacrifice.

He is the true Lamb who took away the sins of the world.
By dying he destroyed our death;
by rising he restored our life."

The liturgy is the unique way we have of being a part of and being made sharers in the whole of the paschal mystery. Through it, especially on each of the days of the triduum, we become partakers and sharers in Christ's passion and resurrection, humiliation and glorification, self-emptying and exaltation, suffering and rising to new life. Through the liturgy the evil, sin, conflict, unbelief, and estrangement from God in our lives is ended. Through the liturgy we share in the goodness and holiness of God; we come to union with him and deeper faith in him. Any separation from God in our human lives is bridged and ended through the reconciliation and the peace of Christ—won for us through his saving, paschal mystery.

Commemoration of the Lord's Entrance into Jerusalem
    The eucharist today is made up of two parts: the commemoration of the Lord's entrance into Jerusalem and the liturgy of the

word and eucharist focusing on his passion and death. The first part, which in the present reform can be a "procession," or a "simple (or) solemn entrance" was late in evolving in the Roman Rite since it was only in the eleventh and twelfth centuries that this custom was firmly established at Rome itself. The procession with palm originated in the fourth century at Jerusalem and was held in the late afternoon. The procession formed at a location outside the city, most often at the Mount of Olives, and was comprised of the bishop, ministers, all the faithful, and especially children.

This custom spread to Spain and Gaul, and it is from there that it eventually spread to Rome. Interestingly, Rome observed this day as the Sunday of the passion of the Lord, whereas the term "Palm Sunday" was introduced much later.

The present Roman usage calls for some commemoration of Jesus' entry into Jerusalem at all Masses this Sunday. The most solemn type consists of a procession of the whole assembly. The priest, wearing a red vestment (either cope for the procession and chasuble for the eucharist proper or a red chasuble for both procession and eucharist). The antiphon, "Hosannah to the Son of David," quoted in the three synoptic texts of the passion is sung as the liturgy begins. This text is taken from the Hallel psalms, used at the Jewish liturgy of Passover, the last part of which is used in our eucharistic liturgy as part of the "Holy, holy, holy" acclamation:

"Hosannah to the Son of David,
the King of Israel.
Blessed is he who comes
in the name of the Lord.
Hosannah in the highest" (Ps 118:26, Mt 21:9).

The prayer for the blessing of the branches (that the people already hold in their hands) is taken from one of two options, the first of which is from the Leonine Sacramentary, rich in its theology and explication of the meaning of the liturgy being celebrated:

"Almighty God,
we pray you
bless (†) these branches
and make them holy.
Today we joyfully acclaim Jesus our Messiah and King.

May we reach one day the happiness of the new and everlasting
   Jerusalem
by faithfully following him
who lives and reigns for ever and ever."

The priest then sprinkles the branches in silence. What is particularly significant in this prayer is that it associates our present liturgy
with an act of faith in Jesus as both Messiah and King and it looks
beyond this present liturgy to our share in the life of God in the
kingdom forever.

The proclamation of the gospel recounting the triumphal entrance now follows, which itself can be followed by a brief homily.
The text for year "A" is from Matthew 21:1–11, which emphasizes
the humility of Jesus (vs. 5). The evangelist quotes Zechariah 9:9
("See, your king shall come to you; a just savior is he. Meek, and
riding on an ass, on a colt, the foal of an ass.") The crowd spreads
cloaks on the road and branches along Jesus' path (vs. 8) and
acclaims him as the "prophet Jesus from Nazareth in Galilee"
(vs. 11).

The gospel of Mark (11:1–10) or John (12:12–16) may be used in
the "B" cycle at this point in the liturgy. Mark's text closely
parallels Matthew's (especially vss. 1–3) and at times adds some
fuller details of what happened. However Mark introduces two
significant themes that differentiate his treatment of the event and
that offer important points for reflection. First, Mark notes that the
cloaks and the reeds are placed "on the road" (vs. 8), which for
Mark carries the technical understanding connected with the word
"way" throughout his gospel. For the evangelist, to follow the
"way" or to go "along the way" of Jesus is to imitate him whose
path led to suffering and death at Jerusalem. To imitate Jesus today
requires that we do more than march in a parade; it requires that
we imitate his humility and resolute journey to suffering at Calvary.
As Jesus made his way to Jerusalem to suffer and die so must the
believer be prepared to follow the same way of Jesus. Second,
Mark explicitly adds an eschatological reference where he speaks of
the "kingdom of our father David to come" (vs. 10). This kingdom
is not a worldly kingdom, as many people of Jesus' time imagined,
but a reign in which the will of the Father will be paramount.

The gospel account from John follows the raising of Lazarus

from the dead; hence the acclaim of the population is part adulation of the man who raised his friend. John also refers to Zechariah 9:9 to show that Jesus is not a political liberator. He will transcend the boundaries of the Israelite nation and be Messiah for all people. He states explicitly that at first the "disciples did not understand all this" (vs. 16) but that they did come to understand "after Jesus was glorified" (vs. 16). This term itself is significant in that in John's account of the passion, Jesus' glorification comes about through his suffering and death.

The account from Luke (19:28–40) draws on the journey motif in his gospel, which sees Jerusalem as the goal (vs. 29). Significantly Jesus approaches the city from Mount Olivet from which one can see all Jerusalem, both the city and the temple. For Luke Jesus' entrance into Jerusalem is the moment he has planned for throughout his gospel. For those who believe in Jesus as Messiah this event ushers in the saving events that inaugurate a new way of relating with God, through Jesus. The profession of faith is not easily made however, for Luke stresses the suffering required of those who would follow the Lord. "Peace" and "glory" are only possible through identification with Jesus' suffering and death.

Following the gospel (and homily), the celebrant may address the community with the words:

"Let us go forth in peace,
praising Jesus our Messiah,
as did the crowds who welcomed him to Jerusalem."

The procession then begins, headed by a thurifer with a lighted thurible, a "cross-bearer (with a cross suitably decorated) between two ministers with lighted candles" followed by the priest, other ministers, and the whole congregation carrying palm branches. The Missal notes that the procession is to be accompanied with antiphons taken from the gospel read, the verses of Psalm 23 or 46, and "a hymn in honor of Christ the King, such as All Glory Laud and Honor."

The gesture of processing and the symbols of palm, incense, and the cross should be emphasized when we come to appreciate what is occurring liturgically. Through these symbols and gestures we participate not in an historical and time-bound drama; rather through them we share in the fullness of what this event means.

As we take palms in our hands to acclaim Christ as Messiah and Lord, we commit ourselves to taking up whatever is necessary for us to join in his suffering and death as well.

Celebration of the Lord's Entrance into Jerusalem

A most important feature of the celebration of the Holy Week liturgy involves the proper use of symbols. Today the distribution of palms as people gather, blessing them with holy water, and carrying them in procession are important aspects of this particular celebration. In addition the rubrics call for a "suitably decorated" cross. This allows for great creativity and imagination, but it is important to keep the cross itself central as that which leads the procession and that which is described in the passion account as the place of Jesus' death. In addition to this symbol, there is the gesture of incensing. The Lord who was acknowledged by the Magi at the Epiphany with the gift of frankincense is the same Lord whose paschal mystery we enter into at the altar, reverenced today with the gesture of kissing and the act of incensation.

The involvement of worshiping assemblies through gesture marks every liturgy (standing, sitting, bowing, touching, and being touched), but today the procession inaugurates a series of liturgies in which all are invited to participate. On Holy Thursday all are involved in the procession to transfer the eucharist to the reposi-tory; on Good Friday all process to reverence the cross, and on Holy Saturday all process behind the paschal candle during the liturgy of light. Where oftentimes liturgical gestures and the use of symbols are reserved to the ministers, these processions are popular and meant for all. Once again, it is through symbols and gestures as well as texts that the liturgy is experienced in its fullness. Gestures and symbols should be especially emphasized this week.

Finally the choice of texts is important for this commemoration because the rubrics state that the introduction before the blessing of the palms and the invitation to process may be from those in the Sacramentary or others composed for the occasion. One approach to adapting the formulas would be to include specific ways this particular community has prepared "by works of charity and self-sacrifice, for the celebration of our Lord's paschal mystery." Also this introduction can serve as a brief overview of what is to occur at the Easter triduum, thus linking this Sunday liturgy with what is to come at the end of the week.

Liturgy of the Eucharist

After the procession and the incensation of the altar, the traditional opening prayer follows. It reflects important theological points and a change of mood for the liturgy. From the triumph and acclamation of Christ as king in the procession, the liturgy now shifts to an emphasis on Christ as a model of humility and as the Lord who fulfilled his Father's will.

The parallel between Jesus' suffering and our witnessing to him by following his example is proclaimed in the liturgy of the Word that follows.

The first reading from the third servant song of Isaiah (50:4–7) has already been used at morning prayer on Wednesday of the fifth week of Lent and will be used on Wednesday of this week both at morning prayer and at the eucharist (vss. 4–9). This affirmation of confidence in God in the midst of suffering should find an echo in our own lives.

"I gave my back to those who beat me, my cheeks to those who plucked my beard; my face I did not shield from buffets and spitting" (vs. 6). Yet, says the servant, despite this ignominy and humiliation "the Lord God is my help, therefore I am not disgraced" (vs. 7).

Most appropriately this text is followed by Psalm 22, with the refrain, "My God, my God, why have you abandoned me?" (vs. 2). That this text will be quoted by Jesus from the cross is one example of the way in which this psalm has been used to influence the formation of the passion narratives.

As is characteristic of this kind of psalm, the prayer describing the trials and suffering endured also contains a prayer of confidence and trust in the Lord. Even when the liturgy emphasizes the reality of the passion and suffering of Jesus, as it does in the liturgy of the Word today, it also emphasizes his confidence and trust in his Father.

The second reading is the familiar hymn from Philippians (2:6–11), which is used as a reading for Masses of the Triumph of the Cross and as a canticle at evening prayer, a usage which will be reiterated at evening prayer on Good Friday and Holy Saturday.

The suffering and exaltation of Jesus reminds us of how suffering can lead to sharing in the glory of God. Jesus took the "form of a slave . . . being born in the likeness of men" (vs. 7). In this "human estate" (vs. 7) he "humbled himself obediently accepting death on a cross" (vs. 8). This reference grounds the liturgical text about Jesus' free acceptance of death when we pray in the second eucharistic prayer: "Before he was given up to death, a death he freely accepted. . . ." The suffering servant of the Father, however, does not wallow in pain and sorrow, for even in the midst of such ignominy he trusts and affirms his faith in God who ultimately will exalt him highly, bestowing on him a "name above every other name . . ." (vs. 9). Thus it is that we proclaim: "Jesus Christ is Lord" (vs. 11).

Verses 8 and 9 of this text are used as the verse before the gospel today and on Good Friday, and stress the fact that "Christ became obedient *for us* even to dying on the cross."

The central text during the liturgy of the word today is the passion account that now follows. Because the texts of the synoptics are read over the course of three years, it is important to interpret these texts in the light of the particular interest and narrative style of each evangelist.

In cycle "A" the passion according to Matthew is read (26:14–27:66). All the synoptic accounts agree that the passion and death of Jesus occurred at the time of the Jewish Passover (vs. 18), here stated to begin on the "first day of the feast of unleavened bread" (vs. 17).

It is in Matthew's text alone that we find the command form in the account of the institution of the Lord's Supper, "Take this and eat it" (vs. 26), and "All of you must drink of it" (vs. 27). Jesus is looking toward the succeeding generations of disciples who, like his first followers at the last supper, obey his command to take and eat/drink, but who also commit themselves to do what the Lord requires of them throughout their lives. It is significant that this gospel ends with the command: "Teach them to carry out everything I have commanded you" (Mt 28:20).

That Jesus will be betrayed by a disciple is first mentioned "in the course of the meal" (vs. 21). This may well be a reference to Psalm 41:10 where the psalmist speaks of betrayal "even by my friend who had my trust and partook of my bread [it is he who] has raised his heel against me." Interestingly the reaction among Jesus' disciples does not focus on one obvious candidate, for they say, "Surely it is not I" (vs. 22), indicating that they realize full well their lack of full commitment to the Lord and that each of them could be his betrayer.

Matthew points out that even though Peter states firmly, "Though all may have their faith in you shaken, mine will never be shaken" (vs. 33), before the chapter ends Peter does deny Jesus (vss. 69–75). The supreme irony is that it is the centurion who at Jesus' death ultimately recognizes him as the "Son of God" (27:54) whereas a chosen disciple, Peter, states "I do not know the man" (26:74).

The weakness of the disciples is also seen in the agony in the garden when Jesus takes Peter, James, and John, the privileged witnesses to the event of the transfiguration, to pray with him, but they fall asleep. The very human portrait of the disciples in this passion account exemplifies our own very human weaknesses.

Significantly while all the evangelists describe Judas' act of betraying Jesus, it is only in Matthew's gospel that Judas repents of what he had done. He tells us that Judas "began to regret his action deeply" (27:3) and stated, "I did wrong to deliver up an innocent man" (vs. 4). Just as in the case of Peter, Judas' act of betrayal leads to regret and remorse. Our own regret and remorse for betraying the Lord in our own lives is part of the essential foundation for our celebration of penance and eucharist.

In cycle "B" the passion according to Mark is read. Once again the passion takes place at the time of Passover and the Feast of Unleavened Bread (vs. 1). This time of special solemn liturgical commemoration and festivity in Judaism is the time when Jesus will bring to completion what the faith of Judaism longed for. From the beginning, however, Mark notes that the establishment of the new covenant in Jesus involves his physical death and burial. The act of anointing Jesus' feet is understood to be a way of anticipating the body's preparation for burial (vs. 8). The way to Jerusalem is the way to suffering and death for Jesus; for his disciples the way of following Christ means participation in real suffering and rejection.

As in Matthew, the disciples protest that "surely not I" (14:19) will betray the Lord. Yet Mark states that it is "one of the twelve" (vs. 20) who will betray Jesus, not just a disciple. These twelve, chosen and called by Jesus to be his followers, represent the twelve tribes of Israel in that it is through them (as it was through Israel) that the world will receive God's revelation and promise of universal salvation. This special position and important vocation makes the fact that the betrayer comes from this number all the more shocking. The reality of betrayal is not at all softened in Mark.

In 14:32–42 Jesus' agony in Gethsemane is emphasized, but through it he calls upon his Father, "Abba," which term indicates an intimate relationship of dependence. Jesus "kept saying 'Abba (O Father), you have the power to do all things. Take this cup away from me. But let it be as you would have it, not as I' " (vs. 36). The very moment when Jesus was weakest before his passion and death is the very moment when he commits himself even more completely to the Father's will. Jesus' example in Mark is most significant because of the evangelist's interest in instructing the community for which he writes. At the very time when suffering for the sake of the gospel seems to be too much, it is precisely then that they, like Jesus, are to submit themselves to the Father's will.

The attitude of Jesus before his betrayer in Mark's account is especially interesting in that Jesus makes no response when Judas addresses him as "Rabbi," or betrays him by an embrace. A bit later Jesus does address his accuser, but only to recall that the arrest at this place and time is done "so that the Scriptures may be fulfilled" (vs. 49).

True to his editorial plan in the gospel, Mark writes about the reality of Jesus' suffering in order to instruct and to comfort the suffering primitive church.

In cycle "C" the passion account according to Luke (22:14–23:56) is read. As the other evangelists have done, Luke also places the betrayal and passion account in the context of the Passover. Jesus begins by addressing his disciples: "I have greatly desired to eat this Passover with you before I suffer" (22:15). Yet Luke shows how Jesus makes this meal the paradigm of the Christian liturgy. In this experience of meal fellowship (stressed throughout Luke's gospel, as seen in chapter 14 and in 15:1–2, for example), Jesus vows not to drink of the wine "until the coming of the reign of God" (22:18). Here Jesus states that the promised kingdom is about to be inaugurated through his passion, death, and glorification. He states that from now on this meal of bread and wine will be "as a remembrance of me" (vs. 19). From now on it will be this cultic act of memorial, remembering what God has done and what he continues to do through Christ, that will stand as a unique and privileged moment of encounter with God. The eucharistic memorial is both a remembrance and a foretaste of what is yet to be.

It has already been pointed out (in the commentary for the Second Sunday of Lent) that Luke's gospel portrays Jesus as praying at the most significant moments of his earthly life. Thus Luke implies that Jesus' followers should be humble, obedient, and prayerful, imitating Jesus in acknowledging dependence on God.

One lesson that can be drawn from Luke's very realistic account of the passion is that prayer, especially liturgical prayer, must be offered by those who are truly committed to the Lord.

The prayer over the gifts, taken from the Leonine Sacramentary, contains a balanced theology reflecting the Roman church's traditional emphasis on the passion today:

"Lord,
may the suffering and death of Jesus, your only Son,
make us pleasing to you.
Alone we can do nothing,
but may this perfect sacrifice
win us your mercy and love."

The prescribed preface for today is that of Passion (Palm) Sunday with the significant center section:

"Though he was sinless, he suffered willingly for sinners.
Though innocent, he accepted death to save the guilty.
By his dying he destroyed our sins.
By his rising he has raised us up to holiness of life."

These phrases are a most significant illustration of the way the liturgy is the unique mediation of Christ's redemption to us. The balance and parallelism here are also striking because they point to the importance of the dying and rising of Jesus as together comprising the single event of salvation. It is this same parallelism that will be seen next Sunday when the first Easter preface states:

"We praise you with greater joy than ever

on this Easter night (day),
when Christ became our paschal sacrifice.

He is the true Lamb who took away the sins of the world.
By dying he destroyed our death;
by rising he restored our life."

The reality of the suffering of Jesus is reiterated in the text of the
communion antiphon: "Father, if this cup may not pass, but I must
drink it, then your will be done" (Mt 26:42). This text is particularly appropriate at this point in the liturgy for it can remind us
that in the eucharist we participate in Christ's suffering and glory; it
gives us strength to accept the cup of suffering that the Father has
apportioned to us as he did to his Son.

The prayer after communion relates our human hunger with our
spiritual hungering for the coming kingdom of God; it demonstrates
the place that the eucharist has in our present lives:

"Lord,
you have satisfied our hunger with this eucharistic food.
The death of your Son gives us hope and strengthens our faith.
May his resurrection give us perseverance
and lead us to salvation."

Celebration of the Eucharist
The tone has shifted from acclamation and exaltation to sober
(but not mournful) reflection on the reality of the passion of Jesus.
The incensation of the altar should be done solemnly, after which
the proclamation of the opening prayer should be careful, deliberate, and paced. This prayer provides the verbal hinge to mark this
shift in tone. The responsorial psalm might be sung to a plaintive
setting with minimal accompaniment; this will indicate the dramatic
change from "All Glory Laud and Honor" to "Why have you
forsaken me?" The fact that there is no greeting before the passion
(as would be customary before the gospel) and that incense is not
to be used indicates very ancient liturgical practice; it is not meant
to indicate a mournful attitude. The reader(s) who will proclaim the
passion should be well aware of their burden of keeping the
congregation's attention through a long text. The use of dramatic
silences between sections of the narrative, some involvement by a

schola singing some of the parts, and the involvement of the congregation in saying the people's parts are ways of making the proclamation more inviting. The rubrics in the Lectionary state that this is the "most important reading" today and that for pastoral reasons the first or second reading (or in some cases both readings) may be dropped in order to emphasize this text. The tradition of the Roman liturgy in observing this as the Sunday of the passion is clearly preserved.

For the intercessions today the introduction and concluding prayer could be composed to reflect the passion narrative. The intentions could be modeled on those assigned for Lent and for the first days of Holy Week in the Sacramentary Appendix.

Those who are marginal to the church and those who are estranged from the church's worship should be prayed for in an understanding way since some who attend the liturgy today are just such people who need particular care and understanding.

The second eucharistic prayer, because of its brevity and its statement of Jesus' suffering, could be used with the preface of the Passion of our Lord. In addition, the reference at the end of the prayer to "All who have done your will throughout the ages" could lead to an introduction to the Lord's Prayer about our being willing to do the Lord's will.

The use of the memorial acclamation "Dying you destroyed our death . . ." would be a way of reinforcing the unity of the paschal mystery and the community's sharing in it through the liturgy.

The Lamb of God could be expanded to include titles of Jesus drawn from the passion narrative and the gospel of the entrance into Jerusalem, "Son of God," "Son of David," etc.

In liturgical tradition the time just before the dismissal was used for announcements. This could be a good place to mention the times and places for the celebration of the liturgies of the triduum.

The solemn blessing of the Passion of the Lord is provided in the Mass formula.

Liturgy of the Hours

Evening Prayer I and II both emphasize the passion of Christ while morning prayer emphasizes Jesus' triumphal entry into Jerusalem.

Significantly, while the psalms at evening prayer are the same used on the Second Sunday of Lent, the antiphons at these hours are changed to reflect the themes proper to this Sunday.

At Evening Prayer I, the first antiphon is inspired by the passion narrative and deals with Jesus' betrayal: "Day after day I sat teaching you in the temple and you did not lay hands on me. Now you scourge me and lead me to the cross." The second antiphon is a statement of confidence in God: "The Lord God is my help; no shame can harm me." The third is based on the Philippians hymn that it introduces (this text is used as the second reading at the eucharist today): "The Lord Jesus humbled himself by showing obedience even when this meant death, death on a cross." These antiphons reflect well the theology of Passion Sunday and remind us of our sharing in Christ's passion and death.

The scripture reading for this evening prayer is the same as that used last Saturday evening, 1 Peter 1:18–21. We are reminded that in Christ we are delivered from a futile way of life (vs. 18), that Christ's blood is that which has saved us and redeemed us (vs. 19), and that in Christ we are fellow believers in the God who raised him and who will in turn raise us up to share in his life forever (vs. 21). It is through the *blood* of the *Lamb* of God that we are saved from *death*, raised to *life* and will one day share God's *glory* forever.

Also significant is the careful wording of the antiphon to the Canticle of Mary, since it uses titles of Jesus that we use to acclaim our faith in him: "Praise to our King, the Son of David, the Redeemer of the world; praise to the Savior whose coming had been foretold by the prophets."

The intercessions offer a well constructed set of petitions that join the theology of this day with our individual and communal needs. We realize that we need to be aware that the Lord's "hour" has come and that we are made new by his passion and death.

The seasonal invitatory to the hours changes today to the text: "Come, let us worship Christ the Lord, who for our sake endured temptation and suffering," which text is used through Wednesday. Appropriately, it demonstrates how our salvation was accomplished through suffering and the passion of Jesus.

The scripture reading from Hebrews (10:1–18) at the office of readings compares and contrasts the sacrifices of the old and new law. Unlike the sacrifices of the old law, Jesus' self-offering happened once for all. This replaces Israel's annual recalling of sins and the sacrifice of bulls and goats (vss. 1,3). Only Jesus' redemptive death, the death of the Lamb of God, "takes away the sins of the world." It is this one sacrifice that has "forever perfected those who are being sanctified" (vs. 13). But for this to be accomplished in us, we need to imitate Christ in offering our wills to the Father.

The text today from Andrew of Crete joins the notion of Jesus' triumphal entry into Jerusalem with our offering of self before God. The scene of the people laying garments and olive branches before Jesus is used to illustrate the author's main point:

"So let us spread before his feet, not
garments or soulless olive branches, which
delight the eye for a few hours and then wither,
but ourselves, clothed in his grace, or rather,
clothed completely in him."

This clothing occurs sacramentally in baptism (as is seen in the rite using the white garment) but it happens spiritually each year as we observe the liturgy of the Lord's passion and death.

At morning prayer the triumphal entrance into Jerusalem is commemorated with the first antiphon and psalm reflecting the gospel's account of what occurred. We proclaim: "Blessed is he who comes in the name of the Lord," (antiphon). Psalm 118 speaks of going "forward in procession with branches even to the altar" (vs. 27), which can be applied to today's liturgy as we carry palms and sing in praise of the Lord.

The second and third antiphons today are inspired by the gospel accounts of Jesus' triumph: "God grant that with the angels and the children we may be faithful and sing with them to the conqueror of death. . . ." "Blessed is he who comes in the name of the Lord; peace in heaven and glory in the highest." This latter text is especially interesting since it also adds a reference from Luke's gospel to "peace" and "glory," realities granted us only because the triumphant Lord suffered and died to bring us salvation.

The short scripture reading is the text from Zechariah 9:9, which has been quoted in the passion narratives. Appropriately the antiphon to Zechariah's canticle at morning prayer involves our welcoming the Lord as he comes to us, while the intercessions speak about our being led to the paschal feast of heaven, our being saved from our sins, and our seeing in the cross of Christ the tree that brought us life and rebirth.

At Evening Prayer II, the emphasis returns to the passion of Jesus. The antiphons speak of Christ being "scourged, treated with contempt" and his ultimate vindication since "God's right hand has raised him up." Reference to the blood shed for our salvation applies this saving act to us: "The blood of Christ washes away our sins and makes us worthy to serve the living God."

The identification between Christ's saving death and our lives is reflected in the third antiphon: "Christ bore our sins in his own body on the cross so that we might die to sin and be alive to all that is good."

The scripture reading is the same as was used last week, the summary statement of Paul from Acts (13:26–30) about the paschal mystery. Despite lack of evidence against him (vs. 28), Jesus' enemies had him executed. Ultimately "they took him down from the tree and laid him in a tomb" (vs. 29) from which "God raised him from the dead" (vs. 30).

The antiphon to the Canticle of the Blessed Virgin speaks of the flock being scattered and Christ's resurrection to new life.

The intercessions point to the parallel between Jesus' death and ours in him, between his resurrection and our sharing new life in him.

Celebration of the Hours

Because Jesus' passion and death is commemorated at both Evening Prayer I and II, a hymn about Christ's passion would appropriately introduce these hours of prayer.

At Evening Prayer I the psalm prayer following the first psalm might be adjusted to reflect the passion more clearly; that which follows the third psalm, however, stands as a good example of liturgical and theological precision.

At Evening Prayer II the psalm prayer following the second psalm might also be adjusted to reflect the passion more clearly.

The scripture reading at this hour could easily be expanded beyond the verses presented here since Paul's summary continues for a number of verses in Acts 13:16ff.

The invitatory today could employ Psalm 95 (the classic invitatory psalm) with the assigned antiphon about Christ's suffering for our sake to introduce the hours today.

The psalmody at the office of readings is the same as that of the Second Sunday of Lent, Psalm 104, and thus allows for silence between sections of the psalm or for antiphons and doxologies at those places.

At morning prayer a hymn acclaiming Christ's entrance into Jerusalem would help introduce the rest of the texts of this hour. If the hymn "All Glory Laud and Honor" is to be used to accompany the palm procession, it would be best to use another at this hour. On the other hand, a hymn acclaiming Christ's triumph on the cross (as opposed to the fleeting triumph experienced as Jesus entered Jerusalem) would be useful at this hour.

Of the psalm prayers given in the text, that which follows the third psalm might well be rewritten in order to commemorate the palm procession and the passion of Jesus.

If the text of the scripture reading is to be expanded, the use of Zechariah 9:9–10 or 9–12 would be logical units (the first of which is used in the *Lutheran Book of Worship* today and the second in the Methodist and Presbyterian Lectionaries for Passion Sunday).

Reflection—"Exaltation: Real and Imagined"

We all like to be praised, recognized, and acclaimed, and from such acknowledgment often comes the impetus to further growth and development. But what is important is honest affirmation and sincere love.

As Jesus entered Jerusalem the crowd welcomed him because of the miracle of raising Lazarus, or because he was an intriguing folk hero. They did acclaim him and they did lay their cloaks in his path, and they did shout "hosannah." But what is equally clear is that their praise was not long-lasting. After all, it is the crowd who some days later cry out, "Crucify him."

The fickleness of the crowd probably shocks us. But does our fickleness before God shock us? Are we aware that we often act like the crowd did? Are we not aware that there are times when we say all the right words in our worship (thanks, praise, glory, hosannah, amen) but that we really mean those things only half-heartedly? The challenge of this Passion Sunday is that we be aware of the difference between real and false exaltation of Christ, and that we learn from the crowd that we can be as fickle as they when it comes to following through in faith and declaring our commitment to him.

The real exaltation for Jesus came from his Father who raised him from the dead. It never came from the crowds at all. What about us? Do we realize that our real and most authentic affirmation really comes from God? Ultimately it is not what friends or neighbors think about us or how they judge us. What really matters is what God knows about us and how he judges us. We know that in following him, we will experience derision as well as acclamation, misjudgment as well as exaltation, suspicion as well as praise.

The journey from self-will to obedience and from superficial recitation of prayers to authentic worship takes more than a week, even if its name is "holy." But this one week, this Holy Week, can make a great difference if through Christ we offer our very selves to God and through Christ receive a share of life in union with God.

MONDAY OF HOLY WEEK

Liturgical Context

It has already been pointed out that a principle that governs the liturgies of Holy Week is that these separate rites are our communal commemoration of and participation in the one paschal mystery of Jesus. The unity of this central mystery of our salvation should be borne in mind when interpreting the texts used on a given day since a common fault when interpreting these liturgies is to view them as completely separate, more like the successive scenes of a play rather than liturgies with one central theme—the memorial of the paschal mystery.

Yet it should also be pointed out that within this unified commemoration, there are varying shades of emphasis each day of the week that point to individual events that led up to the death and resurrection of Jesus. These emphases should therefore be understood within the framework provided by the central focus of the week—our participation in Christ's dying and rising. The separation in time and space between the original events themselves and our day is bridged through the liturgy. The liturgy does not merely recall the historical details of Christ; rather, through it we are able to share in the fullness of Christ's saving mysteries, immersed in the light of his risen glory. Clearly, this is something that the original eyewitnesses could not do. Our celebration of the liturgy makes us full sharers in the whole paschal mystery. As the invitatory to the liturgy of the hours used from Monday to Thursday this week states: "When I am lifted up from the earth.—I will draw all men to myself." Using the Johannine terminology of being "lifted up," this statement demonstrates the unique union that exists, between the believer and Christ that is accomplished through the liturgy.

The immediate context for today's celebration was established yesterday with the emphasis on the passion and death of Jesus. The liturgy from Monday to Wednesday this week continues to reflect the passion, as is stated in the Lectionary Introduction: "In the first half of Holy Week the readings are about the mystery of Christ's passion" (no. 98). The liturgies of the triduum obviously have their own emphases. But over all it is the unity of the paschal mystery and our incorporation into this mystery of faith that is the foundation for what occurs liturgically this week.

Liturgy of the Eucharist

The entrance antiphon today can be understood as the Old Testament believer's plea to God, as the cry of Jesus, the servant of his Father's will, and as the prayer of the contemporary Christian community that admits its need for God as it gathers for prayer. "Defend me, Lord, from all my foes . . . for you have the power to save me" (Ps 35:1–2; 139:8) can only be uttered in honesty and humility by one who has a deep and abiding confidence in the saving power of God.

The opening prayer reflects a typically balanced approach to the paschal mystery since it asks that "by the suffering and death of your Son" (whose passion is especially commemorated this week), we may be strengthened and protected in our weakness. This strength and protection is offered each time we celebrate these sacred mysteries.

Today's first reading begins a series of three that are used at the beginning of Holy Week, about the suffering servant figure in Isaiah. This text from Isaiah 42 (vss. 1–7) emphasizes the attitude of Jesus before his accusers (admitting, however, that this was not the original setting of the reading) as he went to his passion and cross. This "chosen one" is he who "shall bring forth justice to the nations" (vs. 1, and vs. 6 "for the victory of justice"). He is the Lord's "covenant of the people, a light for the nations" (vs. 6). He will open the eyes of the blind and liberate prisoners from confinement. This brief passage recalls the Lenten references to light and the light symbolism that is so central to the Easter vigil.

The responsorial psalm, 27, was already used in Lent on the Second Sunday in the "C" cycle. Here the response itself picks up the illumination theme from the reading by proclaiming that "The Lord is my light and my salvation" (vs. 1).

The Johannine imagery of the verse before the gospel is clear: "Let us greet our king: he alone showed mercy for our sins." In John's gospel it is the kingship of Christ that is revealed at the crucifixion, and Jesus' death coincides with the slaying of the passover lambs.

The gospel today, from John 12 (vss. 1–11), recalls the central affirmation of Jesus as the resurrection and the life after he raised his friend Lazarus from the dead. He stated: "Whoever believes in me, though he should die, will come to life; and whoever is alive and believes in me will never die" (11:25–26). In what are really two separate sections in the narrative, the second part deals with the faith motif (vss. 9–11). There was a "great crowd . . . not only to see Jesus but also to see Lazarus whom he has raised from the dead" (vs. 9). Both Jesus and Lazarus are seen to be enemies of the religious establishment to the extent that both were to be killed "Because many Jews were going over to Jesus and believing in him on account of Lazarus" (vs. 10). The first part of the gospel deals with Mary's anointing the feet of Jesus with oil. While such a gesture would be most uncommon as hospitality to a guest (because feet were washed, not anointed), the use of oil leads John to comment that this was a preparation for Jesus' coming death (vs. 3).

The prayer over the gifts summarizes an important foundation for liturgical prayer, that it is the mercy of God that provides the sacrifice we offer and it is his mercy that will bring us to life eternal.

Once again, using the Johannine notion of "hour," the preface reminds us that Christ's triumph over sin and death is specially commemorated in these days and that we share in his victory over sin and death through the liturgy.

The prayer after communion reminds us that the eucharist is a healing and strength until we come to share salvation in Christ for all eternity. This sacrament is our guide now that gives us the grace to live the faith we profess at the liturgy.

Celebration of the Eucharist

The introduction to the liturgy could briefly introduce the notion of the passion of Jesus as seen in the scriptures today. The fifth set of invocations at the penitential rite can be understood as referring to our incorporation into Jesus' dying and rising through the sacraments of initiation and penance.

For the prayer of the faithful today, the presider could well use the sample formula provided for the first days of Holy Week in the Sacramentary Appendix. In addition there might be petitions for those who witness to faith in Jesus as servant and who work for his justice and peace in the world (see the first Servant Song).

The second passion preface is prescribed for use today.

During the eucharistic prayer the first memorial acclamation ("Christ has died") would be a direct reference to what is commemorated at every liturgy and to what will be especially recalled later this week.

The Lord's Prayer could be introduced by a reference to calling on God as Father in faith with the reliance that marked Jesus' dependence on his Father as he endured the passion.

Invocations to the Lamb of God that refer to the passion of Jesus could be used in addition to the traditional "Lamb of God," should this chant be extended beyond three invocations.

Of the prayers over the people, number 17, about the love that Jesus showed us as "he delivered himself to evil men and suffered the agony of the cross" would be a fitting conclusion to the liturgy.

Liturgy of the Hours

The first reading at the office of readings continues the letter to the Hebrews (10:19–39) used on Passion Sunday; it is fittingly subtitled "Perseverance in faith." We who are saved through the "blood" and "flesh" (vss. 19–20) of Jesus draw near in confidence to God through Christ as high priest (vs. 21). The author then exhorts us to "hold unswervingly to our profession" of faith in him (vs. 23) and to encourage one another to persevere in faith. We who have already been "enlightened" (vs. 32) renew and deepen our commitment to the Lord in these final days of Lent as we observe the liturgy and through it become renewed so as to live out the mystery of God's love for us.

In the text St. Augustine refers to the passion as our "hope of glory" and a "lesson in patience." He speaks of the necessity of Christ's death through which we who live this human life can come to share divine life.

Christ's death then becomes our greatest hope and our greatest glory, for through it we are saved from sin and death. "Though sinless himself [Jesus] suffered for us sinners the punishment we deserved for our sins." It is this aspect of Jesus' passion that draws us near to God in hope.

The psalmody at the office of readings is from Psalm 31 (1–17,20–25), subtitled "A troubled person's confident appeal to God." The structure of the psalm is significant for after acclaiming the Lord as our "rock" and "stronghold" (vss. 1–2), the psalmist describes our weakness and concludes with a note of encouragement and commitment: "Be strong, let your heart take courage, all who hope in the Lord" (vs. 25).

At morning prayer the antiphons are significant as they all refer to Christ's passion. The first quotes Jesus' words, "My heart is nearly broken with sorrow; stay here and watch with me." This invitation to watch and pray recalls the disciples' reaction in the garden of Gethsemane; their lack of attention acts as a counter to what should be our attentive approach to this morning prayer. The psalm that follows, Psalm 42, is also used at the Easter vigil as the response to the reading from Ezekiel 36 (16–28). It can easily be understood to refer to our condition before God when it speaks of our soul "yearning for . . . God" (vs. 1) and of our soul being "cast down" and yet acclaiming "hope in God" who is our savior (vss. 6,12). The second antiphon uses Johannine language to refer to the coming judgment on the world and the definitive driving out of the "prince of this world." From now on it will be Jesus who is the lifegiving Lord of all. The third antiphon reminds us that here and now Jesus alone is the beginning and end of our faith.

The scripture reading from Jeremiah (11:19–20) speaks of the "Lamb led to slaughter" and in the response we affirm that it was "Through your own blood, Lord, [that] you brought us back to God." Already at this early stage of Holy Week we reflect on the notion of blood that will be so important to appreciate as we celebrate the paschal triduum.

The antiphon to the Canticle of Zechariah today uses Johannine language to refer to Jesus as sent by the Father to give life to anyone who accepts him as the Lord.

The intercessions at morning prayer today will be used again on Tuesday and Wednesday of this week. The structure in the petitions is significant in that each one takes a text or incident from the life of Jesus and applies it to our own situation. Thus, after referring to the suffering through which Jesus entered into his glory, we pray that we might come "to the Passover feast of heaven." The petitions refer to initiation and the passion of Jesus by praying that he who "made the cross the tree of life [would] give its fruit to those reborn in baptism." In a reference to penance, the last petition asks that as Jesus forgave the repentant thief he might forgive our sins.

The antiphons at evening prayer use scriptural imagery to refer to Christ's passion. The first states that Jesus "had neither beauty, nor majesty, nothing to attract our eyes" and yet in faith we know that this humiliation is precisely what led to exaltation and triumph over sin and death.

The scripture reading from Romans 5 (vss. 8–9), which was also used last week, comes from the most significant part of the epistle, where Paul reaffirms that Christ died for us "while we were still sinners," and that we now stand justified before God by his blood. As at morning prayer, the intercessions at evening prayer will be used for the first three days this week. The parallel between Jesus' example and our participation in the paschal mystery is seen in our prayer that we might share in the resurrection as well as the passion of the Lord (first petition), that we might experience the saving power of God in our lives as derived from Jesus' passion (third petition), and that we might share in the obedience and patient endurance of Jesus as he willingly accepted death for us (fourth petition).

Celebration of the Hours

The invitatory phrase today about Christ's being "lifted up" and drawing all to himself could be accompanied by Psalm 100, which reiterates our relationship to the Lord and his mercy for us:

"He made us, we belong to him,
    we are his people, the sheep of his flock" (vs. 3).

The confidence expressed here does not ignore the reality of Christ's passion; rather it recalls our status as God's people in and through it. The psalm prayer after the three sections of Psalm 31 referring to a "martyr's strength" could be expanded to refer to our need for the forgiveness of sins and the price for our redemption paid by the passion and death of Jesus.

At morning and evening prayer a passion hymn would suitably introduce each of these hours.

The prayer following the third psalm could be adjusted to refer to the passion of our Lord, as our hope and as that which leads us to share in the joy of Easter. The verses from the Jeremiah reading could easily be extended should a longer reading be desired.

At the conclusion of the intercessions, an introduction to the Lord's Prayer that refers to our being reconciled through the death of Jesus would appropriately continue the parallelism in the petitions between Christ's passion and our present need for his love.

At evening prayer the prayer following the second psalm could be adjusted to refer to the union of Christ with his church through the enduring power of the paschal mystery. The text from Romans 5 can be extended to include more verses from this important section of the letter should a longer reading be desired. As a way of concluding the petitions and introducing the Lord's Prayer, a reference to our need for forgiveness through Christ could precede the communal recitation of the Our Father.

Reflection—"The Faith of a Servant"

When we think of a "servant" we generally think of a person who does something for another. To be of service to another can also mean to help a friend or to aid a relative, especially when that person is ill or suffering in any way. A servant offers service or helps another. He or she does something.

In line with this understanding of what being a servant means, we can readily see why Jesus has repeatedly been called the servant of the Father. It is not just that Jesus did what the Father required of him—it is his trust in his Father's will that made the difference. Jesus' dependence on the Father and humble submission to the passion as the means to accomplish our redemption is as important as the accomplishment of the paschal mystery itself.

The attitude of Jesus the suffering servant and his free acceptance of death make today's liturgy especially instructive for us. What we celebrate in faith is the accomplishment of our salvation through Christ the servant, through Christ the one who trusted in his Father's will. What we celebrate in the sacred mysteries today is our union with Christ, in deed and in faith, so that through him we might serve others freely and in obedience. The point is not just putting up with situations where we are called upon to be of service. In the light of Jesus' example, even the most menial acts of service have redemptive value when we do them in obedience and love. Hence, the faith of the suffering servant as well as the obedience and love of Jesus are virtues that we should imitate and qualities that we should develop.

TUESDAY OF HOLY WEEK

Liturgical Context

The accounts of the passion according to Mark and Luke are no longer read on Tuesday and Wednesday of Holy Week, but are assigned to cycles "B" and "C" for Passion Sunday. The present Lectionary, therefore, gives special emphasis to the passion narratives on Passion Sunday and Good Friday and emphasizes the servant songs from Isaiah and selections from John for the early days of Holy Week. Today's gospel, therefore, assumes great prominence in interpreting the theology and liturgy of this day. The text from John deals with the imminent passion and death of Jesus by referring to his betrayal; hence it continues to set the stage for the unfolding of the passion of Jesus (as will be recounted later in the week). The experience of Jesus in being betrayed serves as a model for believers who, like him, often experience rejection and suspicion because of the faith they profess and live.

Liturgy of the Eucharist

The entrance antiphon from Psalm 27 (vs. 12) is newly chosen for today's liturgy and can be understood as an indirect reference to the betrayal and trial of Jesus: "False witnesses have stood up against me, and my enemies threaten violence; Lord, do not surrender me into their power." Jesus, in fact, endures their false accusations and mock trials as he goes to his passion and death; but instead of having to surrender to their power, through the resurrection Jesus triumphs over them and rises victorious over sin and the forces of evil in the world.

The opening prayer today is traditional; we pray that we might experience the Father's "forgiveness and mercy as we celebrate the passion and death of the Lord."

The second servant song from Isaiah (49:1–6) is the first reading today and also serves as the first reading on the solemnity of John the Baptist. The servant in verses 3 and 5 was called from birth, from his mother's womb (vs. 1) to gather Israel and to bring back Jacob and his inheritance to the Lord (vs. 5) and ultimately to extend salvation to the ends of the earth (vs. 5). The means he used to accomplish this are preaching and proclamation of the Lord's word (vs. 2, like "a sharp edged sword"). Even though this servant may feel that his work has been in vain (vs. 4), he trusts that his reward is with the Lord and his recompense is in God alone. The application to Jesus is easy to see in that he proclaimed and established the kingdom of his Father. In the process he endured rejection, but by trusting in his Father's will he established the reign of God over all nations.

The responsorial psalm (Ps 71) reflects the theme of the servant song by it emphasizing the importance of proclaiming the word that the Lord has uttered in establishing his rule: "I will sing of your salvation" and "my mouth shall declare your justice" (vs. 16). Like the servant we pray confidently that we who have depended on the Lord from our birth (vs. 6) continue to take refuge in the Lord (vs. 1), whom we acknowledge as "rock," "fortress," and "stronghold."

The gospel is introduced by the acclamation: "Hail to our king, obedient to his Father; he went to his crucifixion like a gentle lamb." This short statement is most significant theologically in that it uses Johannine terminology to refer to Christ as "King." It uses the notion of obedience (from Philippians) as a central aspect of his mission, and it concludes with a reference to the important place that the "gentle lamb" has in our understanding of Christ's paschal victory.

The gospel text itself from John 13 (vss. 21–33,36–38) deals with the betrayal of Jesus. These verses follow upon verses 1–15 of the washing of the feet at the Last Supper, which text is traditionally used on Holy Thursday evening. The fact that the betrayal is therefore out of sequence from the way these events occurred historically is itself an example of how the liturgy is not concerned to unfold the passion narrative as a drama; rather it emphasizes important aspects of these texts where they fit liturgically.

Right after Judas' departure, Jesus says, "Now is the Son of Man glorified and God is glorified in him" (vs. 31). The theme of seeing the glory of God revealed in Jesus and our participation in the glory of God through Jesus is a constant and recurring notion in the fourth gospel. The fact that Judas' betrayal will bring about the final and complete glorification of Jesus shows that out of a seemingly disastrous deed God will work for our good by revealing his glory fully in His Son. We are told that God will glorify his Son soon (vs. 32). According to John it is the crucifixion that definitively reveals the glory of God in Jesus.

Another Johannine theme is found in this text where the author relates that Satan entered Judas' heart (vs. 27). For John there is a continual battle between the forces of good and evil (light and darkness, etc.), and the evangelist notes that evil will once again try to overcome good in Christ. While not directly related to this text, we can state that liturgically this recalls the scene of the temptation of Jesus when Satan tempted him three times. This text fittingly was proclaimed on the First Sunday of Lent to instruct us as we began this holy season. This brief reference to Satan reminds us that the conflict will be definitively conquered by Jesus through his passion, death and resurrection.

The evangelist then states simply that "it was night" (vs. 30). Yet when coupled with John's understanding of the battle between good and evil and light and darkness, the reference to night reinforces the fact that now the enemies of Jesus will seek to put an end to his influence and to his reign. The gospel narrative rises to a climax when Jesus confronts Simon Peter with the fact that he will disown him.

The prayer over the gifts, especially in its Latin version, asks that the Lord be pleased with the offerings we present, and that as we partake in them and grow in holiness we might come to share in their fullness (in the kingdom forever).

The communion antiphon in today's liturgy is from Romans 8:32 rather than from the book of the Psalms or the gospel of the day, as is customary.

The prayer after communion continues the eschatological note found in the prayer over the gifts. Through it we ask that God's mercy might strengthen us now and "bring us a share in [his] life forever."

Celebration of the Eucharist

The introduction today could speak about our call to serve God and each other simply and humbly in imitation of the servant in the first reading. Yet we also must admit that we fail and that like Peter there are times when even we disown the Lord. Hence the liturgy is a place to receive the grace we need to bear witness to Christ and to become his faithful servants.

The use of the second form of the penitential rite, about having sinned against the Lord and asking that he show his mercy and love, would be a fitting introduction to the liturgy today.

In addition to the petitions noted in the Sacramentary Appendix for these days of Holy Week, additional prayers could be added that refer to fidelity—that we might grow in faithfulness to the gospel, that married couples might grow in their commitment to love each other until death, and that priests and religious might remain faithful to their vocations.

The second passion preface is prescribed for use today.

The second memorial acclamation ("dying you destroyed our death . . .") would be a way of reiterating our faith in the enduring power of the dying and rising of Jesus.

The Lord's Prayer could be introduced by mentioning our need to pray for the grace to remain faithful to the Lord even as we pray "thy kingdom come, thy will be done on earth. . . ."

As was suggested for the liturgy yesterday, invocations about

Christ's passion could be inserted in the Lamb of God, and number 17 of the prayers over the people would be a useful option today.

Should the presider want to reinforce the eschatological reference in the prayer over the gifts and in the prayer after communion, he might use number 16 of the prayers over the people to conclude the eucharist because of its mention of the Lord's care for his people in "this life" and in the "life to come."

Liturgy of the Hours

The scripture reading at the office of readings today introduces chapter 12 of the letter to the Hebrews. While yesterday's reading was from the end of chapter 10, chapter 11 describing the many Old Testament models of faith is skipped in favor of this reading about perseverance "in running the race which lies ahead" (vs. 1). Our faith and hope is based on the fact that Jesus "endured the cross . . . [and] has taken his seat at the right hand of God" (vs. 2). The author goes on to encourage his readers to accept the discipline that God sends for our benefit (vss. 3,7,10). The discipline, trials, and difficulties in our lives are to lead us to union with the Father, just as Jesus' passion and death led him to final vindication in the resurrection.

Today's patristic text from St. Basil states that Christ came "So that we could be saved by imitation of him and recover our original status as sons of God by adoption." St. Basil says that baptism is the sacrament through which we imitate Christ's death and which symbolizes our breaking with our former way of life. Through this sacrament we participate intimately and really in the event of the paschal mystery of Christ. Significantly, the responsory to this reading consists of verses 3,5, and 4 of the sixth chapter of Romans, which is proclaimed at the Easter vigil as a way of leading to the celebration of sacramental initiation.

At morning prayer today the first two antiphons appeal for God's mercy "from deceitful and impious men," for he has "ransomed my life." That these could be prayers of the servant of God is indicated strongly in the third antiphon: "My servant, the Just One, will justify many by taking their sins on himself." It is the obedience and deeds of the servant that offer us confidence and the strength to persevere in our own lives of faith.

The scripture reading from Zechariah 10 (vss. 10–11a) was also used last Tuesday and is clearly meant to refer to Jesus who was "thrust through" at his crucifixion in order to show the reality of his suffering and the price he paid for our redemption.

At evening prayer the first two antiphons also can be understood as prayers of the servant. The first states that "They insulted me and filled me with dread but the Lord was at my side." The second is a cry to the Lord who will sustain and protect the servant: "Deliver me, Lord, and place me at your side, then let whoever will, lift his hand to strike me." The third antiphon acclaims Christ, of whom it is said: "You were slain, Lord, and by your blood you have ransomed us for God." This coincides particularly well with the text of the hymn from Revelation (4:11; 5:9,10,12), which is prayed this evening:

"For you were slain;
   with your blood you purchased for God
men of every race and tongue,
of every people and nation" (5:9).

The scripture reading from 1 Corinthians (1:27b–30), also used last week at evening prayer, refers to God who has given us life in Christ Jesus. "He has made him our wisdom and also our justification, our sanctification, and our redemption" (vs. 30).

The antiphon to the Canticle of Mary offers a brief reference to Christ's laying down his life and taking it up again for our redemption.

Celebration of the Hours

The invitatory phrase and Psalm 100, as was recommended for use yesterday, would be a suitable way to introduce today's liturgy of the hours. The particularly significant responses to both readings at the office of readings make them useful options for use in celebration today.

At both morning and evening prayer a passion hymn would be a suitable way to introduce these hours of prayer.

The psalm prayer after the first psalm could easily be expanded by making reference to the passion and death of Jesus as the source of the light shining on in the darkness of this world. The psalm prayer after the third psalm could also contain a reference to Christ as the source of all the good that we do. In addition, the short scripture reading from Zechariah could easily be expanded if a longer reading is desired. Since the same intercessions are recommended for prayer today as were used yesterday, some substitutions or additions might be in order, especially petitions about initiation and those to be baptized at Easter.

Reflection—"The Obedience of the Servant"

Throughout Lent the scripture readings have asserted again and again that Jesus was obedient to his Father's will and that for us to lead gospel-oriented lives we too must imitate such obedience. Today's scripture texts reaffirm the importance of the servant's obedience and note two characteristics of his service that should mark our self-offering to God. First, the servant has a lifelong occupation and, second, he perseveres through periods of aridity and apparent uselessness. In both cases it was the servant's obedience that made him favored in God's sight.

The lifelong vocation to serve God and our neighbor is seen clearly in the servant song where in two places he states that he was chosen from the womb for this task. From human generation he was destined to lead his people to a deeper awareness of God in their midst. It is no different with ourselves. From the moment of our spiritual regeneration, our spiritual birth, we have the mission to manifest our baptismal faith commitment each day that we live. Like the suffering servant of Isaiah we are to dedicate ourselves to humble and obedient service day by day. Clearly, our experience tells us that such a burden is heavy. Sometimes we muse and fantasize about "time off for good behavior." We would prefer to take a vacation from the faith (and perhaps we have) rather than to face the demands that living the faith implies. The vocation is lifelong, but its burden is light when we realize that it is God who has called us and God who sustains us in faith.

This leads to the second characteristic of the servant—perseverance. We live in an age of institutionalized "newness" and cultural escapism. The products we label "new" today are soon replaced by "all new" and even "better" models. In fact, we have become so accustomed to newness and change that when things remain stable for a time we easily get bored—a disease for which our culture provides ample diversion.

But in our spiritual lives is it really the "new" or the "different" that we need? The virtue of the servant was his "staying power." The fact that the servant did not give up but persevered was an essential part of his vocation and mission.

Even when the cast of characters with whom we live and work does not change, we must remain faithful to our responsibility to love all in Christ. Even when we would prefer a new set of circumstances in which to live, unmarried instead of wedded, unvowed instead of committed, independent instead of part of a household, the example of the servant serves as a model for us to persevere. But we do it in the knowledge that the God who called us to these states in life is the God who sustains us in love, commitments, and responsibilities.

WEDNESDAY OF HOLY WEEK

Liturgical Context

Today the revised liturgy presents the Matthean account of Jesus' betrayal, thus effectively ending the semicontinuous reading from John that has occupied this second part of Lent. It also leads to the celebration of the paschal triduum on the following days. Like the other texts proclaimed and liturgies celebrated, it is part of our continued and progressive commemoration of Jesus' passion, death, and resurrection. As part of these events the betrayal is given a place of significance.

Liturgy of the Eucharist

The fact that the former Roman usage assigned the passion narrative for proclamation today is still reflected in the entrance antiphon from the familiar Christ hymn of Philippians 2 (vss. 10,8,11). This text was chosen to reflect the passion narrative because it emphasizes the attitude of Jesus in becoming "obedient for us even to death, dying on the cross." This text is fittingly retained for use in the present reform because it emphasizes that the liturgical commemoration this week center on the paschal mystery as a whole.

The opening prayer emphasizes the reality of Christ's suffering ("accepted the cross") and our participation in the salvation he won through his death and resurrection ("and freed us from the power of the enemy").

The first reading from Isaiah (50:4–9) was used as Sunday's first reading. As we hear it today, it completes the series of texts concerning the servant of the Lord that have been read on the first days of this Holy Week. In it the call to proclamation as an essential part of his role is noted again: "That I might know how to proclaim to the weary a word that will rouse them" (vs. 4). That the mission of the servant involved his free acceptance of the Lord's will for him is noted in the firm declaration: "I have not rebelled, have not turned back" (vs. 5). Even amid real suffering (vs. 6) the servant acclaims the Lord as his help (vss. 7,9), as the one who still upholds him (vs. 8). These verses offer comfort to those who suffer for the sake of Christ and especially to those whose lives witness to the message of the gospel. In the words of the responsorial psalm, we trust in the Lord despite our suffering and pray: "Lord, in your great love, answer me" (Ps 69:14).

The gospel from Matthew (26:14–15) has already been reviewed in the commentary for Passion Sunday "A" cycle. The assignment of these verses to this Wednesday of Holy Week points out the important role that Judas played in the unfolding of the passion of Jesus. The fact that there is the potential for Judas in all of us gives this text a certain urgency. One of the reasons we celebrate the liturgy is so that we can grow in faith and be more firmly allied with the Lord.

In the prayer over the gifts we ask that we may one day share in the eternal life Christ won for us.

The notion of Jesus' sacrifice is reiterated in the communion antiphon today, also from the gospel of Matthew (20:28): "The Son of Man did not come to be served, but to serve, and to give his life as a ransom for many."

The fact that Jesus' death was the price for our salvation is reaffirmed in the prayer after communion.

Since we are still very human and live on this earth straining for more complete union with God, we can take comfort in today's prayer after communion, which asks that our faith would grow as a result of our sharing in the eucharist and that our hope might be confirmed in the life it promises.

Celebration of the Eucharist

The introductory rites today could include a brief comment about Judas' act of betrayal and our own actions that at times belie our faith in God.

The communal recitation of the "I confess" with the phrase "in what I have done and in what I have failed to do" would itself underscore our failings and our need for grace and healing.

Tuesday's verse before the gospel could be used today since it deals with Jesus' attitude as he faced his impending death "like a gentle lamb . . . [and] obedient to his Father."

Among the intercessions today, petitions could be made for those who suffer physically and emotionally, and those with terminal illnesses.

As has been the case since Monday, the preface assigned for use today is the second of the Passion of the Lord, with the significant text:

"The days of his life-giving death and glorious resurrection are
    approaching.
This is the hour when he triumphed over Satan's pride,
the time when we celebrate the great event of our redemption."

The second eucharistic prayer could be used today because of its brevity and because it will likely not be used again until Easter week. Its reference to the death that Jesus accepted freely would make it coincide well with the verse before the gospel and with the attitude reflected in the triduum liturgies.

The second introduction to the Lord's Prayer, about calling on God as Father, would be an appropriate option today since the latter part of the first reading and the responsorial psalm speak of the presence of the Lord with his people, especially in their need.

Number 16 of the prayers over the people could be used as the conclusion to the liturgy because it adds a fitting eschatological note to the liturgy; in it we pray that we might be brought "to the life to come" in Christ.

Liturgy of the Hours

Following the same invitatory used on Monday and Tuesday, today's reading at the office of readings from Hebrews 12 (vss. 14–29) deals with our becoming united to God through Christ, the fulfillment of the hopes and promises of the old covenant. Beginning with examples of the kind of disobedience to God in the Old Testament that should not be imitated (vss. 14–17), the major section of the reading deals with a contrast between the old and new covenants. As is typical for the author of this letter, the rites and sacrifices of the old law are used as types of the person and ministry of Jesus. He is the "mediator of a new covenant" whose "sprinkled blood speaks more eloquently than that of Abel" (vs. 24). The author encourages his readers to "hold fast to God's grace, through which we may offer worship acceptable to him in reverence and awe" (vs. 28).

The second reading from St. Augustine's treatise on John brings out the deep significance of the eucharistic meal we celebrate in memory of the Lord Jesus. The same kind of meal used to commemorate the passover of Israel is now used to commemorate the paschal victory of Jesus. It is especially by identifying with the death of Jesus as his final and supreme act of witness to the Father that the Christian martyrs became one with and in him. Through his body and blood poured out for us, we receive the forgiveness of our sins and the strength to bear witness to him in our lives.

At morning prayer the antiphon to the first psalm (Ps 77) reflects a confident stance before God as we pray: "In the day of my distress I reached out with my hands to seek the Lord's help." The psalm prayer that follows contrasts the old and new covenant and so places this Old Testament prayer in a relationship to our present liturgical celebration.

The antiphon that introduces the second psalm (canticle from 1 Sm 2:1–10) reflects the theology of Romans 6, the classic text about baptism that is used at the Easter vigil: "If we have died with Christ, we believe that we shall also live with Christ."

The final psalm of praise (Ps 97) speaks of the glory of God, and its antiphon associates ourselves with Christ in whom "we have been sanctified and redeemed."

The antiphon to Zechariah's canticle speaks of Jesus' sacrifice as the perfect offering to God: "His blood purifies us from sin and makes us fit servants of the living God."

At evening prayer the first antiphon reiterates the gospel since it sets up the betrayal of Jesus: evil men said, "Let us make the just man suffer; he sets himself against our way of life." The text of the psalm (Ps 62) urges confidence and trust in the Lord:

"In God alone is my soul at rest;
  my help comes from him.
He alone is my rock, my stronghold,
  my fortress: I stand firm" (vss. 1–2).

The unique mediation of Jesus is the subject of the second antiphon: "He took all our sins upon himself and asked forgiveness for our offenses." That the work of redemption is for all peoples, not just Israel, is reiterated in the recurring verse to Psalm 67:

"Let the peoples praise you, O God;
let all the peoples praise you."

The specific role that blood played in the old covenant rituals is reiterated again in the third antiphon: "In Christ we have found deliverance; through his blood, the forgiveness of our sins." This is a particularly fitting introduction to the hymn from Colossians (1:12–20) since it deals with Christ as the firstborn (and of us therefore as reborn in him) and as the one who saved us from "the power of darkness" (vs. 12). The unmistakable baptismal references here should not be forgotten as the text is prayed on this last day of Lent before initiation at the Easter vigil.

The scripture reading from Ephesians (4:32–5:2) deals with our response to the new covenant in Jesus as experienced in and through baptism. We are to forgive others as we have been for-given in Christ.

The antiphon to the Canticle of Mary emphasizes the coming passion of Christ since it states: "My hour is close at hand; I and my disciples shall celebrate the Passover in your house." With this text the drama of Jesus' approaching death heightens. Soon the liturgies of the triduum will unfold, through which we become real sharers in the dying and rising of Christ.

Celebration of the Hours
The invitatory verse can appropriately be accompanied by the recitation of Psalm 24 with its significant reminder that the ones to

climb the mountain of the Lord are those whose hands are sinless and whose hearts are clean. As Lent draws to a close, these sentiments should serve to remind those who gather for worship that they come in their need to be forgiven their sins by the Lord they worship.

At the office of readings the psalm prayer after Psalm 52 could be changed to reflect more adequately our being made sharers in the life of God through Christ, whose word prunes away what is barren and unworthy of his kingdom.

At both morning and evening prayer a passion hymn would serve well as an introduction to the hour. At morning prayer the psalm prayer after the third psalm could be changed to reflect more adequately the light/darkness motif that will be so strong at Easter initiations. Since the scripture reading for this hour is the same as that assigned for the eucharist today, another section of the servant songs from Isaiah would be a fitting choice.

At evening prayer the first psalm prayer could be changed to reflect the peace and reconciliation we have received through Christ, our only hope and source of true rest and peace.

The scripture reading from Ephesians could easily be extended beyond the verses presented should the community want a more thorough exploration of the meaning of baptism.

Reflection—"The Trust of the Servant"

As the servant of his Father Jesus functioned in a relationship of trust. He learned obedience through what he suffered and he was subject to his Father in such a way that he had to trust in him completely. There was no betrayal of his Father's will. But paradoxically, he himself was betrayed by one of his company. Where there should have been a confidential relationship between Jesus and the twelve, the gospels tell us that Judas broke that sacred trust and was disloyal to his Master and Lord.

Where do we find ourselves? Do we take the route of reliance on God and trust in him as is imaged for us by Jesus? Or do we take the route of expedience, self-aggrandizement, and disloyalty that is imaged by Judas? Are we imitators of the Lamb of God or of the spy who betrayed his Master?

What the liturgy presents for us today are texts and prayers that assume that we trust in God as did Jesus, and that like him we are willing to be servants of his Father. Will these texts be contradicted in the lives we lead outside the liturgy? The choice is ours. The hour is fast approaching when we will renew baptismal promises and receive the paschal communion of the Lamb of God. Will these be true signs of conversion and of trust?

There were two servants—Jesus and Judas. One trusted and the other betrayed. Whom shall we imitate?